ESSENTIAL SKILLS EVERY TEEN SHOULD KNOW

The Ultimate 3-in-1 Life Skills, Money Skills and Digital Skills Survival Book for Teenage Boys & Girls

FERNE BOWE

Copyright © 2024 Ferne Bowe

Published by: Bemberton Ltd

All rights reserved. No part of this book or any portion thereof may be reproduced in any form by any electronic or mechanical means without permission in writing from the publisher, except for the use of brief quotes in a book review.

The publisher accepts no legal responsibility for any action taken by the reader, including but not limited to financial losses or damages, both directly or indirectly incurred as a result of the content in this book.

ISBN: 978-1-915833-61-7

Disclaimer: The information in this book is general and designed to be for information only. While every effort has been made to ensure it is wholly accurate and complete, it is for general information only. It is not intended, nor should it be taken as professional advice. The author gives no warranties or undertakings whatsoever concerning the content. For matters of a medical nature, the reader should consult a doctor or other health care professional for specific health-related advice. The reader accepts that the author is not responsible for any action, including but not limited to losses both directly or indirectly incurred by the reader as a result of the content in this book.

View all our books at **bemberton.com.**

TABLE OF CONTENTS

BOOK 1. LIFE SKILLS FOR YOUNG ADULTS

7	**Introduction**
9	Chapter 1. Managing Your Money & Budgeting
21	Chapter 2. The Basics of Saving & Investing
27	Chapter 3. A Simple Guide to Renting
31	Chapter 4. Cooking & Food Skills
45	Chapter 5. Living a Healthy Lifestyle & Caring for Your Mental Health
55	Chapter 6. Personal Healthcare & Basic First Aid
65	Chapter 7. Maintaining Relationships: Social Skills, Networking and Communication
73	Chapter 8. How to Manage a Home
83	Chapter 9. Organization & Time Management
91	Chapter 10. Problem-Solving & Decision-Making Skills
95	Chapter 11. Kickstarting Your Career

BOOK 2. MONEY SKILLS FOR TEENS

107	**Introduction**
109	**Part One: Understanding Money — The Basics**
109	Chapter 1. Money (Really) Matters
115	Chapter 2. Banking 101
123	Chapter 3. Credit Reports — Why Your Credit Score Matters!
131	Chapter 4. Jobs & Money
139	Chapter 5. Keeping It Private — Frauds and Scams

145 **Part Two: Budgeting and Savvy Spending**

145   Chapter 6. Budgeting — Making a Plan (and Sticking to It)

153   Chapter 7. Spending — How to Get More for Less!

161 **Part Three: Borrowing, Debt, and Big-Ticket Item Purchases**

161   Chapter 8. Introduction to Borrowing Money and Debt

171   Chapter 9. Big-Ticket Item Purchases

175   Chapter 10. An Introduction to Car Ownership

179   Chapter 11. An Introduction to Home Ownership

183 **Part Four: Your Way to Wealth**

183   Chapter 12. Saving — Your Rainy Day Fund

191   Chapter 13. Investing — Building Wealth

205 **Part Five: The Future of Money**

207   Chapter 14. From Cash to Cashless

213 **Let's get started!!!**

BOOK 3. DIGITAL LIFE SKILLS FOR TEENS

217 Introduction

219   Chapter 1. The Digital Evolution: How Technology Transformed Our Lives

225   Chapter 2. Understanding Digital Safety: How to Protect Yourself Online

241   Chapter 3. Digital Conduct: How to Behave Responsibly Online

261   Chapter 4. Communicating in a Digital World: How to Interact Effectively Online

275   Chapter 5. Finding and Handling Information: Smart Strategies for the Digital Age

289   Chapter 6. Digital Commerce: How to Be a Savvy Online Shopper

305   Chapter 7. Finding Balance: How to Manage Screen Time and Well-Being

317 **Conclusion**

LIFE SKILLS FOR YOUNG ADULTS

How to Manage Money, Find a Job, Stay Fit, Eat Healthy and Live Independently

Everything a Teen Should Know Before Leaving Home

FERNE BOWE

BEMBERTON BOOKS

SOMETHING FOR YOU

Thanks for buying this book. To show our appreciation, here's a **FREE** printable copy of the "Life Skills for Tweens Workbook"

WITH OVER 80 FUN ACTIVITIES JUST FOR TWEENS!

 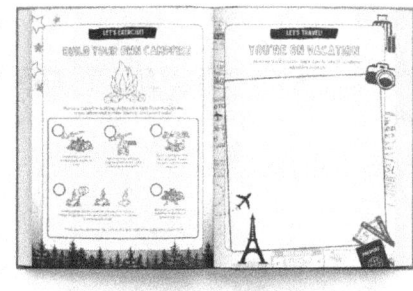

Scan the code to download your FREE printable copy

INTRODUCTION

Congratulations, you're a young adult! You've made it and are about to embark on the next phase of your life. You're about to become independent and leave the nest. But before you do, there are some things you need to know. Things that they don't teach you in high school. Things that will help you succeed in the real world.

We're talking about life skills.

We all know that life skills are important, but what exactly are they? Life skills are the abilities and knowledge that we need to help us navigate through everyday life. They include everything from time management and decision-making to communication and relationship building, to cooking and budgeting. They are all the practical skills that we need to function independently.

So why are life skills so important? Because they give us the ability to tackle anything that comes our way. They prepare us for adulthood's challenges and help us become well-rounded, successful individuals.

Think about it this way, would you rather be stranded on a deserted island with someone who knows how to build a shelter and start a fire, or someone who can recite all the state capitals? We all know the answer to that.

Learning life skills is essential for every young adult. Unfortunately, many of these skills are not taught in school. They are learned outside of the classroom, through experience and trial and error. You won't sit an exam on how to rent your first apartment, or how to save smart, but these are all essential life skills that you need to know.

That's what this book is for. It's a practical guide that will give you the tools you need to succeed in the real world. And while it's designed to be read cover to cover, you can also dip in and out of it as you need to. So, if you're looking for advice on how to manage your finances, you can head straight to that chapter. Or, if you need some tips on relationships, then that's where you'll find them. Furthermore, you'll find key information highlighted in bold throughout the book, so that you can easily scan and find what you're looking for.

So, what are you waiting for? It's time to learn the life skills that will help you thrive in the real world!

Disclaimer: The information in this book is general and designed to be for information only. Whilst every effort has been made to ensure it is accurate it is for general information only and is not intended nor should it be taken as professional advice. For matters of a medical nature, please consult a doctor or other healthcare professional for any specific health-related advice. For money matters, you should consult with a professional financial advisor before making any major decisions regarding your finances.

CHAPTER 1:

MANAGING YOUR MONEY & BUDGETING

Leaving home and heading out into the big wide world is an exciting time—but it can also be daunting, especially when it comes to money and budgeting. It's essential to learn the skills outlined in this chapter before you leave home to handle your finances responsibly and avoid any potential problems down the road.

This chapter will discuss some of the most essential money and budgeting skills that every young adult should learn. We'll cover everything from creating a budget to managing your expenses wisely. So whether you're just starting in college or about to graduate, read on for some essential tips!

Please note, that information in this chapter is for information only and should not be taken as professional financial advice. You should consult with a financial advisor before making any major decisions regarding your finances.

WHAT IS BUDGETING & WHY IS IT IMPORTANT?

Learning how to budget is the most critical money management skill. A budget allows you to track your expenses and ensure that you're not spending more than you can afford. It also helps you plan for the future and save for important goals like a car or a down payment on a house.

HOW TO CREATE A BUDGET

There is no one "right" way to create a budget—it depends on your individual needs and circumstances. Here are some tips on how to get started:

- **Start by calculating your monthly expenses.** This includes all your outgoings, from your rent to your grocery bill. Write these down in a budget worksheet or on a piece of paper. You may find it helpful to split these into two categories. Fixed expenses, such as rent or car payments, don't change month-to-month. Variable expenses, like groceries or entertainment, vary from month to month. You might find it helpful to break these into necessities & wants. Necessities are things like food, shelter, and clothing—while wants are things like cable TV or that new party outfit.

- **Next, calculate your income**. This is the total amount of money you bring in each month and includes all of the money you earn from wages, investments, and other sources of income. Say, you make $200 waiting tables at the weekend, and your allowance is $300. Your total monthly income would be $500.

- **Now it's time to create your budget**! Look at your expenses and see what you can afford to spend each month. If your total monthly costs are more than your total monthly income, you'll need to make some adjustments. You may need to cut back on some of your wants or find a way to increase your income. On the other hand, if your total monthly expenses are less than your total monthly income, you can use the extra money to save or invest.

- **Make sure you have some "emergency" funds to fall back on**. This is your insurance and will cover unexpected expenses if your budget falls short, or your circumstances unexpectedly change.

- **Be patient**! It may take a little time to tweak your budget and make it work. But with a bit of effort, you'll be able to successfully manage your finances.

Finally, be sure to **revise your budget** regularly as your income and expenses change.

HOW TO CHOOSE A BANK AND OPEN A BANK ACCOUNT

To budget effectively, you need to choose and open a bank account. This is an important way to manage your money and take charge of your financial responsibilities.

First, you must choose the bank and account that suits you best.

There are many different financial institutions and bank accounts out there, so it's worth shopping around as many offer incentives to new customers. Some accounts charge a monthly fee if you don't bring in a certain amount each month. Still, there are perks attached to these accounts like higher interest rates, free overdrafts, discounts, gifts, or free insurance. While others offer only online customer service, which may not suit everyone.

Before you make your decision, research and compare what's on offer. It's important to determine what's important to you.

To open your account, you usually have to:
- Apply using an application form on the bank's website
- Pass the identity and security checks (sometimes this means visiting the bank, while some will complete online security checks)
- Put some money into your account to activate it.

Each month, you should receive a statement from your bank. Most banks give you the option to receive online statements or a paper statement by mail.

HOW TO READ A BANK STATEMENT

It's a good habit to check your bank statement regularly to keep on top of your expenses, and to ensure you are not subject to fraud. You can usually check your transactions, via mobile banking apps or online accounts.

When checking your statement, you should:
- Look at each transaction to ensure that anything you've spent or bills have come out and are deducted from the balance
- Check that you recognize each transaction and its amount. If there are any you don't recognize, make a note of these.
- Make a note of any regular fees, direct debits, or bills you pay monthly, so you know what to expect when it comes to your money. This way, you can budget wisely.
- Trace any transactions or amounts you are unsure of and enquire about them
- Cancel any unnecessary monthly payments. Simply log into your online account, select your bank account, and click the menu. You should then see options to view your regular monthly direct debits and/or standing orders. You can click on them to view, edit or cancel.

KNOW YOUR PAYMENTS: DIRECT DEBITS, STANDING ORDERS, AND RECURRING PAYMENTS

Direct debits and standing orders are regular payments set up on your bank account that come out regularly (usually on a specific date), every month.

Standing orders are set up by you, and you can change them or cancel them at any time. An example might be your monthly rent.

Direct debits are set up by the company you're paying (for example, your utility bill or gym membership), and are pulled from your bank account. They can only be changed or canceled with the company's permission.

Recurring payments are set up on your debit or credit card and are charged on a pre-arranged payment schedule. The money is automatically charged to your card on the agreed date. An example of a recurring payment would be if you subscribed to a monthly streaming service, and they charged your card on the same date each month.

MANAGING YOUR MONEY WISELY

Once you have a budget in place, it's essential to follow it closely. This means making sure that you don't spend more than you can afford each month and saving for the future.

Here are a few tips on how to manage your money wisely:

- **Avoid impulse buying.** If you see something you want, wait a few days before deciding whether or not to buy it. This will give you time to think about whether or not you really need it.
- **Create a savings goal.** It's important to have a savings account for emergencies. Still, it's also a good idea to save for specific items like a car or a down payment on a house. No matter how low your income, aim for 20% of your income to be saved each month. Pay yourself first—before you pay any of your other bills, make sure you put money into your savings account.
- **Use cash instead of credit cards.** Credit cards can be tempting, especially when you're short on money. But they can also lead to debt if you're not careful. Use cash whenever possible to track precisely how much money you're spending.
- **Use a debit card instead of a credit card.** When you use a debit card, you're spending the money that you already have. Whereas when you use a credit card you're borrowing money

that you may not be able to pay back. This helps you to stay within your budget, and it also helps you avoid getting into debt.

- **Cancel Amazon Prime & delete shopping apps from your phone**. If you have a hard time resisting the temptation to buy things, delete shopping apps from your phone. This will help you to avoid temptation.

- **Eat in instead of eating out**. Eating out can be expensive, especially if you're doing it often. Try to cook at home as much as possible to save money.

- **Look for discounts and deals**. There are plenty of ways to save money on everyday items. Look for bargains at stores, coupons online, and sales at your favorite retailers. Many stores offer discounts for students, so be sure to take advantage of them.

- **Buy used**. One way to save money on big-ticket items is to buy them used. You can find used cars, furniture, and even clothes at garage sales, consignment shops, and online marketplaces like eBay or Craigslist.

- **Skip the upgrade**. Do you need a new phone with a better camera? Make do with what you have until you can afford to upgrade. This goes for other big-ticket items as well. If you don't need the newest model, save your money and buy the older one.

- **Cancel recurring monthly subscription services**. Many of these services offer free trials and then automatically revert to a monthly or annual recurring subscription. Check your bank statements, and cancel those that you don't use or need.

- **Deal with financial stress head-on**. If you're feeling overwhelmed by your finances, don't try to ignore the problem. Deal with it head-on and come up with a plan to fix it.

HOW TO MAKE MONEY

There are plenty of ways to make extra money if you need it. Here are a few ideas:

- **Start a side hustle**. A side hustle is a job or project you do in your spare time. It can be anything from freelance writing to dog walking.

- **Sell unwanted items online**. If you have any extra clothes, furniture, or other items lying around, sell them online to make some extra cash.

- **Get a weekend job**. If you need more money quickly, consider getting a weekend job. This can be anything from working in a restaurant to driving for Uber.

- **Rent out a room in your house.** If you have an extra room in your house, rent it out to make some extra cash. This can be a great way to cover your expenses, especially if you're unsure what you want to do after college.

- **Invest in stocks or mutual funds.** Consider investing in stocks or mutual funds if you have some money to spare. This can be a great way to make money over time, and it's a relatively low-risk investment.

- **Start a blog or online business.** If you're interested in starting your own business, consider starting a blog or online business. This can be a great way to make money while working from home.

- **Become a tutor.** If you're good at a particular subject, consider becoming a tutor. You can offer your services online or in person.

- **Donate plasma.** Donating plasma is a great way to make extra money without doing much work. You can usually donate twice a week and earn up to $400 a month.

- **Participate in online surveys.** Many websites pay you for completing online surveys. This is a great way to make some extra money without leaving your house.

- **Start a savings challenge.** A savings challenge is a great way to motivate yourself to save money. Choose a goal, like saving 20% of your income each month or saving $1,000 in six months, and then work towards it.

Managing your money can seem like a daunting task, but if you take it one step at a time, you'll be able to successfully manage your finances.

BORROWING: CREDIT CARDS, DEBT AND MORTGAGES

There may be times when your monthly income doesn't cover your expenses, and you need to borrow money to make ends meet. Or you may want to buy a new car or home, and you need to finance the purchase with a loan.

Borrowing, debt, and loans are perfectly normal and common. Most people have some form of debt (e.g. a mortgage, student loan, credit card debt). The key is to understand the implications of borrowing money and manage your debt responsibly so that it doesn't become a burden.

WHAT ARE CREDIT CARDS?

Credit cards can be handy if used wisely. They can help you build your credit rating. Sometimes they provide a period of interest-free credit which can be useful if you want to buy something urgently but don't have enough money in the bank.

However, they are an expensive method of borrowing unless you pay back the full balance every month.

The interest you pay on a credit card is called APR. Let's explore what that means.

> ### What is APR?
> APR stands for **Annual Percentage Rate.** It's the interest rate you're charged on a loan, credit card, or other borrowing product. The APR is the cost of borrowing money, expressed as a percentage of the amount you borrow. For example, if you're charged an APR of 12%, that means it costs you $12 to borrow $100 for one year.
>
> Remember, APR only covers interest, so any further fees or fines are not included in this. On certain products, APR can be extremely high. For example, the APR on some credit cards can be over 30%. This is why it's important to understand what you're being charged and to keep up with your monthly payments.

Many people prefer to use an overdraft or a bank loan as they are less expensive for longer-term borrowing.

OVERDRAFTS AND LOANS

An **overdraft** is a loan from your bank that lets you spend more money than you have in your account. Most banks will allow you to do this, but you have to agree to the amount before going overdrawn. They may also charge you fees and interest on the amount you've overdrawn. Many people use overdrafts as an emergency fund to tide themselves over until they get paid.

A **loan** is when you borrow money from a lender and agree to pay it back over a period of time. The borrower pays interest on the loan and this is added to the amount you need to repay. The borrower pays a fixed amount each week or month until the loan is repaid in full.

BUYING A HOUSE: HOW DO MORTGAGES WORK?

Buying a home can give you security and a place to call your own. But it's not always easy to get on the property ladder and is a big financial commitment. Though you may not be quite ready to take that step now, it helps to understand how mortgages work so you can make an informed decision when the time comes.

A mortgage is a loan that you take out to buy a property. The property is used as collateral, which means that if you can't repay the loan, the lender can repossess the property and sell it to recoup their money. There are two different types of mortgage—interest only and repayment.

> **Interest-only mortgages**
> With an interest-only mortgage when you pay your mortgage each month, you are only paying the interest and nothing off your mortgage balance. This means that your debt will not reduce, and you'll still owe the full balance of your mortgage at the end of your mortgage term.
>
> **Repayment mortgages**
> With a repayment mortgage when you make monthly repayments, you cover the interest and a contribution towards your mortgage balance too. This means, your debt will reduce and at the end of the term, your balance will be paid and you will own your property outright. Repayment mortgages are usually repaid over 25 years, but this can depend on the lender.

HOW MUCH CAN I BORROW?

The amount you can borrow will depend on your monthly income, monthly expenses, employment status, and credit history.

Most lenders apply a debt-to-income ratio. They want you to comfortably be able to cover your mortgage payments each month, so don't want you to spend more than 31–36% of your monthly income on your housing debts. This includes not just the repayment of the mortgage, but also insurance, and taxes.

- **For example:** *If you earn $3,500 per month, the maximum amount you can afford to spend on your mortgage is $1,085-$1,260.*

You can reduce your monthly mortgage payments and afford more houses if you can put down a larger down payment. The down payment is the amount of money you pay upfront when you purchase the property.

> **Another example:** *If you're buying a $200,000 house and you have a 20% down payment of $40,000, your monthly payments will be lower than if you had a 10% down payment of $20,000.*

This is because you're borrowing less money and so will have to pay less interest each month.

You can use a mortgage calculator to work out how much you could afford to borrow, and what your monthly payments would be.

CREDIT PROFILE

Your credit score is a calculation that represents your creditworthiness. It's used by lenders to decide whether or not to give you a loan, and at what interest rate.

Your credit score is based on your credit history, which is a record of your past activity, including the types of credit you already have and your repayment behavior.

The better your credit history, the higher your credit score will be and the more likely you are to be approved for a loan at a favorable interest rate.

It's a good idea to check your credit report regularly, to ensure that the information collated is correct. You can do this via one of the main credit reporting agencies online for free.

WHAT AFFECTS YOUR CREDIT PROFILE?

Several factors can affect your credit score, including:

- **New credit applications.** Applying for multiple credit products at the same time can negatively impact your credit score.
- **The mix of credit products.** A good mix of well-maintained products (eg. credit cards, loans, etc.) can improve your score
- **Your payment history,** and whether you have been paying your bills on time.
- **The amount of debt you have.** Too much debt will impact the amount you can borrow.

- **The age of your credit history or accounts**. The older your credit history, the better your credit score will be.

> **Top Tips to Improve Your Credit Score**
> - *Make all regular payments on time.* This shows lenders you are reliable and responsible
> - *Check your credit report for errors* and report any you find
> - *Don't use too much credit,* stay well below your limit—use about 30% of your credit if you can keep old accounts open. This demonstrates a long, well-managed, credit history

Borrowing money is a part of life for most people but by keeping on top of your repayments, and understanding the ins and outs of borrowing, you can ensure it doesn't become a burden.

HOW TO AVOID FRAUD AND SCAMS

With the rise of online shopping, social media, and online banking, there has also been a rise in fraud and identity theft.

Fraudsters are opportunists and will target anyone they think they can easily scam. They often create fake websites, phone numbers, or social media profiles to trick people into giving them personal information and money. It's important to be aware of the different types of scams so that you can protect yourself from them.

Some common types of fraud include:

- **Phishing**—this is where fraudsters pose as a trusted person or organization to trick you into revealing personal information or login details. They typically do this by sending a text, instant message, or email.
- **Vishing**—this is where fraudsters use automated voice messages or calls posing as a legitimate company. The aim is to collect your personal information, such as credit card details, your PIN, or any digital passcodes or passwords.
- **Social engineering**—this is where fraudsters try to deceive people by manipulating them into disclosing confidential or personal information. This is also known as psychological manipulation.
- **Online scams**—these are becoming more and more common and take many forms. They can occur through emails, websites, social media, and even over the phone. When fake goods or trials are offered. For example, some scams involve copycat official websites, where the fraudsters create a website that looks very similar to a legitimate one. Other scams involve fake prize draws, holiday accommodation, and even online dating. The goal of the fraudster is always the same: to trick people into sharing personal information, login details, or financial data.

Although there are many scams out there, don't worry there are some simple steps that you can take to reduce your risk.

Online Safety Tips

 Never share passwords
Never share your passwords or PIN with others, especially via text, email, cell or in person

 Use strong passwords
Include symbols, numbers, capital letters and never reuse passwords across different sites.

 Turn on 2FA
Where possible, turn on two-factor authentication. Consider using a password manager tool, such as LastPass.

 Limit your info
Limit the personal information you display on your public social media accounts. This includes your address, date of birth and age etc.

 Listen to your gut
If it doesn't feel right or it sounds too good to be true, don't go through with it - hang up, or don't click the link, and report the email. You should also contact your bank too!

 Stop and think
Before clicking on any links in an email, text, or message. Always check the domain name & the email address matches the name of the person or business.

Now that we've covered managing your money, it's time to take it that step further in chapter 2, by discussing the basics around saving and investing!

CHAPTER 2:

THE BASICS OF SAVING & INVESTING

What's the one thing you've always dreamed of buying but haven't had the money to purchase? A car? A new bike? A trip abroad?

Saving and investing for the future is one of the most important things you can do for yourself. By setting aside money when you're young, you'll have time to let your money grow over time. And if you continue to save consistently, you can achieve your financial goals and make your dreams a reality.

Please note, that information in this chapter is for information only and should not be taken or construed as financial advice. Whilst every effort is made to ensure the information is accurate it is no substitute for professional advice. You should consult with a financial advisor before making any major decisions regarding your finances.

HOW TO SAVE SMART TO GET AHEAD

When you save money, you're essentially putting it aside to use in the future. You can save for various purposes, such as retirement, a rainy-day fund, or a down payment on a house. While saving may sound boring, it's one of the smartest things you can do. It's your path to financial independence.

Saving is an accomplishment and it's something to be proud of. Not only do you have the satisfaction of knowing that you're doing something responsible for your future, but you can also enjoy the peace of mind that comes with knowing you have money saved up in case of an emergency.

There are a few different ways to save money. Many banks offer **instant access savings accounts** that allow you to earn interest on your deposited money without access restrictions. The rate of interest you make will depend on the type of account and the bank where you invest your money. Typically, you'll earn around 2% interest for an instant access savings account.

Meaning if you invest $100 and the interest is 2% at the end of the year, your investment will be worth $102.

This is a great low-risk investment option if you don't want to tie up your money for an extended period.

> **TOP TIP: Automate Your Savings**
> One of the smartest ways to save is to set up a system where a certain amount of money is transferred from your checking account to your savings account automatically each month. This can be a great way to make sure you're always saving for the future, without having to think about it.

Depending on your goals, you may also want to consider investing.

HOW INVESTING WORKS

Investing is essentially putting your money into something with the expectation of earning a return. It's a way to grow your money over time and it can be a great way to reach your financial goals.

When you invest, you're buying assets such as stocks, bonds, or real estate. These assets usually offer higher returns than savings accounts but have higher risk levels. This means there is a risk that your investments could lose money if the market takes a downturn.

22 ESSENTIAL SKILLS EVERY TEEN SHOULD KNOW

Before deciding if investing is right for you, you should **consider your goals, financial situation, and risk tolerance**.

You should also set yourself a limit—don't invest all of your money and be sure to consider your investments carefully. Many people find it useful to seek advice from a financial advisor or an investment expert.

If you're saving for a holiday, a car, or a new gadget, a savings account could be a better option than investing. On the other hand, if you're comfortable taking on more risk and have a longer time horizon, you may want to consider investing in stocks or mutual funds.

These assets often offer higher returns but come with more risk. The key is to remain invested, even when the market drops. The longer you're willing to invest, the more likely you will see positive returns. And if you start early, you'll have plenty of time to let your money grow via the magic of compounding.

THE WONDERS OF COMPOUND INTEREST

Compounding is one of the most powerful tools you have to save money. This is because compound interest allows your money to grow exponentially over time.

When you earn through compounding, your **interest is added to your initial investment**, so both the initial sum and the interest make interest.

> *Let's take a look at an example:*
>
> *Assume you invest $1,000 in a savings account that pays 5% compound interest. At the end of the first year, your investment will be worth $1,050.*
>
> *In the second year, you earn the 5% interest on $1050, so at the end of that year, your investment will be worth $1,102.50.*
>
> *And at the end of the third year, your investment will be worth $1,157.63.*

As you can see, your investment grows at a much faster rate.

The key is to start saving at a young age, so you have longer to enjoy the benefits of compound interest.

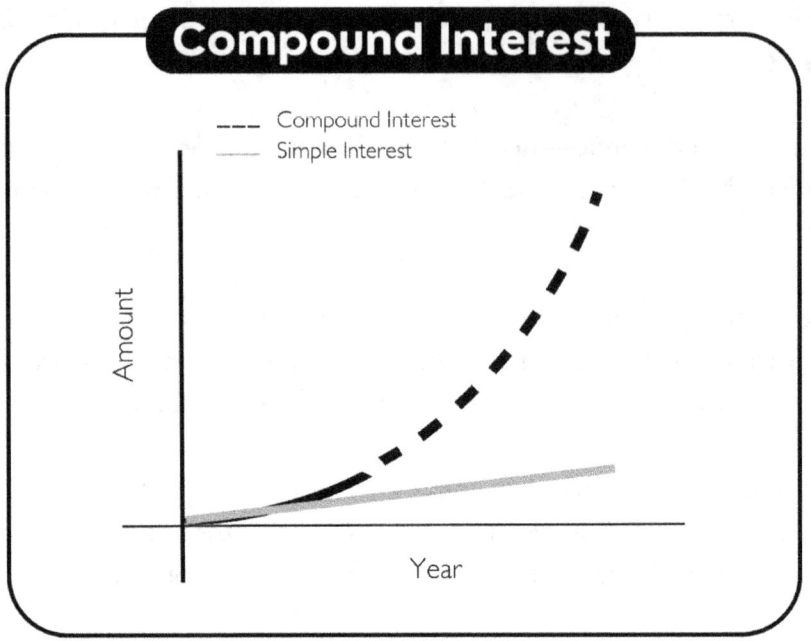

> **Let's take a look at another example:**
>
> Imagine 20-year-old Jon invests $1,000 today and leaves it untouched until he retires at 70. If he earns 7% interest every year, Jon's $1,000 will have turned into $29,457 by the time he's 70.
>
> But let's say Annie waited until she was 30 before she invested $1,000. Even if she earned the same 7% interest, her investment would only grow to $14,974 by the time she retires at 70.

The longer you wait to start investing, the more difficult it becomes to catch up.

If you don't have a large lump sum to put away now, **small monthly contributions make a massive difference in the long run.** Even if you can't afford to invest a lot of money each month, your contributions will still add up over time.

> For example, if Jon invests $20 per month until he's 70, he'll have invested a total of $12,000. But his investment will be worth more than $100,000 thanks to compound interest (on a 7% interest rate).

That's the power of starting early and letting your money grow over time!

That's the power of compound interest!

HOW TO INVEST IN STOCKS AND SHARES

You're never too young to start investing. One of the best things about stocks is that you don't need a lot of money to get started. But it's important to understand the risks involved before you start investing.

When you buy a stock (or share), you're buying a piece of a company. If you own Apple stock, for example, you own a small piece of the company. The **price of a stock goes up and down** depending on how well the company is doing. If the company does well, the stock price will go up. If the company does poorly, the stock price will go down. This means that **there is a risk that you could lose money if you invest in stocks**.

There are a few different ways to invest in stocks. You can buy shares in individual companies, or you can invest in mutual funds or exchange-traded funds (ETFs).

A mutual fund is a collection of stocks from different companies, while an ETF tracks an index, such as the S&P 500, which is a collection of 500 of the largest US companies.

When you invest in a mutual fund or ETF, you're spreading your risk across many different companies. This means that if one company performs poorly, it won't have a huge impact on your overall investment.

When it comes to stocks and shares, it's important to remember that there's no such thing as a guaranteed return. The key is your time horizon: the longer you're willing to wait, the more likely you are to see a positive return.

The key to being a successful investor is staying calm and not reacting to short-term market movements. Avoid looking at your investments daily. **Try to think long-term, and you'll be more likely to make intelligent investment decisions.**

As Warren Buffett, one of the most successful investors of all time, says: "Be fearful when others are greedy, and be greedy when others are fearful."

When it comes to investing, there are no guarantees. However, if you're patient and willing to take a little bit of risk, stocks can be a great way to grow your money over time.

How to Start Investing

If you're ready to start investing, there are a few things you need to do first.

1. ***Figure out how much money you can afford to invest.*** Remembering investing is a long-term game, so you should be comfortable locking your money away for at least 5 years. There's a saying that you should only invest what you can afford to lose.

2. ***Choose the investments you want to make.*** There are many different types of investments to choose from, so take some time to think about what's right for you.

3. ***Open a brokerage account.*** A brokerage account is where you buy and sell stocks, mutual funds, and other securities.

4. ***Make regular contributions.*** This will help you build your investment portfolio over time.

5. ***Stay invested for the long term.*** Don't panic and sell your investments if the stock market goes down. The key to successful investing is patience and discipline!

CHAPTER 3:

A SIMPLE GUIDE TO RENTING

When you first leave home and get a place of your own, you may decide to rent. Renting a property means you live in a property that belongs to someone else (the landlord). You (the tenant) pay them an agreed fee, (the rent) usually on a monthly or weekly basis. It's common for you to agree to a specific period for renting and to sign a contract (the Lease); for example, most people rent for either a 6 or 12-month period.

If you plan on renting a property, there are some things you need to know…

WHAT YOU NEED TO KNOW

When renting your first place, you should **do your research** to ensure the property and the neighborhood fit your lifestyle. **Location is key**. If you like to go out and party, you'll want to live in a neighborhood with lots of nightlife. If you're more of a homebody, opt for a quieter neighborhood. Equally, what you might save on rent you'll spend on transportation costs if you live too far from your work or college.

Another thing to consider is **who you'll be living with**. Will you be renting alone or with friends?

Renting with friends reduces the cost. For example, if the monthly rent is $2000, splitting it four ways brings each person's cost down to $500 per month. Just ensure everyone sharing the place gets on well together, especially when entering a lease agreement for 6 months or more.

Renting can be expensive. Make sure you know how much you can afford to spend each month on rent. You'll also need to find out what's included in the rent (e.g., water, electricity, heating) and what isn't (e.g. internet, parking). You'll also need to factor in the cost of a security deposit, which is usually one month's rent.

The security deposit is a way for the landlord to protect themselves in case you damage the property or stop paying rent.

If you want to rent a property for $2000 per month, you'll likely have to pay a $2000 security deposit plus $2000 rent upfront before you move in—that's a whopping $4000!

KNOW YOUR LANDLORD

There are different types of landlords that you may rent from and it's useful to know who you're dealing with.

- **Private landlords** are individuals who own a property and rent it out themselves without any support from a property company or rental agency.

- **College or university landlords** are typically an accommodation team based within the college or university. The team manages properties owned by the university and takes charge of all related rentals.

- A **property agent** is a company that handles real estate professionally for clients. They manage everything related to managing the property from finding tenants to fixing any problems that may arise. Most agents carry out financial background checks on potential tenants.

· ·

IF YOU HAVE A PROPERTY IN MIND

Once you find a property you like, you first must sign a **lease agreement, pay your security deposit, and then start paying your rent**.

Your landlord will provide you with the written lease agreement before you move in. This document will outline the terms of your rental agreement, such as the rent amount, length of the lease, and any special conditions. It's important to read through the lease agreement carefully and ask questions if you don't understand something. You should also keep a copy for yourself so you can refer to it whenever necessary.

Your landlord may also provide an **inventory list**. This is a list of all the items in the property when you move in, along with their condition. Make sure to check the list carefully and note any damage or missing items, so you're not held responsible for them later on. The return of your security deposit will hinge on the condition of the property and the inventory list when you leave.

WHAT HAPPENS AFTER YOU MOVE IN?

When you move into your new place, you should keep the property clean and tidy. This will help you maintain a good relationship with your landlord and avoid any penalties. Of course, things may break down sometimes; **if you report them and take responsibility, the landlord is likely to be more understanding.**

As a tenant, **you are responsible for paying your rent on time each month**. If you can't pay the rent, talk to your landlord ASAP—they may be able to work out a payment plan with you. Late payments can result in eviction, so it's important to stay on top of your rent.

You are responsible for paying your bills on time when you live in a property. This includes your electricity, water, internet, and cable bills. Paying online is often the simplest option, but there are many other options available.

As soon as you move into a new property, you must arrange to put the **utility bills** in your name. This can be done by contacting the utility company and providing them with your name and address. You may also wish to arrange extra services, such as cable TV or broadband. Most companies offer package deals that include several services at a discounted price.

CHAPTER 4:

COOKING & FOOD SKILLS

Cooking and food skills are an essential part of life. They can help you save money, stay healthy, and impress your friends and family. Learning basic cooking is a good habit that leads to a lifetime of enjoyment, good food, and healthy eating habits.

This chapter will cover the basics of cooking: cooking different types of foods, reading recipes, and mastering basic skills in the kitchen. With a little bit of practice, you will be able to cook delicious and healthy meals for yourself and your loved ones!

....

YOUR COOKING TECHNIQUE GLOSSARY

To get you started, there are a few basic cooking techniques that every student chef should know. These techniques will help you prepare different foods and make your dishes look and taste better.

- **Sautéing** is a technique used to cook food quickly in a small amount of oil or butter. To sauté, place the food in a pan over medium-high heat and stir frequently.
- **Braising** is a technique used to simmer meat or vegetables in a small amount of liquid. Place the food in a pan or pot and cover it with liquid to braise. Bring the liquid to a simmer and cook until the desired doneness is reached.
- **Roasting** is a technique used to cook food in an oven. To roast, place the food on a baking sheet or roasting tray and cook at a high temperature.
- **Blanching** is a technique used to cook vegetables quickly in boiling water. To blanch, place the vegetables in a pot of boiling water and cook for 1–2 minutes. Remove the vegetables with a slotted spoon and put them in ice water to stop cooking.

- **Poaching** is a technique used to cook delicate foods in a liquid such as broth, milk, or wine. To poach, place the food in a poaching pan or pot and bring the water to a simmer. Cook until the desired doneness is reached.

- **Grilling** is a technique used to cook food over an open flame. Place the food on the grill grate and cook until the desired doneness is reached. Be sure to brush the food with oil or melted butter to help it stay moist and prevent it from sticking to the grate.

Now that you know the basic cooking techniques, you can try cooking various dishes! Be sure to experiment and have fun in the kitchen. With a bit of practice, you will be able to cook like a pro!

HOW TO READ A RECIPE

A recipe is a set of instructions that tells you how to make a particular dish. It can be helpful to read a recipe through before beginning to cook, so you know what ingredients you will need, what order to prepare the ingredients in, and how long it will take to cook.

When reading a recipe, here are some things to look for:

- **The number of servings the dish will make or the serving size**
  Serving size refers to the amount of food that a particular recipe will make. Most recipes list the serving size in the header or first paragraph. This is important because it will help you decide how much to make. You may want to halve or quarter the recipe if you are cooking for fewer people.

- **What ingredients are needed**
  All recipes list the ingredients needed to make the dish. Check you have all of the ingredients on hand before you start cooking, or you may be running to the store in the middle of making dinner!

- **Preparation time**
  Most recipes list how long it will take to prepare the dish. This can help decide what to make for dinner. If you are short on time, choose a recipe that takes less time to prepare or cook.

- **Cooking time**
  Just like preparation time, **cooking time is usually listed in most recipes.** This can help you plan your meal. If you have a dish that needs to cook for an hour, you may want to start it early to be ready when you are done cooking everything else.

- **What tools and equipment are needed**
  Some recipes require special tools or equipment, such as a food processor. **Check what is required before you start.**

- **The directions or method**
  The directions for a recipe tell you what order to prepare the ingredients and how to cook the dish. They are usually written in a step-by-step format. Be sure to follow the directions, or you may end up with something that doesn't taste very good!

HOW TO MASTER BASIC KITCHEN SKILLS

Now that you're cooking for yourself and you understand recipes, it's essential to know basic kitchen skills and to get the essential tools. Here are a few tips to help you get started.

- **Wash your hands**
  Before you do anything in the kitchen, wash your hands with soap and warm water. This will help keep you and your food safe from bacteria.

- **Measuring Ingredients**
  Mastering basic recipes requires proper measurement of ingredients. You will need to be familiar with the different types of measuring cups and spoons to do this.

When measuring liquid ingredients, use a liquid measuring cup or jug. These cups usually have markings on the side that will help you measure the exact amount you need.

When measuring dry ingredients, be sure to use a dry measuring cup. These cups are typically graduated in ounces or milliliters.

When measuring solid ingredients, it is best to use a kitchen scale. This will help you get an accurate measurement, especially when dealing with large quantities.

By using the correct type of measuring cup or spoon for the job, you will end up with accurate measurements and successful recipes.

Kitchen Conversion Chart

gr	tsp	tbsp	fl oz	cup	pint	quart	gallon
15	3	1	1/2	1/16	1/32	-	-
28	6	2	1	1/8	1/16	1/32	-
57	12	4	2	1/4	1/8	1/16	-
85	18	6	3	1/3	-	-	-
115	24	8	4	1/2	1/4	1/8	1/32
170	36	12	6	3/4	-	-	-
227	48	16	8	1	1/2	1/4	1/16
908	-	64	32	4	2	1	1/4
-	-	256	128	16	8	4	1

- **Knives**

  A good set of knives is an essential kitchen tool. They will make the preparation of meals much easier and faster.

  When choosing knives, look for a set that includes a paring knife, which is good for peeling and slicing fruit; a chef's knife, which is good for chopping vegetables; and a bread knife, which is good for slicing bread.

  Be sure to keep your knives sharpened. A sharp knife is a safe knife.

- **Cutting Board**

  Choose a board made from a durable material, such as wood or plastic. Keep your cutting board clean and sanitize it after each use.

  Cutting boards come in different colors, for different purposes, to prevent cross-contamination of bacteria.

  - White boards are used for bread and dairy (eg. cheese)
  - Green boards are used for cutting vegetables, fruit, and salad.
  - Yellow boards are used for cutting cooked meat.
  - Blue boards are used for cutting fish.
  - Red boards are used for chopping raw meat.

- **Pots and Pans**
  Every kitchen needs a good set of pots and pans. When choosing pots and pans, select ones that are made of durable materials such as stainless steel or cast iron.

  Be sure to choose pots and pans that are the appropriate size for the job. For example, a small saucepan is not going to be very useful when cooking for a large group of people.

  It is also important to have several different sizes of pots and pans on hand. This will give you the flexibility to make a variety of different dishes.

- **Cooking Utensils**
  In addition to pots and pans, you will also need a few basic cooking utensils. These include things like wooden spoons, spatulas, and tongs.

  When choosing cooking utensils, look for ones that are made of durable materials such as stainless steel or silicone. These materials will withstand the heat of the stove and are less likely to melt or warp.

HOW TO COOK ON A BUDGET

Cooking for yourself is usually cheaper than eating out at a restaurant. Here are a few tips to help you stay on budget when cooking independently.

- **Plan your meals.**
  If you plan out your meals for the week, you will be less likely to order takeout or buy food from the grocery store. Planning meals also helps you use up all of your ingredients, saving you money.

  To plan your meals, simply write out a list of all the meals you want to eat for the week. Then, make a grocery list of all the ingredients you will need to make those meals.

- **Cook in bulk.**
  If you have time, cook a large batch of food that can be eaten throughout the week. To cook in bulk, simply double or triple the recipe that you are making. Once the food is cooked, portion it into individual servings and store it in the fridge or freezer.

  Then just reheat it when you are ready to eat. This will save you time and money since you won't have to cook every day.

- **Shop for bargains at the grocery store sale section.**
  Most grocery stores have a section where they sell food on sale, often when it is close to its expiration date. This is a great place to find inexpensive groceries that you can use in your recipes. Be sure to check out this section regularly, as you can stock up on staples like grains, pasta, and canned goods when they are on sale. Just ensure you only buy items you will use so they don't go to waste.

- **Avoid processed foods.**
  Processed foods are often expensive and not very healthy. Instead, try cooking meals using fresh ingredients. This will save you money, but it will also give you the nutrients your body needs.

- **Use leftovers.**
  If you have leftovers from a previous meal, don't throw them away! Instead, put them in the fridge and eat them for lunch or dinner the next day.

- **Compare the prices of different brands.**
  Not all brands of the same product are created equal. Compare the prices of different brands to find the best deal. Supermarket brands are usually cheaper than premium household brands often with minimal difference in quality.

- **Buy in bulk.**
  If you will use a particular ingredient frequently, buy it in bulk. This will save you money in the long run. Staples such as rice, pasta, and olive oil can often be found at a discount if you buy them in large quantities.

- **Make your lunch for college or work.**
  Making your lunch is a great way to save money and eat healthily. If you brown-bag it, you can save even more money by cooking extra food at dinner and bringing the leftovers for lunch the next day.

HOW TO STORE FOOD

Once you have cooked your meals, or bought your groceries you will need to store the food properly to prevent it from spoiling. Here are a few tips on how to store food so that it stays fresh:

- **Refrigerate perishable items.**
  Perishable items such as meat, dairy, and seafood should be stored in the fridge. These items will go bad quickly at room temperature, so it's important to keep them cold. As a simple rule,

if the items you bought were in the fridge at the grocery store, they should go back in the fridge when you get home.

- **Freeze items for longer storage.**
  If you won't be using an item right away, you can store it in the freezer. This is a great way to store meat, fish, and vegetables so that they don't go bad. It's also a great way to keep your bulk-cooked meals fresh so you can eat them later. To freeze your food, simply place it in a freezer-safe container and store it in the freezer.

  To thaw your food, place it in the fridge the night before you plan to eat it. Always check the food is fully thawed before cooking.

  Important: Whilst it is generally ok to thaw foods, cook them, and refreeze the cooked version, it is not recommended to refreeze food that has already been thawed.

  > *For example: if you have frozen a raw steak, you can defrost it, cook it, and then refreeze the cooked steak. However, if you have defrosted the steak and it has been sitting in your fridge for a few days, do not refreeze it.*

- **Store dry goods in a cool, dry place.**
  Dry goods such as grains, pasta, and flour should be stored in a cool, dark place. The pantry is usually the best spot for these items. These items will last for several months when stored properly.

Following these storage tips will help you keep your food fresh and prevent it from spoiling. Just be mindful of expiration dates, as some foods will only last for a short period, even when stored properly.

HOW TO MAKE A GROCERY LIST

The key to meal planning and saving money, is to **create a list before you go grocery shopping**. Lots of people don't do this, and as a result, they often end up buying things they don't need, or forget items that they do need. If you want to stick to your budget, planning your meals and creating an organized list is a MUST.

> **Making a list doesn't have to be time-consuming if you follow the three golden rules:**
>
> 1. *Have an ongoing, 'to buy' list* and keep it in an accessible place. As you run low on items, make a quick note of it on your list. This is NOT your actual shopping list, but it will help you compile it. When you decide to buy the item, simply add the item to your shopping list and cross it off the 'to buy' list.
>
> 2. *Keep an inventory* of the items you always need, such as flour, pasta, rice, and oil. While this is time-consuming the first time you do it, your inventory can be maintained easily, with a quick weekly update. If you know what you have, it's easier to create both your list and meal plan.
>
> 3. *Write your weekly meal plan* BEFORE you compile your shopping list. This will help you to determine what ingredients you NEED to buy that week.

By following the three golden rules, you can be sure that your list will be both comprehensive and efficient—saving you time and money.

When you're ready to write your list, you should look at your meal plan and consider what you may need for each meal. Check your inventory to see what you already have and write a list of the things you need to buy to make each meal. Don't forget to cross-check this with your ongoing 'to buy' list.

When your list is complete and you're shopping for your items, don't forget to compare the prices across the different brands to see if savings can be made.

MASTERING BASIC RECIPES

Cooking is all about experimentation. The more you experiment, the better you will become at creating delicious and healthy meals. By mastering a few simple recipes and learning to cook staples, such as eggs, rice, and pasta, you will be able to cook a variety of different meals in no time. Here are a few recipes to help get you started.

HOW TO COOK A MEAN BREAKFAST

Breakfast is the most important meal of the day. It kick-starts your metabolism and provides the energy you need to get through the day.

There are endless possibilities for breakfast. Here are a few of our favorites.

BOILED EGG

A soft-boiled egg is a quick and easy breakfast option. Place 1–2 eggs in a pot of boiling water, then cook for 5 minutes. Remove the eggs from the pot with a slotted spoon, then place them in a bowl of cold water.

If you are cooking eggs straight from the fridge, add a minute or two of cooking time.

OMELET

An omelet is a classic breakfast dish that can be made with a variety of different ingredients.

Serves: 1   Prep Time: 5mins   Cooking Time: 5mins

Ingredients:
- 2–3 Eggs
- Optional Filling—cheese, ham and vegetables

Directions:
1. Beat 2–3 eggs in a bowl, then pour them into a hot skillet, ensuring they don't burn on the bottom.
2. Cook for 2–3 minutes until the bottom is set, then add your desired fillings. Cheese, ham, and vegetables all make great additions to an omelet.
3. Once the fillings are added, fold the omelet in half and cook for an additional minute or two, or until the middle is cooked.

SCRAMBLED EGGS

To make scrambled eggs, follow the recipe above, and stir the eggs gently with a wooden spoon while cooking. Cook until the eggs are soft-firm.

PANCAKES

Pancakes are a delicious way to start your day.

Serves: 8	Prep time: 7mins	Cooking Time: 10 mins

Ingredients:
- 1 cup of flour
- 2 tablespoons of sugar
- 2 teaspoons of baking powder
- ½ teaspoon of salt
- 1 Egg
- 1 cup of milk
- Optional Toppings!

Directions:
1. Mix 1 cup of flour, 2 tablespoons of sugar, 2 teaspoons of baking powder, and ½ teaspoon of salt in a bowl.
2. Add 1 egg and 1 cup of milk, then stir until the batter is smooth.
3. Pour ¼ cup of batter onto a hot griddle, and cook for 2–3 minutes per side until the pancakes are golden brown.
4. Serve with your favorite toppings, such as maple syrup, jam, or berries.

BREAKFAST SMOOTHIE

A breakfast smoothie is a great way to combine your favorite fruits and vegetables in one delicious healthy drink.

Serves: 1+	Prep Time: 5 mins

Ingredients:
- Fruit or Vegetables—Be creative with what you have!
- ¼ cup of yogurt
- ½ cup of milk

Directions:
Simply blend 1 cup of fresh or frozen fruit, ¼ cup of yogurt, and ½ cup of milk in a blender until thick and creamy. The key with smoothies is to be creative, don't be afraid to combine different fruit, vegetables, and flavor combinations. For example, adding a handful of spinach or kale for an extra boost of nutrients.

EASY MAIN MEALS

Main meals are important too, and there's no reason why they can't be quick and easy. By mastering one or two simple sauces you can adapt them to make a variety of different dishes. Here are a few simple recipes to get you started:

PASTA WITH TOMATO SAUCE

Tomato sauce is a versatile sauce that can be used in a variety of different dishes.

Serves: 4   Prep Time: 5mins   Cooking Time: 15mins

Ingredients:
- 1 Onion, chopped
- 2 Garlic cloves, chopped
- 1 can of diced tomatoes
- 1 teaspoon of sugar
- 1 tablespoon of herbs—such as basil or oregano
- Salt and pepper to taste
- Pasta

Directions:
1. Sauté 1 chopped onion and 2 cloves of garlic in a tablespoon of olive oil until they are softened.
2. Add 1 can of diced tomatoes, 1 teaspoon of sugar, and 1 tablespoon of chopped fresh herbs, such as basil or oregano.
3. Simmer the sauce for 15 minutes, then season to taste with salt and pepper.
4. In the meantime, to cook the perfect pasta, simply bring a pot of water to the boil, then add 1 tablespoon of salt. Add the pasta and cook for 2–3 minutes less than the instructions on the packet. Drain the pasta, then add it to the tomato sauce.
5. Serve with grated cheese and a side salad.

TACO MEAT SAUCE

Taco meat is another versatile sauce that can be used in a variety of different dishes, such as tacos, burritos, or nachos. It can also be used as a topping for salads or pasta dishes. If you don't have the individual spices, replace them with a packet of taco seasoning.

Serves: 4   Prep Time: 5mins   Cooking Time: 10mins

Ingredients:
- 1 chopped onion
- 1 chopped garlic clove
- 1 pound of ground beef
- 1 can of diced tomatoes
- 1 teaspoon of chilli powder
- 1 teaspoon of cumin
- Salt and pepper to taste
- Taco shells or tortillas
- Optional extras: shredded cheese, lettuce & sour cream

Directions:
1. Saute 1 chopped onion and 1 crushed garlic clove in a tablespoon of olive oil until they are soft.

2. Add 1 pound of ground beef to the onion and garlic mixture breaking it up as you add it. Fry on medium heat until the beef has browned (keep turning it and do not let it burn).

3. Drain any excess fat, then add a can of diced tomatoes, a teaspoon of chili powder, and a teaspoon of cumin. If you like your chili hot, add more chili powder or fresh chilis according to taste.

4. Season with salt and pepper to taste.

5. Simmer for 10 minutes, then add taco shells or tortillas and serve with shredded cheese, lettuce, and sour cream.

MEAT-FREE VEGETARIAN OPTION

If you want to create a vegetarian or vegan option, simply replace the ground beef with a meat substitute. Good meat substitutes include using a vegan mince replacement, or you could use grated carrots, finely sliced celery, red lentils, or shredded cabbage instead.

15 MINUTE SOUP WITH LEFTOVERS
....

Soups can make a healthy and nutritious meal. They are quick and easy and can contain almost anything and are a great way to use up your leftovers.

Serves: 4   Prep Time: 10mins   Cooking Time: 25mins

Ingredients:
- Any vegetables you have available or any leftovers you have from other meals—chop them up into small cubes.
- Two bouillon cubes
- Chopped garlic or onion (optional)

Directions:
1. Saute your prepared vegetables in a saucepan for 5–10 minutes.
2. Add water to the pan, enough to cover the vegetables.
3. Bring to a boil, and sprinkle in the bouillon cubes.
4. Stir well and turn down the heat.
5. Simmer for 10–15 minutes or until the vegetables are soft.
6. Add salt and pepper to taste.
7. Serve (with bread if you wish)!

5 WAYS TO SPRUCE UP YOUR SOUP

- To turn your soup into a broth, add two tablespoons of dried broth mix (red lentils and barley).

- Add pasta to your soup, if you want a more filling meal.

- You can also add any leftover meat to your soup, such as chicken, bacon, or beef if you prefer a meaty flavor—make sure you heat through thoroughly before serving.

- Spice up your soup by adding a sprinkling of chili powder, curry powder or paste, or cumin seeds.

- Combination of ingredients that make great soup:

  - Butternut squash, potato, onion, and a teaspoon of curry powder for spicy butternut squash soup.

  - Leek and potatoes work well, along with bacon (optional). This works well as a thicker soup, so be sure to add the cornstarch mix mentioned above.

  - Broth mix, peas, carrots, onion, and diced peeled potatoes make an excellent broth, and again, the corn start mix makes it thicker and creamy, especially if you use milk instead of water. Chicken or lamb leftovers are great additions to any broth!

CHAPTER 5:

LIVING A HEALTHY LIFESTYLE & CARING FOR YOUR MENTAL HEALTH

Living a healthy lifestyle is important for your physical and mental health. It's important to ensure you take care of your own needs, so you have the energy to allow yourself to live the life you want. As well as feeling better, if you eat healthily and take regular exercise you will be at lower risk of developing health conditions in the future. You'll also find you build up your immune system and are more likely to get over sicknesses bugs and viruses quickly.

When we eat and drink, our bodies take in energy from our consumption, and this is measured in calories. We need this energy to keep us alive and to keep our body running in an efficient, healthy, way.

Our bodies use energy for everything from breathing to circulating blood, to digesting food. Even when you're asleep or resting, your body is still using energy to maintain all of its vital functions.

Calories are just units of measurement that we use to track the amount of energy that we are taking in from food and drink, and the amount of energy that we are using through activity.

The recommended daily intake (RDI) of calories for men is 2,500, and for women it is 2,000. However, this will vary depending on age, weight, height, and activity level.

For example, a person who works as a sports coach has a physical job, and therefore they are more likely to need more calories than a person who works in an office. Of course, using our brain power requires energy too, so that person would still need their fair share of calories too.

The most important thing you can do is to **make sure you're eating a healthy and balanced diet of nutritious foods from all the food groups.**

HOW TO GET THE ENERGY YOUR BODY NEEDS

The body derives calories (energy) from nutrients. The three main nutrients that provide energy are:

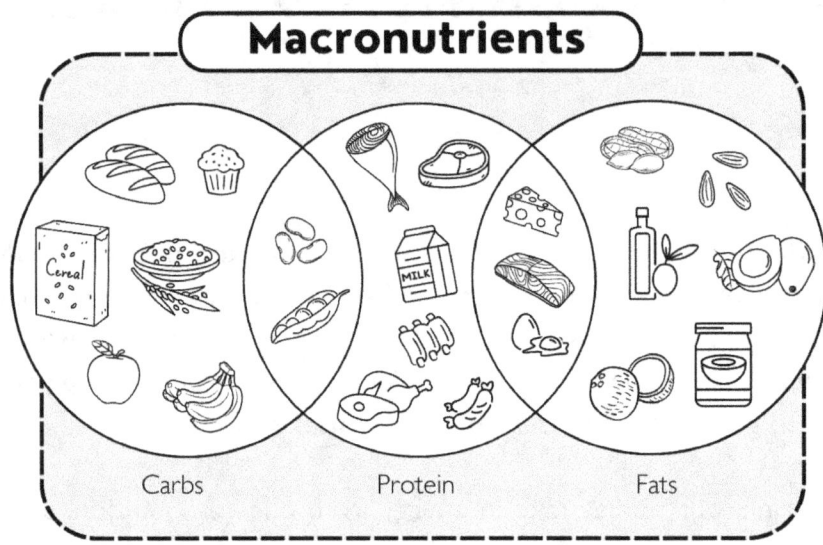

CARBOHYDRATES

Carbs are broken down into glucose, which the body uses for energy. They are most commonly found in grains, bread, pasta, rice, potatoes, fruit, vegetables, and cereals. They are also found in sugary foods such as candy, cake, and cookies.

FATS

Fats are a concentrated source of energy and are also needed for other functions in the body such as making hormones, and cell membranes, and breaking down other nutrients. For example, Fat is a source of fatty acid that helps the body absorb vitamins A, D, and E. The body cannot produce fatty acids itself, so our bodies would be unable to absorb these without any fat.

Therefore, a small amount of fat is required as part of a healthy diet, but too much can lead to health problems.

The two primary fats found in food are saturated fats and unsaturated fats.

- **Saturated fats** are found in animal products such as butter, cream, meat, and cheese. They can also be found in some plant oils such as coconut oil, palm oil, and cocoa butter.

- **Unsaturated fats** are found in plant oils such as olive oil, rapeseed oil, sunflower oil, and soya bean oil. They are also found in oily fish such as salmon, mackerel, and herring. Unlike saturated fats, 'good' unsaturated fats can help reduce your cholesterol levels and lower your risk of developing heart problems.

PROTEINS

Proteins are needed to grow and repair your body tissues. Your body breaks down protein into amino acids, which are the building blocks of your muscles.

Proteins are found in meat, fish, eggs, beans, and lentils. They are also found in dairy products such as milk and cheese.

As well as carbs, fats, and protein, the body also needs micro-nutrients in the form of vitamins and minerals.

ESSENTIAL VITAMINS AND MINERALS

Vitamins and minerals are essential nutrients needed in small amounts to keep the body healthy and functioning correctly. These nutrients are in various foods, including fruits, vegetables, whole grains, dairy products, and meat. While most of us get enough nutrients if we eat a balanced diet, occasionally, we need to take supplements.

There are several types of vitamins and minerals, but we'll explore some of the most common below:

- **Vitamin A** is in cheese, eggs, oily fish, milk, and yogurt. It helps your body fight infections and illness, helps to keep your skin healthy, and is also good for vision.

- **Vitamin B** has many different types. The role of B vitamins is to help release energy from the food we eat. They are also important for our body's general health and well-being.

- **Vitamin C** is in citrus fruits, tomatoes, peppers, broccoli, and Brussels sprouts. It helps to protect cells and keeps them healthy.

- **Vitamin D** is in oily fish, eggs, and fortified foods such as cereals and fat spreads. It helps the body absorb calcium, required for healthy bones and teeth.

- **Vitamin E** is in vegetable oils, nuts, and seeds. It helps to protect cells from damage.

- **Calcium** is found in dairy products such as milk, cheese, and yogurt. It is also found in green leafy vegetables, such as broccoli and cabbage. Calcium is needed for healthy bones and teeth.
- **Iron** is found in meat, poultry, fish, beans, lentils, and fortified cereals. It helps make red blood cells, which carry oxygen around the body.

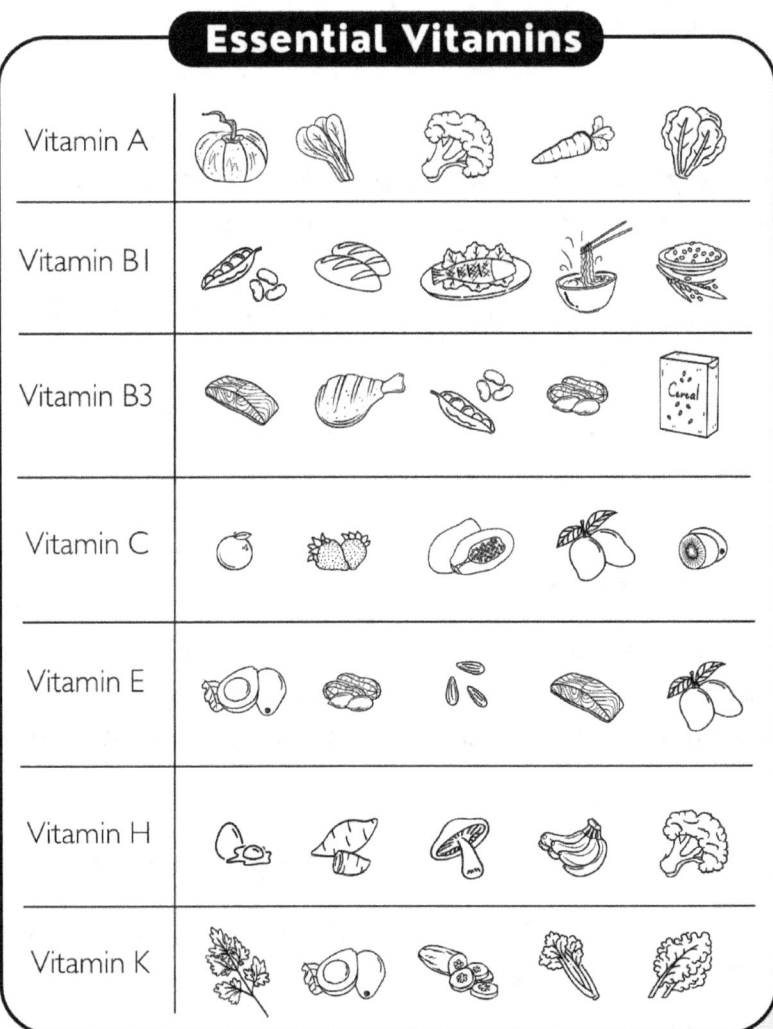

HOW TO EAT A HEALTHY AND BALANCED DIET

A healthy and balanced diet includes a variety of nutrient-rich foods your body needs to function so that you feel your best, have good energy levels, and maintain your health.

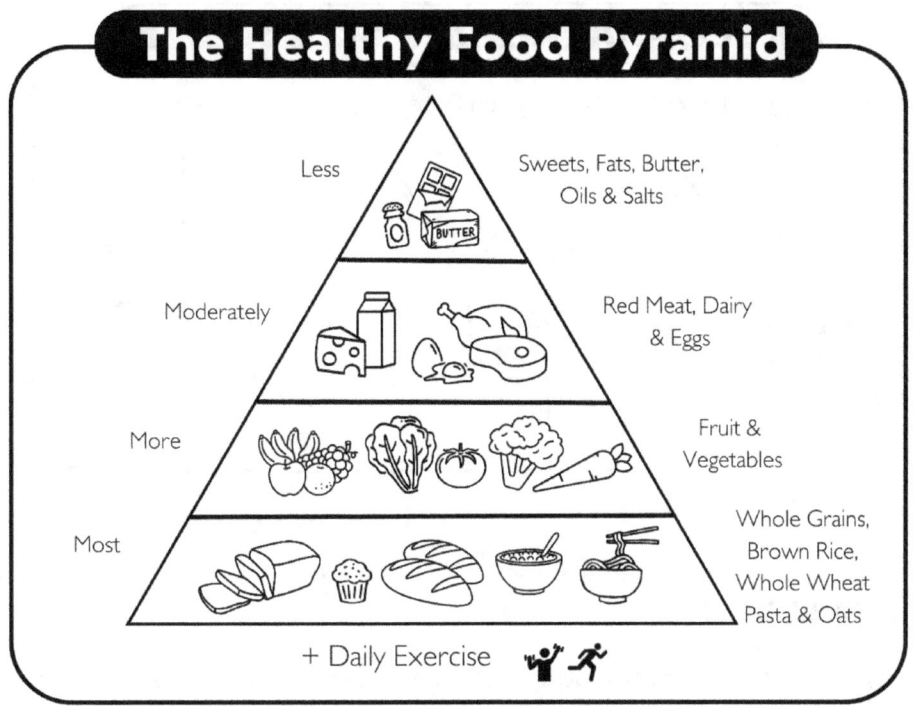

A healthy diet should consist of all the food groups:

- **Fruit and Vegetables**: you should aim to eat at least five portions of a variety of fruits and vegetables each day. This is because they are a good source of vitamins and minerals, as well as dietary fiber.

- **Starchy Foods**: you should eat starchy foods such as potatoes, rice, pasta and bread. They provide a good base for your meals and are high in fiber.

- **Protein Meat, Fish, Eggs, Beans, and Lentils**: include a variety of meat, fish, beans, and lentils in your diet as they are rich in protein and other nutrients.

- **Dairy**: products such as milk, cheese, and yogurt provide calcium which is essential for strong bones and teeth.

- **Fats**: oils and spreads provide essential fatty acids and are a good energy source.

Remember that **we all have different energy needs depending on age, gender, activity levels, and weight**.

When it comes to portion sizes, a good rule of thumb is to fill up around one-third of your plate with starchy foods, one-third with vegetables or salad, and the final third with meat, fish, or beans.

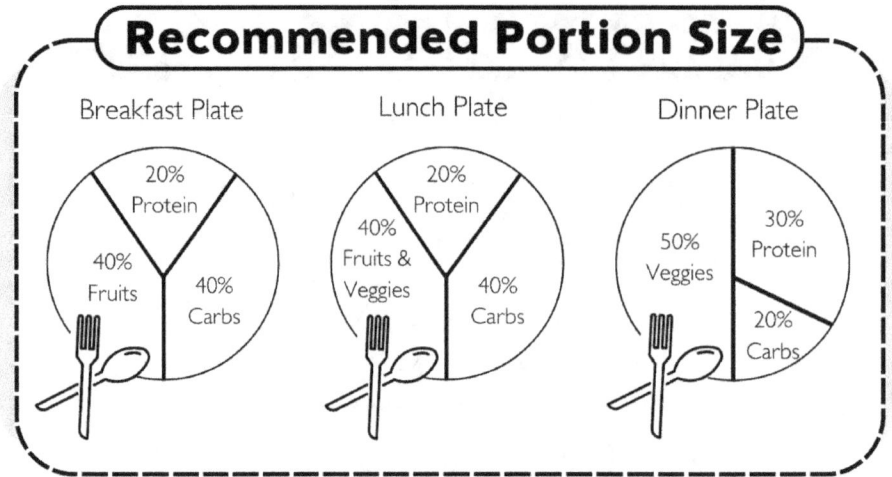

WATER AND HYDRATION

Water is essential for having a healthy body and mind. **Every single cell in our bodies needs water to function properly**. Water helps transport oxygen and nutrients around the body, regulates our body temperature, protects our organs, and aids digestion.

We need to drink around 8 glasses of water per day to stay hydrated. To ensure you are getting enough water, try to drink a glass of water with every meal and snack. You can also carry a water bottle with you when you are out and about. Your daily recommended intake can be met by drinking fluids, eating water-rich foods such as fruits and vegetables, and from water found in other drinks such as tea and coffee.

Avoid sugary or fizzy drinks, as they can cause tooth decay, and the sugar can give you an energy high followed by an energy low. Try to stick to water or other unsweetened drinks.

HOW TO READ FOOD LABELS

Food labels contain a lot of valuable information that can help you make healthier choices. Here are some things to look out for:

- **The list of ingredients**: tells you what is in the food. The first ingredient listed is usually the main one, and the last ingredient listed is typically present in smaller amounts. So if sugar is one of the first few ingredients, then the food is high in sugar.

- **The nutrition information panel**: gives you information on the energy (calories), fat, saturates, sugar, and salt content of the food. It is important to remember that the serving size listed on the label is not necessarily the same as the portion size you would eat. For example, a packet of biscuits may say that it contains eight servings, but if you eat the whole pack, you would need to multiply the nutrition information by 8.

- **The % Reference Intake (RI)**: tells you the percentage of an adult's recommended daily intake provided by one serving of the food. For example, if a product contains 20% of the RI for sugar, one serving provides 20% of the sugar an adult should eat in a day.

- **The use-by date**: gives the date up to which you can use the food without it going off.

Of course, the importance of diet and nutrition is only one part of the puzzle when staying healthy. Being physically active, getting enough sleep, and managing stress are important factors.

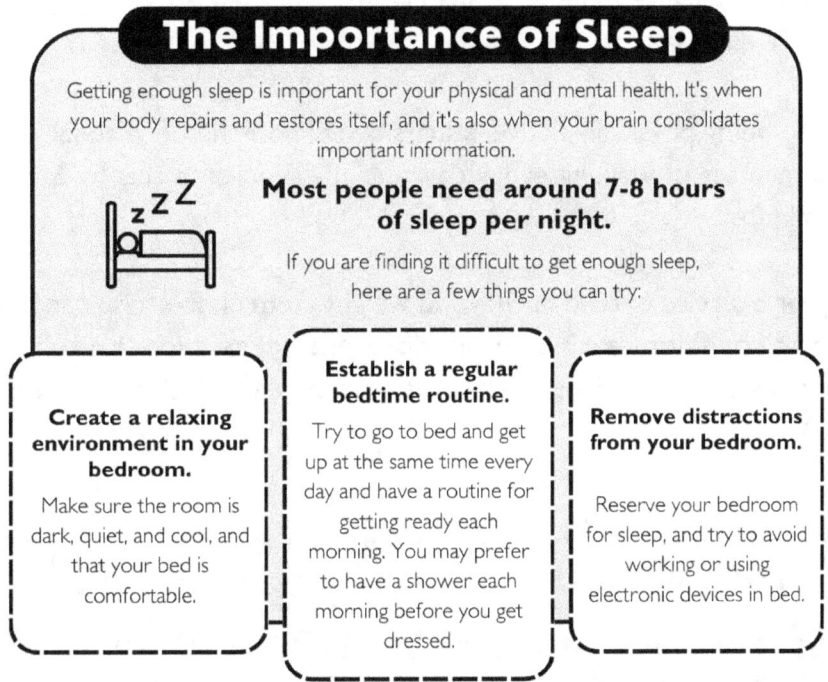

HOW TO STAY FIT

Taking part in regular exercise is important for your physical health and well-being. It can help to reduce your risk of developing health conditions. It can also help to keep your weight under control and can improve your mental health and mood.

You should aim to take part in two types of exercise: aerobic exercise and strength training.

AEROBIC EXERCISE

Aerobic exercise is any activity that gets your heart rate up and makes you breathe more heavily. It includes activities such as walking, running, swimming, and biking. Aerobic exercise helps to improve your cardiovascular fitness, and can also help to reduce stress and anxiety.

STRENGTH TRAINING

Strength training is any activity that works your muscles and helps to improve your muscle strength. It includes activities such as lifting weights and doing bodyweight exercises. Strength training helps to improve your bone density and can also help to reduce the risk of injuries.

The best way to stay fit is to be physically active every day. Adults should aim for at least 30 minutes of moderate-intensity physical activity on most if not all, days of the week. Moderate-intensity activities include walking, swimming, and cycling. You can also do a combination of different activities to reach your daily goal.

If you are not used to being physically active, start slowly and build up gradually. For example, you could start with 10 minutes of walking every day, and then increase this by 5 minutes each week until you reach 30 minutes.

The benefits of regular exercise extend far beyond weight control. Exercise can also help to reduce the risk of developing conditions such as heart disease, strokes, type 2 diabetes, some types of cancer, and osteoporosis. It can also help to improve mental health, including reducing stress, anxiety, and depression.

HOW TO COPE WITH EMOTIONS

To remain healthy, you also need to manage your feelings, in a healthy way. We all know that there are ups and downs in life. There are times we handle heart-breaking moments, and glorious ones too. We need to be ready to handle disappointments, stress, and times of crisis. People who don't have healthy coping skills, often develop unhealthy ones.

HOW TO DEAL WITH STRESS

Stress is our body's response to demands placed on it. It is a normal human emotion that we all experience from time to time.

The best way to describe stress is to imagine you have a bucket inside your body that collects your everyday stresses.

Your bucket collects stresses to do with work, finances, home life, relationships, and health. We all have a different-sized bucket, and we all manage stress differently, so something you see as being stressful, another person will not, and vice-versa. When a lot of things happen, our bucket fills, causing us to feel anxious, tired, low and emotional, burnt out, and snappy or irritable. When we begin to feel like this, we must relieve the stress by turning on a tap and letting some of it out, or the bucket will overflow and we will become unwell.

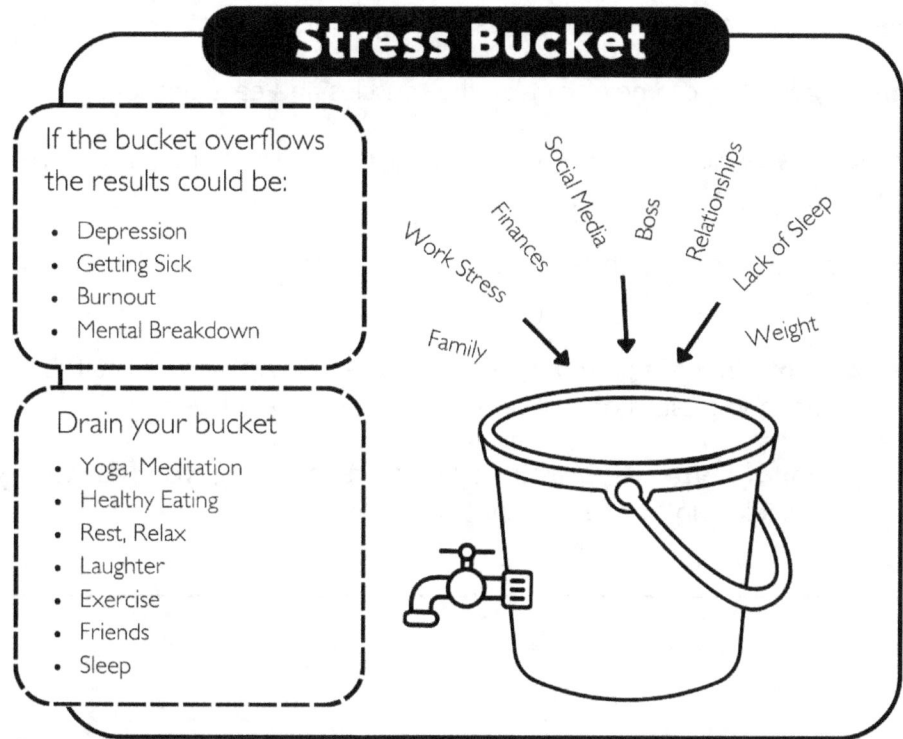

There are many different ways to let stress out of our buckets. Some people exercise, some people meditate or do yoga, some take long baths, some listen to music or read books—there is no one right way to do it. It is important to find what works for you and to do it regularly before your bucket begins to overflow.

Do whatever you need to do to let the stress out of your bucket!

Here are some tips on how to empty your stress bucket:

1. **Exercise**—this can be anything from a brisk walk to a more intense workout at the gym. It releases endorphins which have mood-boosting effects.

2. **Relaxation techniques**—such as yoga, meditation, or deep breathing.

3. **Connect with nature**—go for a walk in the park, sit in the garden, or spend time near water.

4. **Spend time with loved ones**—positive social interactions can help reduce stress levels.

5. **Do something you enjoy**—whether it's reading, cooking, painting, or another hobby.

6. **Get a massage**—this can help to relax the muscles and ease tension.

7. **Make time for yourself**—even if it's just 10 minutes a day, make sure you have some "me time" to do something you enjoy.

8. **Be assertive**—say "no" to things that you don't want to do or that will cause you undue stress.

9. **Learn to accept the things you can't change**—this can be difficult, but holding onto resentment and frustration will only add to your stress levels.

10. **Seek professional help**—if your stress levels are impacting your day-to-day life, it may be time to seek help from a therapist or counselor.

TALK ABOUT IT!

The more we learn to talk about how we feel, the better our mental health can be. This isn't a sign of weakness. It's empowering as it helps you take control of your well-being.

We all have disappointments and crisis points in our lives, so it's natural to feel down, anxious, or stressed from time to time. It's only when these feelings become prolonged and begin to impact your daily life that they become a problem. **Talking about how you feel can be the first step in managing stress, anxiety, or depression.**

Remember **you are not alone**. Feeling stressed, disappointed, or in crisis is common, and many people feel just like you do. There is no shame in seeking help. **Talk to a trusted friend, family member, doctor, counselor, or therapist**. The sooner you reach out for help, the sooner you can begin to feel better and move on.

CHAPTER 6:

PERSONAL HEALTHCARE & BASIC FIRST AID

Most young adults are healthy and don't have to think about their health very much. However, it's important to be proactive about your health and to know how to take care of yourself if you do become ill. This chapter will teach you the basics of accessing healthcare and administering first aid.

While every effort is made to ensure the information here is accurate, it is for general information only and is not intended nor should it be taken as medical advice. Please consult a doctor or other healthcare professional for any specific health-related advice.

HEALTHCARE IN THE UNITED STATES

The healthcare system in the United States can be confusing, but as a young adult, you have many options available to you. Below we outline some of the key healthcare resources and options available to you:

CHOOSING NOT TO HAVE INSURANCE

Choosing not to have insurance (or being uninsured) is of course your choice, but be aware that in certain States **you may be penalized** at the end of the year on your taxes. The penalties vary by State so check your local laws if you need to file an exemption or not. In addition, healthcare costs are often much higher for those without insurance, so you may end up paying a lot out of pocket if you need to go to the doctor or hospital.

- **Healthcare Through Your Parents' Insurance**
  If you are under the age of 26, check your parents' insurance as you may be covered under their plan. This just requires a quick phone call to your parents' provider.

- **Healthcare Through Your School**
  Some colleges offer students healthcare insurance while attending the university. This option is typically for foreign students, but it is offered by some colleges to Stateside students. **Talk to your college to get more details.**

  In addition, most colleges offer discounted healthcare services to their students on campus. These services typically include check-ups, prescriptions, and some specialist care. Again check with your college the level of services on offer.

- **Getting Insurance Through Your Employer**
  Most employers offer health insurance for full-time employees. In most cases, this is either free (if your employer pays the whole premium) or more affordable (if you have to pay part of the premium), than finding your insurance. Often, there are added benefits such as reduced cost or even free eye or dental care. However, if you lose or leave your job, you will lose this health plan.

- **Getting Insurance Through the Government (Medicaid/Medicare)**
  If you are not able to afford private health insurance, you may be eligible for Medicaid or Medicare. Both programs offer a wide range of medical services, including doctor's visits, hospital stays, emergency care, and prescription medications. To find out if you qualify for these programs, you should speak to your state Department of Health Services or visit their website.

- **Getting Insurance Through a Private Company**
  This health care you get on your own through any private health insurance company you wish. It allows for more tailoring to your needs than any of the other plans but can be costly.

WHEN CAN I GET INSURANCE?

In most cases, you can only enroll for insurance during what's called an "open enrollment period" or if you have a "qualifying life event."

"Open Season/Enrollment" refers to a period each year when you can enroll in a new health plan or update existing plans. This varies State by State but tends to be at the end of each year. During this period you can sign up for a healthcare plan from a private healthcare provider. You can find information on health insurance plans in your state with a simple Google search.

Before signing up, **it's a good idea to consider what coverage you may need for the coming year.** For example, if you are planning on having a baby, you will want to make sure your plan covers maternity care.

Outside of the open enrollment period, you can only sign up for a health insurance plan if you have a qualifying life event. This includes events such as getting married, having a baby, or losing your job.

Once you have your health plan, it can take anywhere from 2 weeks to 90 days to activate. This time frame is sometimes referred to as a gap in coverage. If you require medical attention during this time, your health plan may not reimburse the cost. Check the terms and policies of your plan for specific details.

SEEING A DOCTOR

Firstly, you need to find out if a doctor is 'in your network'. **Your insurance company will have a list of doctors that you can see**, and these are called in-network doctors. If you go to see a doctor who is not on this list, it is called an out-of-network doctor. Going to see an out-of-network doctor will usually cost you more money.

If you do not have health insurance, you will have to pay for your healthcare yourself. You can still go to the doctor, but it will cost you more money.

NEW PATIENT INTAKE OR WALK-IN

If you have never seen the doctor before, you will need to do a new patient intake. This is where the doctor will ask you questions about your medical history and your current health. They will also likely ask for your medical history, insurance, and financial information. To make a doctor your PCP (Primary care physician) **you will usually need to do the New Patient appointment** then call your insurance and have them list that Doctor as your PCP.

If you have seen the doctor before, you can usually just make a walk-in appointment.

PCP VS. URGENT CARE VS. SPECIALIST VS. ER

You will usually see your primary care physician (PCP) if you have a general health concern. If you have a specific health concern, you will usually be referred by your PCP to a specialist. For example, if you have a heart condition, you will see a cardiologist.

Urgent care is for when you need to see a doctor but it is not an emergency. For example, if you have an earache and need medicine for it, but you can't see your doctor for two days. It's not severe enough for the ER, but the pain is too much for a two-day wait.

The emergency room is for when **you need to see a doctor right away** because it is an emergency.

HOW TO REGISTER WITH A LOCAL DOCTOR IN THE UK

Registering for a doctor in the UK is recommended *as soon as you move into a new area and have a permanent address.* You can register with any GP (general practitioner) in your area, even if they are not your local surgery. To do this, you will need to fill out a registration form, which you can get from your surgery or online. You will need to provide your contact details, date of birth, and National Insurance number. Once you have registered, your GP is your first port of call for all your healthcare needs.

HOW TO MAKE AN APPOINTMENT WITH A GP

If you need to see a GP, you can either call your surgeon or go online to book an appointment. You will usually be able to see a GP the same day if it's an emergency. If it's not an emergency, you will be given an appointment usually within a week or two.

HOW TO PERFORM BASIC FIRST AID

Being able to perform basic first aid is an important life skill.

First aid is the initial care given to someone who has been injured or who is suddenly unwell. This could be anything from a minor cut or bruise to a more serious injury such as a broken bone. It should be administered as soon as possible after the injury or illness has occurred. It is not intended to be a substitute for medical care, but it can often help to stabilize the patient until professional help arrives or can be sought.

Let's explore some common first-aid scenarios and what you can do to help.

HOW TO DEAL WITH CUTS AND GRAZES

If you have a cut or graze, it is important to clean the wound as soon as possible to prevent infection.

1. **Rinse the wound** with clean water for several minutes.

2. **Apply pressure** if the bleeding is constant.

3. To prevent infection of the wounded area, **apply an antiseptic cream** or ointment, if you can do so, and by the manufacturer's instructions.

4. **Place a sterile dressing over the wound** and secure it in place with adhesive tape or a bandage.

5. If the bleeding is constant and does not stop after 10 minutes of applying pressure, **seek medical attention** immediately.

HOW TO REMOVE A SPLINTER

Splinters are also common injuries and can usually be removed easily. If left, they can cause infections under the skin. Therefore, it's important to remove splinters in the safest, cleanest, way. To do this, you should follow the steps below:

1. **Clean the area** around the splinter with warm water and soap.

2. **Use a needle or tweezers** to carefully remove the splinter.

3. If the splinter is embedded deeply, **seek medical attention**.

4. **Apply an antiseptic cream** or ointment to the area and cover with a sterile dressing.

5. **Change the dressing regularly** to prevent infection.

HOW TO DEAL WITH FAINTING

Fainting occurs when you lose consciousness for a short period, usually due to a drop in blood pressure. It can be caused by several things, including low blood sugar levels, standing for a long time, or the sight of blood. It can also be a symptom of an underlying medical condition.

If someone faints, it is important to try to revive them and then seek medical attention if they do not regain consciousness.

1. **Lie them down on their back and raise their legs** above heart level. This will help to increase blood flow to the brain.

2. **Give them plenty of space**, reassure them, and have them sit up slowly.

3. If they do not regain consciousness, **seek medical attention** immediately.

HOW TO TREAT A BURN

Burn injuries are common, and can range from mild to severe. Burns occur when your skin comes into contact with a heat source, such as boiling water or a hot stove.

While minor burns are treatable it's advisable to see a medical professional for more serious injuries.

1. For minor burns, **hold the affected area under cool running water for at least 10 minutes** to reduce swelling. Avoid applying ice or anything ice cold, as this could further damage the skin. You should also avoid greasy substances or creams.
2. **Seek medical attention** immediately if the burn is severe or if it covers a large area of skin.
3. For all burns, **avoid breaking any blisters** that have formed, as this could lead to infection.

HOW TO DEAL WITH CHOKING

Choking occurs when an object becomes lodged in your throat or windpipe, blocking airflow. Choking is a common medical emergency, but it can also be very scary. If someone is choking, it is important to act quickly and try to dislodge the object.

1. **Encourage them to cough**—this may help to dislodge the object.
2. **Give them up to five back blows** between their shoulder blades with the heel of your hand.

    To perform back blows, you should:

    - Place one arm around the person's chest, and bend them over at the waist.
    - Give 5 blows to the back using the bottom of your hand, striking in between the shoulder blades.

3. If this does not work, **try up to five abdominal thrusts** (also known as the Heimlich maneuver)

    To perform the Heimlich maneuver, you should:

    - Stand behind the person who is choking, with one foot in front of the other to help you balance (if it's a child, you may need to kneel).
    - Place your arms around their waist, and tilt them forward slightly
    - Make a fist with one of your hands and place it just above the navel of the person.
    - With the other hand, grab the fist and then thrust this into the stomach with a quick, upward movement, just as if you're trying to pick the person up.

- Repeat 5 times.

4. Repeat these steps until the object is dislodged.

5. **Seek medical attention** if they are still choking or if they become unconscious.

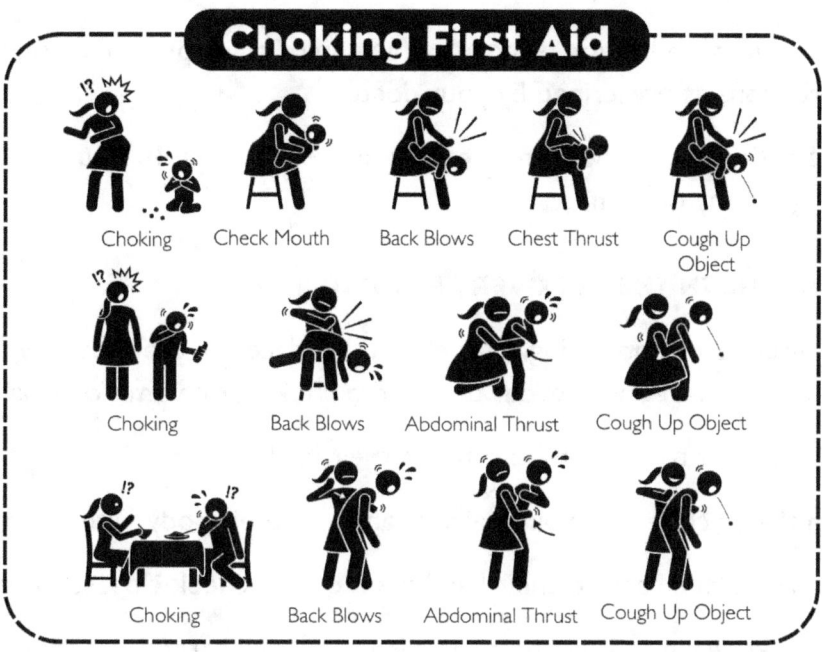

HOW TO DEAL WITH A SPRAIN OR BROKEN BONE

A sprain occurs when you stretch or tear a ligament—the tissue that connects bones. A broken bone occurs when your bone is either cracked or broken completely. Both injuries can be extremely painful and should be treated immediately.

It's important to remember that **a broken bone always requires medical attention**. A doctor understands how the bones heal and work and will provide you with the best advice when it comes to such an injury.

If you think someone has broken bone, follow these steps:

1. **Assess the situation.** Do you need to phone an ambulance or can the person be taken to an accident and emergency facility?

2. If possible **immobilize the injured limb** with a sling or splint to prevent further damage.

3. **Seek medical attention** as soon as possible.

If you think someone has **sprained** their ankle, wrist, or knee, follow these steps:

1. **Apply ice** to the area for 20 minutes every two hours. If you don't have an ice pack, a pack of frozen peas will do.

2. **Keep the injured limb elevated** above heart level to reduce swelling.

3. Take over-the-counter medication, such as paracetamol or ibuprofen, if you can, ensuring you follow the instructions as prescribed by your doctor.

4. **Seek medical attention** if the pain does not improve within 48 hours or if there is severe swelling, bruising, or any deformity.

HOW TO PUT SOMEONE IN THE RECOVERY POSITION

If someone is unconscious but breathing, they should be placed in the recovery position. This will help to keep their airway clear and prevent them from choking on vomit or inhaling their tongue.

1. Kneel on the floor, next to the person lying on their back.

2. Extend the arm that is closest to you at a right angle to their body with their palm facing up.

3. Fold the other arm to the back so their hand rests on the cheek closest to you.

4. Bend the person's knee which is farthest away from you and carefully roll the person onto their side by pulling the bent knee towards you. The bent knee should be at a right angle.

5. Their bent arm should be supporting their head, while their extended arm will prevent you from rolling them too much.

6. Tilt back their head, lift their chin, and check that nothing is blocking their airway.

7. Stay with them, and monitor their condition until help has arrived.

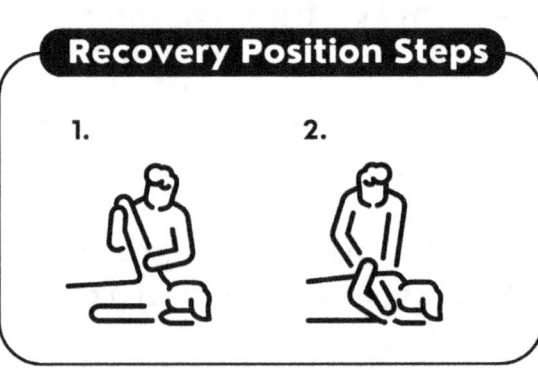

HOW TO BUILD A FIRST AID KIT

A first aid kit is an essential item to have in your home, as it contains all the supplies you need to deal with minor injuries and illnesses. While you can buy complete sets, it can be helpful to build your first aid kit so that you can tailor it to your specific needs.

Here are some **essential items to include in your first aid kit**:

- A range of Band-Aids (different shapes and sizes)
- Small, medium, and large gauge dressings—make sure they are sterile
- Triangular bandages
- Bandages and gauze
- Adhesive tape
- Antiseptic wipes or cream
- Painkillers
- A thermometer
- Tweezers
- Medical Scissors
- A first aid manual
- Cream or spray to relieve bites and stings
- Antihistamines

If you have any specific medical conditions, make sure to include any medication or supplies that you need. It is also a good idea to keep a list of emergency phone numbers in your kit, as well as copies of important medical documents such as your insurance card.

CHAPTER 7:

MAINTAINING RELATIONSHIPS: SOCIAL SKILLS, NETWORKING AND COMMUNICATION

One of the most important things you will do in your life is to build and maintain relationships. This includes **family, friends, partners, and work colleagues**. The people close to you will have a big impact on your life, so it is important to nurture the relationships that you have. This means making time for the people in your life, communicating effectively, and constructively resolving conflicts.

BUILDING RELATIONSHIPS

HOW TO MAKE A GOOD FIRST IMPRESSION

The first step to building any kind of relationship is to make a good first impression. Whether it's a first date, a job interview, or meeting your future in-laws, you want to make sure that you put your best foot forward.

This means **being polite and friendly**, dressing appropriately, and **being on time**. Remember a smile goes a long way. Greeting someone with a smile and making eye contact shows that you are interested in them and open to communication. **Being positive and upbeat** will also make you more likable.

If you are shy or introverted, it can be helpful to **have some conversation starters in mind**. This way, you won't be caught off-guard if there is a lull in the conversation. Common conversation starters include asking about their day, talking about current events, or discussing mutual interests.

Finally, **don't forget your manners**, both in person and online. Saying please and thank you, holding the door open for someone, or sending a thank you card after receiving a gift are all examples of good manners. **These small gestures make you memorable** and show that you are considerate of others and appreciate their efforts.

HOW TO REMEMBER A NAME

The chances are you know someone good at remembering names. They can meet someone new and recall their name days, weeks, or even years later. While some people are naturally good at this, remembering names is like any other skill—it can be learned and practiced.

How to Remember Names Easily

- When you meet someone, pay attention to their name and try to **repeat it in your head a few times.**

- Try to **use it in conversation** a few times.

- Try to associate the name with something that is meaningful to you. Linking the name with a **mental image or a story** to help you remember better.

- **Write the name down** as soon as you meet someone.

- You can also try using **mnemonic devices.** For example, if you meet someone named Karen, who works as a nurse, you could think of her as "care-in" Karen because she is always taking care of others.

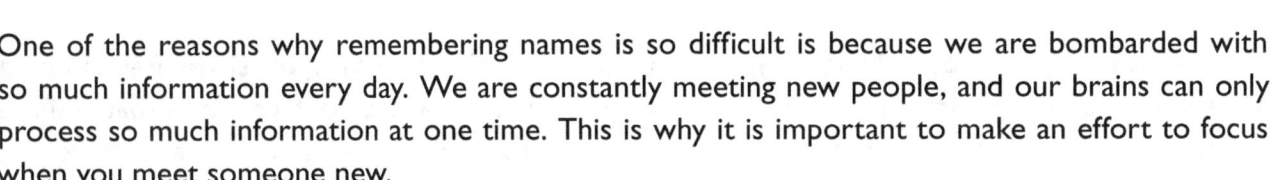

One of the reasons why remembering names is so difficult is because we are bombarded with so much information every day. We are constantly meeting new people, and our brains can only process so much information at one time. This is why it is important to make an effort to focus when you meet someone new.

When you meet someone, pay attention to their name and **try to repeat it in your head a few times**. It can also be helpful to repeat their name back to them or **use it in conversation** a few times. Try to **associate the name with something** meaningful to you and already imprinted in your brain. For example, if you meet someone named Harry, you could think of the story of Harry Potter. Linking the name with a mental image or a story will help you to remember it better.

Another tip for remembering names is to **write them down** as soon as you meet someone. This way, you will have a visual reminder of the person's name and can refer back to it if you forget.

You can also try using mnemonic devices, which are methods for remembering information that **links the information to something else** that is easier to remember. For example, if you meet someone named Karen, who works as a nurse, you could think of her as "care-in" Karen because she is always taking care of others.

Finally, don't get discouraged if you forget a name or two. It happens to everyone. Just apologize and move on. The important thing is to make an effort to remember the names of the people you meet.

Now that you've mastered first impressions and remembering names, it's time to move on to the next step—strengthening relationships.

STRENGTHENING RELATIONSHIPS

How to Listen Effectively

Listening is one of the most important skills you can develop, both personally and professionally. **Much of what you learn in life is through listening**. When you listen, you can gather information, understand other points of view, and build relationships.

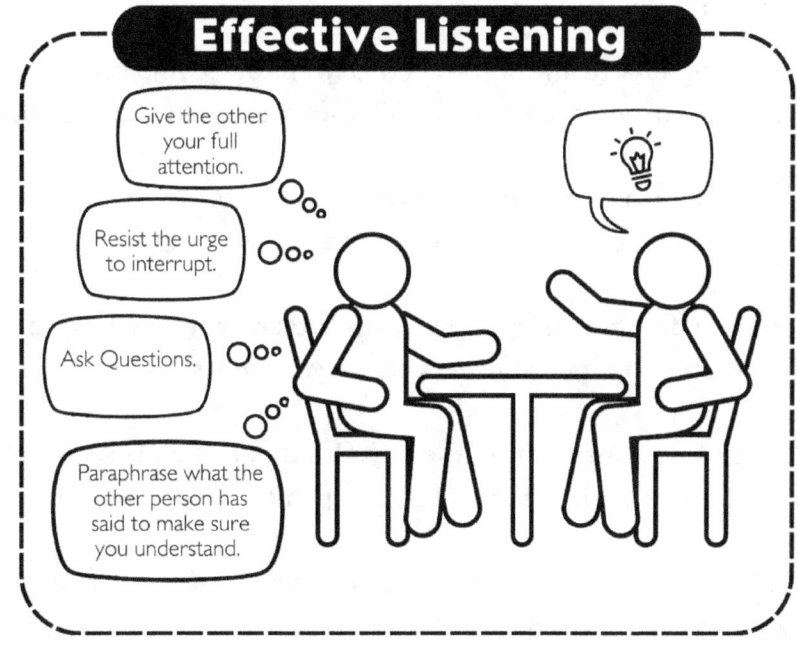

When you are listening to someone, it shows. You make eye contact, nod your head, and give them verbal cues that you are engaged in the conversation. You might even find yourself mirroring their body language.

Active listening can be difficult, especially if you are tired or distracted. However, it is important to make an effort to listen to what the other person is saying. This means not just hearing the words, but understanding the meaning behind them.

LIFE SKILLS FOR YOUNG ADULTS

There are a few things you can do to be a better listener. First, make sure that you **give the other person your full attention**. This means putting away your phone, making eye contact, and maintaining an open body position.

Second, try to **resist the urge to interrupt**. It can be tempting to jump in and share your own opinion, but it's important to let the other person finish what they're saying.

Third, **paraphrase what the other person has said** to make sure you understand. This involves repeating back what you have heard in your own words. For example, you could say, "So what you're saying is that you're feeling overwhelmed by your workload."

Finally, **ask questions**. This shows that you are interested in what the other person is saying and want to know more. Listen twice as much as you talk, and make sure to give the other person your full attention.

Now that you've learned the basics of communication, it's time to move on to the next skill—teamwork.

HOW TO WORK IN A TEAM

Working in a team can be a great way to accomplish more than you could on your own. It also allows you to share the load, delegate tasks, and build relationships.

However, teamwork doesn't always come naturally. It can be difficult to learn how to work effectively with others, especially if you are used to working alone.

You can do a few things to be a better team member. First, **be a good communicator**. This means being able to listen to others, share your ideas, and compromise when necessary.

Second, you need to **be able to take direction**. This doesn't mean that you have to do everything that your team leader says but be open to input from others.

Third, you need to **be able to work with different types of people**. This means understanding and respecting the differences in others, even if you don't always agree with them.

Fourth, **be flexible**. Things change all the time in a team environment, so you need to be able to adapt to new situations.

Finally, you need to **be able to work under pressure**. This means meeting deadlines, handling stress, and staying calm in difficult situations.

If you can master the art of teamwork, you'll be well on your way to success in any field.

HOW TO BUILD YOUR NETWORK

With the advent of social media, networking, and communication have become easier than ever before. However, there is still an art to building relationships and communicating effectively.

If you want **to build a strong network, it is important to be active and engaged**. This means participating in conversations, sharing your own experiences and thoughts, and being supportive of others. It is also important to be genuine and authentic in your interactions. People can see through phony behavior, and it is difficult to build trust with someone if you are not being real.

In addition to being active and engaged, it is also important to **be helpful**. When you are helpful, people are more likely to want to help you in return. Offer your expertise and advice freely, and be willing to **go out of your way to assist others**. Remember, what goes around comes around.

Keep a list of people you meet and their contact information. Follow up with people after you meet them, and stay in touch even if you don't have anything specific to say. Just a quick "thinking of you" message can go a long way in maintaining relationships. Sometimes **the personal touch of a handwritten note or a phone call can make all the difference**. And, don't forget the importance of **face-to-face communication**. In today's world, it is easy to rely on text messages, emails, and social media, but nothing can replace good old-fashioned human interaction.

Finally, **don't be afraid to ask for what you want**. If there is someone you would like to meet or something you would like to achieve, reach out and ask for assistance. The worst that can happen is that they say no.

Building a strong network takes time and effort, but it is worth it. A strong network will provide you with support, advice, and opportunities when you need them.

HOW TO WRITE A PROFESSIONAL EMAIL

Emails can be quite informal, which is great if you're contacting friends and family, but what about when you need to communicate with a potential employer or other professional? In these cases, try to make sure that your email is clear, concise, and free of any errors.

Here are a few tips for writing a professional email:

- **Use a clear and concise subject line**. This will help the recipient know what the email is about.

- **Keep it short and to the point**. No one wants to read long, rambling emails.

- **Use proper grammar and spelling**. This shows that you are taking the email seriously.

- **Appropriately address the recipient**. For example, if you're writing to David Kennedy, you would write "Dear Mr. Kennedy." If you don't know the person's name, it's fine to use "To whom it may concern" or "Dear sir/madam."

- **Avoid using abbreviations or slang**. Again, this is a formal communication, so you want to use proper language.

- **Use a professional sign-off and signature**. For example, "Sincerely" or "Best wishes" as your sign-off, and for your signature include your name, job title (if appropriate), and contact information.

By following these simple tips, you can make sure that your professional email makes the right impression.

HOW TO CELEBRATE FAMILY MEMBERS AND NEVER FORGET A BIRTHDAY

It can be difficult to keep track of all the important dates in your life, let alone remember to celebrate them. However, when you leave home it's important to show your loved ones how much you care, and one way to do that is by making sure you never forget a birthday.

Here are a few tips for celebrating family members and never forgetting a birthday:

- **Keep a calendar**. This will help you keep track of all the important dates in your life.

- **Set reminders**. Whether it's a reminder on your phone or a note in your planner, make sure you have some way to remind yourself of upcoming birthdays at least a week in advance.

- **Make a list**. Write down the birthdays of all your immediate family members and close friends in one place so you can refer to them when needed.
- **Get creative**. If you're struggling to come up with gift ideas, think outside the box. The personal touch of a homemade card or gift can go a long way.

By following these simple tips, you can make sure you never forget another important date again.

BUILDING FOUNDATIONS FOR HEALTHY RELATIONSHIPS

As young adults, we are often inundated with messages about what a "healthy" relationship looks like. Whether it's on social media, in magazines, or on TV, we are constantly bombarded with images and stories about perfect relationships.

But what does a healthy relationship look like?

There is no one-size-fits-all answer to this question, as every relationship is different. However, there are some key characteristics of healthy relationships that we can all strive for.

Some of the key characteristics of healthy relationships include:

- Mutual respect
- Trust
- Communication
- Support
- Equality

In a healthy relationship, **both partners should feel valued and respected**. There should be **trust between you**, and **you should both feel comfortable communicating** openly with each other. You should also feel supported by each other, and you should share equality in the relationship.

Of course, no relationship is perfect, and there will be times when things are not as smooth sailing as we would like them to be. But if you can work through these times together, and you still feel respected, valued, and equal in the relationship, then this is a good sign that you have a healthy relationship.

There are many different types of relationships, and no one type is better than another. What matters most is that you feel happy and safe in your relationship. If you are ever feeling unsafe or uncomfortable in a relationship, it's essential to reach out for help. Talk to a trusted friend or family member, or contact a service that offers support and advice.

No matter what type of relationship you are in, remember that **you deserve to be treated with respect and equality. We all have a right to a healthy and happy relationship**.

CHAPTER 8:

HOW TO MANAGE A HOME

As you begin to live on your own, you'll quickly realize that there's a lot more to managing a home than just cleaning and cooking. There are also repairs, maintenance, and learning to use household appliances. It can be a lot to handle, but don't worry—we're here to help. In this chapter, we'll give you some tips on how to manage your home so you can keep everything running smoothly.

HOW TO USE HOUSEHOLD APPLIANCES

HOW TO USE AN OVEN

Using an oven is pretty simple—you just set the temperature and timer and wait for your food to cook. However, there are a few things you should keep in mind to ensure that your food turns out perfectly.

- **Preheat the oven.** This is especially important if you're baking, as it helps the food cook evenly.

- **Read the recipe and get the right temperature** for your oven. Every recipe is different, so make sure you know what temperature you need to set your oven at.

- **Adjust your interchangeable oven racks**, depending on what the cooking instructions say. For example, if it says to cook the food on the top rack, then make sure you adjust your oven racks accordingly.

- **Know when to open the door.** Every time you open the door, heat escapes and it takes longer for the food to cook. So only open it when necessary.

- **Never leave food unattended.** This is a safety hazard and it's also a surefire way to ruin your food.

HOW TO USE A DISHWASHER

Dishwashers are a great way to get your dishes clean quickly and easily, but there are a few things you should keep in mind to ensure that they come out in good condition.

- **Read the manual.** The first thing you should do is read the manual for your dishwasher. This will tell you how to use it properly and how to maintain it.

- **Pre-wash your dishes.** You should always pre-wash your dishes before putting them in the dishwasher. This helps to remove any food particles that could clog the machine or end up on your dishes.

- **Load the dishwasher properly.** It's important to load the dishwasher properly so that your dishes come out clean. There are usually specific racks for different types of dishes.

- **Use the right detergent.** Make sure you use the right type of detergent for your dishwasher. Some dishwashers have specific types of detergents that they need to work properly.

- **Don't overload the machine.** As it could stop the spinner that distributes the water and cleaning fluid effectively.

- **Select a wash cycle.** Insert the dishwasher tablet or cream into the tablet compartment which is usually located on the inner part of the door, and then start the dishwasher. Usually, the eco cycle is good enough to clean your pots but familiarize yourself with your machine and choose the most appropriate cycle.

- **Care for your machine.** It's important to clean the dishwasher filter regularly. This helps to prevent a build-up of food particles and keeps your machine running smoothly. You should also add salt into the machine compartment every few months to help it run effectively.

HOW TO DO YOUR LAUNDRY

Doing your laundry is often seen as a rite of passage for young adults. Up until now, you might have relied on your parents or guardians to do this for you, but now it's time to learn how to do it yourself.

It's not always as simple as throwing your clothes in the washing machine and forgetting about them, though.

HOW TO USE A WASHING MACHINE

Using a washing machine is pretty straightforward—you just add your clothes, detergent, and water and set the machine to the right cycle. However, there are a few things you should keep in mind to ensure that your clothes come out clean and in good condition.

- **Read the care labels**. The care labels on your clothes will tell you what cycle to use and the maximum temperature the water should be. If clothes are heavily soiled, they will need a hotter wash, whereas if the clothes are reasonably clean, you could use a low-temperature or quick wash. The faster the wash and lower the temperature, the less energy you're using.

Wash	Do not wash / Hand wash only / Machine wash normal / Machine wash gentle / Wash at or below 30°C / Wash at or below 40°C / Wash at or below 50°C / Wash at or below 60°C / Wash at or below 70°C / Wash at or below 95°C
Iron	Iron any temp steam / Low temperature / Medium temperature / High temperature / Do not iron / Do not steam
Bleach	Do not bleach / Do not bleach / Bleach / Non-chlorine bleach
Dry	Tumble dry normal / Tumble dry low heat / Tumble dry medium heat / Tumble dry high heat / Do not tumble dry / Tumble dry no heat
Dry Clean	Do not wet clean / Any solvent / Petroleum solvent only / Any solvent except tetrachloroethylene / Wet cleaning / Dry clean / Do not wet clean / Reduce moisture / No steam / Low heat / Short cycle

- **Separate your clothes**. You should always separate your clothes by color and fabric type. This helps to prevent them from bleeding or getting damaged in the wash.

- **Add the detergent**. Make sure you add the right amount of detergent—too much and your clothes will be stiff and hard, too little and they won't be as clean as you want them to be.

LIFE SKILLS FOR YOUNG ADULTS

- **Don't overload the machine.** It's important to not overload the washing machine, as this can damage your clothes and the machine itself. As a rough guide: A small load will be a third of the drum, and a medium load will be half of the drum. A full load is when the drum is packed three-quarters full.

- **Choose the right cycle.** Different fabrics need different washing cycles, so make sure you use the correct one for your clothes. For example, if you're washing delicate items, you should use the delicate cycle.

- **Remove clothes after washing.** Once the washing cycle is done, it's important to remove your clothes from the machine as soon as possible. Leaving them in there for too long can cause them to start growing mold or mildew, and may make them smell.

Now you have clean clothes, let's look at the most effective ways to dry them.

HOW TO USE A TUMBLE DRYER

Tumble dryers are a great way to get your clothes dry quickly, but there are a few things you should keep in mind.

- **Read the care labels.** The care labels on your clothes will tell you if they can be tumble-dried or not. If they can, it will also tell you what cycle to use. Not all clothes can be tumble-dried, so check first, as this could make your clothes shrink, be damaged, or misshapen.

- **Spin your clothes before you put them in the tumble dryer.** The more water that's removed from your clothes before they go in the tumble dryer, the quicker they will dry.

- **Use the right cycle.** Different fabrics need different drying cycles, so make sure you use the correct one for your clothes. For example, if you're drying delicate items, you should use the delicate cycle.

- **Don't overload the machine.** It's important to not overload the tumble dryer, as this can damage your clothes and the machine itself.

- **Look after your dryer.** Depending on your dryer, you may need to clean the filter after each use. This helps to prevent a build-up of lint, which can be a fire hazard. You may also need to empty the water container that collects the water from your clothes.

Finally, you don't need to tumble dry all of your clothes. Some clothes, like jeans, can be hung up to dry. This will not only save you money on your electricity bill, but it will also help your clothes last longer.

HOW TO REMOVE STAINS

Stains are another important part of doing your laundry. You need to treat stains as soon as possible, otherwise they will set and be much harder to remove. There are all sorts of stain remover products on the market, but not everything works on every stain.

> Here are a few stain-removal tips:
>
> - **Use dish soap.** Dish soap is great for removing grease stains. Just apply some to the stain and scrub it with a brush or sponge. Soak the item before washing it as normal.
> - **Use toothpaste to remove grass stains.** That's right. If you have a grass stain, just apply some toothpaste to the area and scrub. Rinse it off and then wash it as normal.
> - **Make your stain remover for those difficult-to-remove stains.** Make a paste, using an equal part of white vinegar, to an equal part of baking soda, and apply it to the stain. Leave it for 10-15 minutes and then add to a bucket of water with detergent and two tablespoons of vinegar. Soak overnight and then wash as normal.
>
> **TOP TIP:** This homemade stain remover is also effective on carpet stains. Use a toothbrush or scrubbing brush to scrub the paste mixture into the stain, and then wash out with soap and water.

HOW TO CLEAN YOUR HOME

Keeping your home clean and tidy is an important skill. It is good for your health and wellbeing, and it will also make a good impression on guests.

Here are some simple tips that will help you keep your home clean:

- **Develop a cleaning routine and stick to it.** Having a set routine will help you to keep on top of the cleaning and ensure that nothing is missed. If you live in a shared house allocate specific tasks to each person every week. For example, one person could be responsible for hoovering, while another person is responsible for cleaning the kitchen.

- **Don't let the dirt and mess build up.** The more you leave it, the harder it will be to clean. Do a little bit every day and it will soon become part of your routine. This is particularly true for washing up. It's much quicker to wash up after each meal, rather than leaving it all until the end of the day.

- **Invest in good quality cleaning products.** Cheap cleaning products may be tempting, but they are often not as effective and don't last as long. It is worth spending a little bit extra on products that will do a better job.

- **Make your own cleaning products.** There are all sorts of recipes for cleaning products that you can make yourself, using things like vinegar, lemon juice, and bicarbonate of soda. Not only are these environmentally friendly, but they are also usually much cheaper than shop-bought products.

Cleaning your home doesn't have to be a chore. By following these simple tips, you can develop a routine that is quick and easy to follow.

How to Make Your Surface Cleaner

Making your surface cleaner is easy and much cheaper than buying shop-bought cleaners. You can make a simple surface cleaner using white vinegar, water, half a lemon, and essential oils.

To make a surface spray, you will need:

- A spray bottle
- 1 cup of white wine vinegar
- 15 drops of an essential oil (peppermint, orange, lemon, or lavender will work well)
- The juice of half a lemon
- 1 cup of water

Method:

Add the ingredients to the spray bottle and shake gently.

Use this cleaner to wipe down surfaces in your home. It is particularly effective at removing grease and grime.

How to Make Your Window Cleaner

Window cleaners can be expensive, but you can easily make your own using vinegar and water.

Mix 1 part white vinegar with 2 parts water in a spray bottle. Spray onto windows and wipe clean with a cloth.

You can also add a few drops of essential oil to your window cleaner to give it a nice scent.

HOW TO CHANGE YOUR BEDDING

You spend around eight hours a day in bed, and though you may not know it or see it, your bedding can harbor all sorts of bacteria. That's why it's important to change your sheets and pillowcases regularly every 1–2 weeks.

Here's how to do it:

1. Remove all of the old bedding from the bed, including the sheets, duvet cover, and pillowcases.
2. Wash all of the bedding following the care instructions. Generally, bedding should go on a hotter wash to kill any bacteria.
3. Once the bedding is clean, put it back on the bed, starting with the bottom sheet.
4. Turn your duvet cover inside out and put each top corner on the corner of your quilt or duvet, then turn the duvet cover the right way, over the quilt or duvet cover. You may need to keep a tight hold of the corners while doing this, and then once you have it in place, simply hold the corners and give the cover a firm shake.
5. Put your pillows back in their pillowcases and plump them up.

Your bed is now fresh and clean, and ready for a good night's sleep! Finally, it's a good habit to get into making your bed each day... no matter how bad your day has been, coming home to a made bed can make all the difference.

HOW TO UNCLOG A SINK

Sometimes, your sink may get clogged, and this means it's unable to drain effectively. There are some things you can do to fix this yourself, which means you will not have to pay for a plumber.

- First, you should try to use boiling water.
- Pour around half a gallon of boiling water directly into the drain.
- Let it sit for a few minutes to see if this does the trick.
- If not, you can try using a plunger.

Place the plunger over the drain and make sure there is enough water in the sink to cover the rubber part of the plunger. Push and pull the plunger up and down vigorously for around 30 seconds. When you remove the plunger, see if the water drains quickly, and if not, repeat the process.

There are powerful chemical drain cleaners available if you are still having issues, but you could also make your own with a mix of vinegar and baking soda. Simply remove any water from the drain and pour in one cup of baking soda, followed by one cup of white vinegar. Cover the drain and leave the mixture for 15 minutes. Next, remove the stop and run the hot tap or use the boiling water to break up the clog.

HOW TO UNCLOG A TOILET

If your toilet is clogged, don't panic! There are a few things you can do to try and fix it yourself before having to call a plumber.

The most effective way to unclog a toilet is to **use a plunger**.

- Simply insert this into the toilet bowl and cover the hole at the bottom, so the plunger is fully submerged.
- Slowly, pump the plunger up and down over the hole, and then build up the speed until you are pumping vigorously.
- To check if the toilet is unblocked, simply flush.
- Repeat as necessary until the blockage is cleared.

> **How to Make Your Drain Cleaner**
>
> There are some drain cleaners you can buy for your toilet too, but you can also make your own. Wear rubber gloves, then add 1 cup of baking soda and 2 cups of vinegar to the toilet. The mixture will fizz. Pour half a gallon of hot water into the pot—it's best to pour this from your waist level as the force can help unclog the blockage. Make sure the water isn't boiling as this can crack the toilet. Leave the mixture overnight if possible, and then flush the next day.

BASIC SEWING

If an item of clothing needs stitching or fixing, it can be expensive. Sometimes it's best to try to mend it yourself. Hand sewing is fast and easy, so it's worth giving it a try.

You will need a basic sewing kit of threads (in different colors, especially black and white), scissors, and at least one sewing needle.

HOW TO SEW ON A BUTTON

You will need:

- Thread
- A needle
- A button

Method:

1. **Thread your needle and knot the end.**
2. **Push the needle up through the fabric from the back,** making sure to come up through one of the holes in the button.
3. **Push the needle down through the other hole in the button.**
4. **Repeat steps 2 and 3** a few times to secure the button in place.
5. When you're happy that the button is secure, **knot the thread on the back** of the fabric and snip off the excess.

There you have it! You've now successfully sewn a button onto an item of clothing.

HOW TO MEND A HOLE IN FABRIC

You will need:

- Thread
- A needle
- A piece of fabric or patch (optional)

Method:

1. **Unravel your cotton thread from the spool**—you should choose the thread that is closest to the color of the fabric you are stitching. When you've unraveled enough, cut the thread from the spool.

2. If you're using a patch, **place it over the hole** so that the good side of the fabric is facing out.

3. **Thread your needle and knot the end.** To do this Thread the cotton through the eye of the needle (the loop at the top of a sewing needle). Tie the ends of the thread in a knot at the bottom a couple of times, to ensure it's secure. Now you're ready to stitch.

4. **Start sewing at the edge of the hole**, making small stitches close together. To do this, push the needle up through the fabric from the back (wrong side). Push the needle down through the other side.

5. **Repeat steps 2 and 3** around the entire edge of the hole.

6. When you're happy that the patch or hole is secure, **sew back and forth in the same place a couple of times**, and then knot the thread on the back of the fabric and snip off the excess.

There you have it! You've now successfully mended a hole in the fabric.

CHAPTER 9:

ORGANIZATION & TIME MANAGEMENT

Being organized can save you time, money, and a lot of stress. On a practical level, it can also make your space look neater and more inviting. When we are disorganized, it can lead to lost items, late fees, and a general feeling of being overwhelmed. **Developing good organization skills,** managing your time effectively, and prioritizing your tasks are key to leading a productive and stress-free life.

START WITH A CLEAN BEDROOM

When you first leave home, your bedroom may double as your living room, home office, and even dining room. Try to keep it clean and organized to be a sanctuary for you—a place where you can relax and unwind after a long day.

1. **Create designated spaces.** If your bedroom is a dumping ground for all of your stuff, it's time to change that. Create designated spaces for different items—a place for your clothes, a place for your school things and books, etc. This will help you to keep things organized and tidy.

2. **Create a workspace.** If you don't have a designated workspace in your bedroom, it's time to create one. It could be a desk or table, but this will be where you can do your homework, work on projects, etc. Try to avoid using it for other tasks, such as eating or watching TV. Your workspace should be uncluttered and clear of any distractions to help you to stay focused and organized.

3. **Get rid of the clutter.** Take a good look around your room and get rid of anything you don't need or use. This will clear up some space and make it easier to keep things tidy.

4. **Invest in some storage solutions**. If you don't have enough closet space, consider buying a dresser or some shelving to store your things. This will help you to keep your things organized and off the floor.

5. **Make your bed every day.** Taking a few minutes each day to make your bed will go a long way in making your room look neat.

6. **Do a "10-minute tidy" every night.** Before you go to bed, take 10 minutes to pick up any clutter that may have accumulated during the day.

7. **Prepare for tomorrow today**. Get your clothes and school supplies ready for the next day before you go to bed. This will help you avoid scrambling in the morning and make it easier to get out the door on time.

HOW TO CREATE A PRODUCTIVE WORKSPACE

Creating a productive workspace is essential if you want to be able to focus on your studies and get work done. It doesn't have to be big or elaborate—**just a simple, uncluttered space where you can sit down and concentrate on your task**. You may have a dedicated room that you can use as your workspace, or you may have to create a space in your bedroom. Either way, there are a few things you can do to make sure it's conducive to productivity.

Firstly, it's a good idea to **pick somewhere solely for work**—a place where you can sit down and focus without any distractions. This means that you should **avoid using your bed or sofa** as a workspace, as it's too easy to get comfortable and fall asleep! If you don't have a dedicated room for your workspace, try to create a space that is separate from the rest of your bedroom so that you can mentally 'switch off' when you're finished working for the day, and 'switch on' when it's time to study.

It's also important to **make sure your workspace is well-lit**. Natural light is always best, so try to position your desk near a window if possible. If you don't have access to natural light, make sure you have a good-quality lamp to light up your work area.

Make your workspace comfortable. This means having a comfy chair and a suitable desk or table at the correct height. The likelihood is you will be at your desk for long periods, so **make sure you're comfortable to avoid any strain on your back or neck.** Your computer should be at eye level, and your arms should be at a 90-degree angle when you're typing. You may find that a standing desk is more comfortable for you, or that you prefer to work in short bursts with regular breaks—there is no 'correct' way to do it, so find what works best for you.

Finally, your workspace should also **be uncluttered and organized**. This means having a place for everything and keeping your desk tidy. A messy desk can be a distraction, and make it harder for you to focus on your work. Invest in some storage solutions, such as baskets or boxes, to help you keep things tidy. And try to avoid working from your bed, as this can make it harder to focus and be productive.

ORGANIZING AND STORING DOCUMENTS

As you get older, you'll acquire a lot of paperwork and documents, such as school records, medical records, tax documents, bills, etc. Try to keep these organized so that you can easily find them when you need them. The best way to do this is to **create a filing system**.

You can either buy a pre-made filing system or create your own using labels and folders. Start by creating a main folder for each document category (e.g. school, medical, tax, etc.) Then, create sub-folders for each document within that category. For example, you might have a 'school' folder with sub-folders by subject or topic.

Label your folders clearly so that you can easily find what you're looking for. Date each document and file by date, so your most recent documents are at the top. Try to keep on top of it by **regularly sorting files** and purging any outdated or unnecessary documents.

Filing digital documents is much the same as filing physical documents. Start by creating folders for each category of document, then sub-folders for each document within that category. **Date your documents so that you can easily find what you're looking for**. For example, you might have a folder on your computer called 'Medical Records' with sub-folders for ' immunization records', 'doctor visits', and 'prescriptions'. A document within 'immunization records' might be labeled 'MMR immunization—date'.

You can also use online storage services, such as Google Drive or Dropbox, to store and organize your documents. These services allow you to access your files from any device with an internet connection, which can be handy if you need to retrieve a document while you're on the go. Remember to **back up your files regularly** in case of a technical malfunction or power outage.

BACKING UP FILES

No matter how organized and well-maintained your computer is, things can always go wrong. Hard drives can crash, power outages can happen, and accidental deletions are not uncommon. That's why it's important to regularly back up your files.

Backing up your files means making copies of them and storing them in a safe place, such as an external hard drive or a cloud-based storage service. If something happens to your computer, you can rest assured knowing that you have a backup of all your files.

There are a few different ways to go about backing up your files. **You can do it manually**, which means making copies of your files and storing them in a safe place regularly. Or **you can use automatic backup software**, which will make copies of your files and store them in a safe place without you having to do anything. Some operating systems, such as Windows and macOS, even come with their built-in backup software.

No matter which method you choose, the important thing is to make sure that your backup files are stored safely, such as an external hard drive or a cloud-based storage service. And remember to check that your backup files are up-to-date.

TIME MANAGEMENT

One of the most essential life skills that every young adult should learn is time management. Time management is all about **using your time wisely** to get the most out of each day. It's a skill that can be learned and practiced, and it will come in handy both in college and in the working world.

MANAGING STUDY AND WORK

When you are studying or working, it's vital to manage your time wisely. To manage this effectively, you should make full use of your diary. **Use your diary to mark down deadlines, upcoming events, and any other important dates**. This will help you stay on top of things and make sure that you don't miss anything important.

You should also **break down big tasks into smaller**, more manageable chunks. For example, if you have a project due in two weeks, break the project down into smaller tasks that you can complete each day. This will make the project seem less daunting and will help you prioritize your time effectively.

Make a plan and stick to it, and while it's easy to take things on, **be careful that you don't take on too much**. Many people find the 'working backward' technique useful for managing their time. This involves starting with the end goal in mind and working backward to figure out what steps you need to take to achieve it. For example, if your goal is to finish a project by the end of the week, **start by figuring out what tasks need to be completed** each day to reach that goal.

Finally, **schedule some free time into your day**. This may seem like a waste of time, but it's crucial for your mental and physical health. Make sure to schedule some time each day to relax and do something that you enjoy. This could be anything from reading a book to going for a walk. The important thing is to find time each day to unwind and recharge.

HOW TO PRIORITIZE EFFECTIVELY

It can be difficult to prioritize, as you are ultimately deciding between one task and another. However, some general tips can help you when it comes to prioritizing.

Make a list of all your tasks. Identify which of the tasks are urgent and time-sensitive. Then identify the important tasks that are not necessarily urgent, but still important to do. Once you have identified the urgent and important tasks, you can start to prioritize them.

Some people find it helpful to **use a priority matrix** when figuring out which tasks to prioritize. This is a visual way of representing the urgency and importance of each task. The tasks are placed into one of four quadrants, based on their urgency and importance.

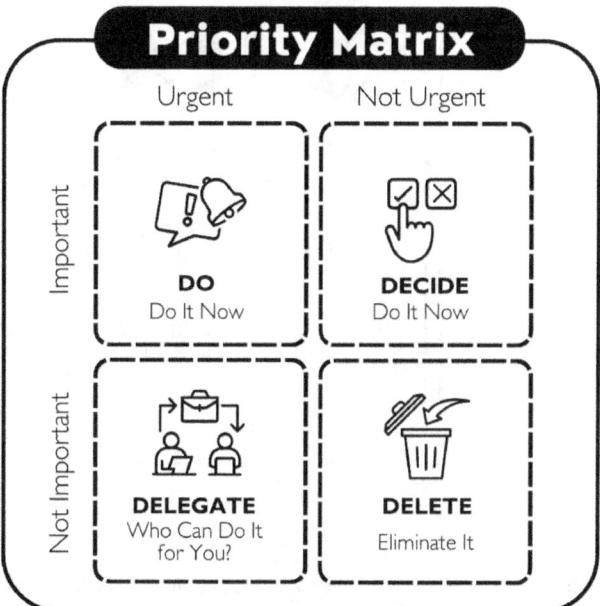

- The **first quadrant** is for tasks that are **both urgent and important**. These are the tasks that you should prioritize first.

- The **second quadrant** is for tasks that are **important but not urgent**. These are the tasks that you should schedule in your diary or to-do list.

- The **third quadrant** is for tasks that are **urgent but not important**. These are the tasks that you should delegate to someone else.

- The **fourth quadrant** is for tasks that are **neither urgent nor important**. These are the tasks that you can eliminate from your to-do list altogether.

Once you have prioritized your tasks, it's important to stick to your plan. Don't let other tasks that come up distract you from the task at hand. It can be challenging to stay focused, but if you can maintain your focus, you will be able to accomplish your goals more efficiently.

GOAL SETTING

When setting goals, you should always think first about the result. What is it you want to achieve? What are you aiming for? When do you want to hit your goal? It's helpful to be invested in the goal, so ensure it's something you want—if it's not, it's unlikely you will be willing to put the time and effort into achieving it.

Once you have a goal in mind, you need to ensure it's SMART. This means it must be Specific, Measurable, Attainable, Relevant and Time-bound.

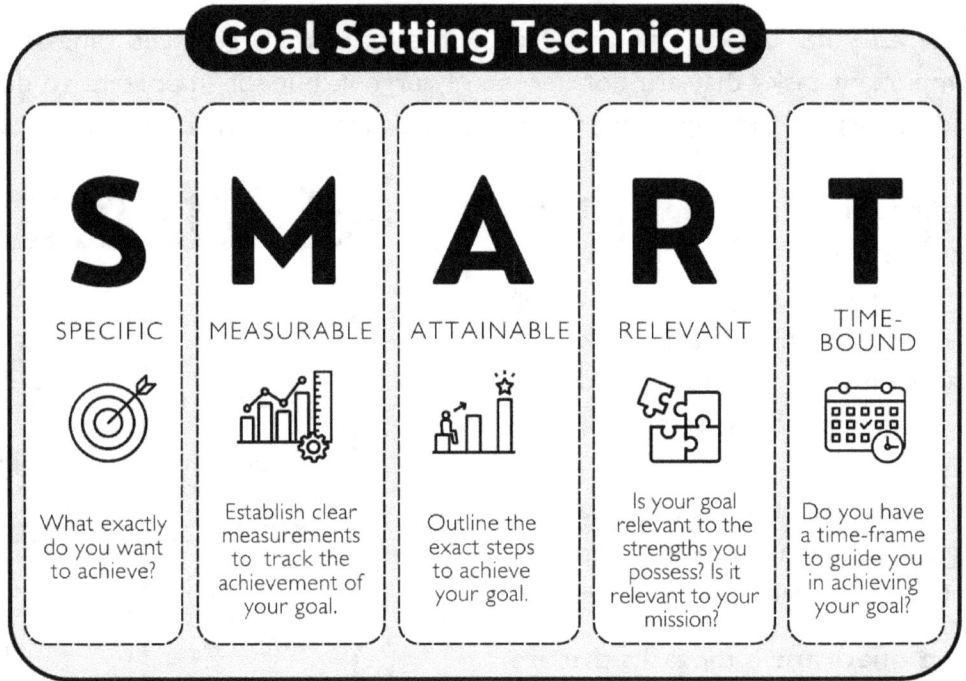

For example, if your goal is to complete a history assignment that is due in four weeks, your stated goal might be:

'I will complete my history assignment by reading one chapter of my textbook each day.'

In the above example, the goal is specific (reading one chapter of the textbook), measurable (I will mark each day off in my calendar as I complete it), attainable (I can realistically read one chapter per day), realistic (I have four weeks to complete the assignment) and time-bound (my assignment is due in four weeks).

Now it's time to break your goals down. You can do this by asking yourself several questions as you start at your end goal, and work backward.

For example, if your goal is to complete an assignment in four weeks, you might ask yourself the following:

- How many pages do I need to read each day?
- What steps must be completed before I start reading?
- When will I complete my research and outline?

By answering these questions, you'll have a better understanding of what needs to be done to complete your goal.

By breaking your goals down into smaller, more achievable steps and ensuring that they are SMART, you can set yourself up for success and effectively manage your time. With the right approach, anyone can learn to effectively manage their time and make the most of each day.

CHAPTER 10:

PROBLEM-SOLVING & DECISION-MAKING SKILLS

Every day we face a multitude of decisions, big and small. Some of these decisions are easy to make, while others may be more difficult. The same goes for problem-solving. Some problems are easy to solve, while others may be more challenging.

Problem-solving and decision-making are closely linked. Problems often present us with a dilemma, and we must use our decision-making skills to choose the best course of action.

In this chapter, we're going to take a look at some of the skills that you need to make decisions and solve problems effectively.

PROBLEM-SOLVING SKILLS

Problems are a part of everyday life and rather than ignoring them, it's best to tackle them head-on before they escalate. They can be small, like trying to figure out what to wear to your friend's party, or they can be big, like trying to decide which college to attend.

No matter the size of the problem there is a process that you can follow to help you solve it. This process is

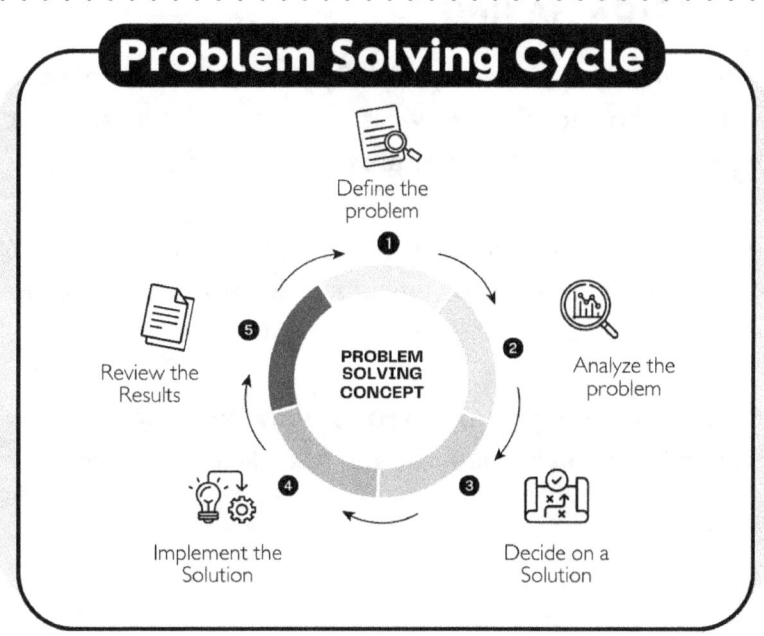

known as the **'problem-solving cycle.'** This is a skill you can carry with you in everything you do. It will help you in your career, your personal life, and your studies.

- **The first step in the problem-solving cycle is to define the problem**. This may seem like an obvious first step, but take the time to determine what the problem is. Once you have identified the problem, you can start to brainstorm possible solutions.

- **The second step is to analyze the problem and evaluate the possible solutions**. Once you have generated a list of possible solutions, it's time to evaluate them. Consider the pros and cons of each solution. What are the risks and potential benefits of each solution?

- **The third step is to choose the best solution**. After evaluating the possible solutions, it's time to choose the one that you think is best.

- **The fourth step is to implement the solution**. Once you have chosen the best solution, it's time to put it into action. This may involve steps such as buying the supplies you need or telling your friends and family about your decision.

- **The final step is to review the results**. How did you do? What would you do differently next time? Making mistakes is all part of the process; try to look back objectively at what you have done and how you might change things next time around.

It's important to remember that not all problems can be solved. And sometimes, the best solution is to do nothing at all.

DECISION MAKING

We make decisions every day, big and small. Some of these decisions are easy to make and require little or no thought, like what to eat for breakfast. Other decisions may be more complex, and require us to weigh up the pros and cons of each option.

Making big decisions can feel like a huge responsibility. You may feel anxious, stressed, and even unsure of yourself. But remember, decisions are empowering. They allow you to take control of your life and create the future that you want.

There is no 'right' or 'wrong' way to make a decision. But there are some steps that you can follow to help you make the best decision for you.

- When faced with difficult decisions, the first step is to **take some time to think about what you want**. What are your goals and values? What is important to you? Once you have a good understanding of what you want, you can start to consider your options.

- The next step is to **gather information about your options**. This may involve researching or talking to people with expertise in the area. Consider the 'What Ifs'. What if you make this decision? What are the risks and potential benefits? What if you don't make this decision? You might find it useful to write a list of the pros and cons of each option. Often by writing down our thoughts and feelings, we can start to see the situation more clearly.

- The third step is to **make a decision**. Once you have gathered all the information you need, it's time to decide. Trust your gut and go with your instincts. But also be prepared to change your mind if new information comes to light.

- And finally, once you have made your decision, **it's time to take action**. This may involve steps such as buying the supplies you need or telling your friends and family about your decision.

Remember, making decisions is empowering. It allows you to take control of your life and create the future that you want. So next time you're faced with a difficult decision, don't be afraid to trust your gut and go for it!

BETTER DECISION MAKING

Better decision-making comes from experience. The more you practice making decisions, the better you will become at it. Equally knowing yourself and what is important to you will also help you make better decisions.

- Firstly, **consider your characteristics and personality type**. Are you an impulsive person or do you like to take your time? Do you like to take risks or play it safe? Knowing your personal preferences can help you understand how you might approach making a decision.

- Secondly, **think about the situation you are in and what is important to you** at that moment. What are your goals and values? What do you want to achieve? Understanding what is important to you will help you make better decisions.

- Thirdly, **slow down and take your time**: When you are faced with a difficult decision, it can be tempting to just go with your first instinct. But it's important to slow down and take the time to think about your options. Don't be pressured or rushed into making a decision.

- Finally, **don't be afraid to make mistake**s—we all do! Just learn from them and keep going.

Making decisions is a normal part of life. The more you practice, the better you will become at it. And by understanding yourself and what is important to you, you can make better decisions for yourself.

HOW TO SAY NO

In our fast-paced, constantly connected world, it's easy to overcommit and take on more than we can handle. So learning to say no, is a crucial skill every young person should learn.

Saying no can be difficult, especially if we don't want to disappoint other people. But it's important to remember that we can't do everything and that **it's okay to say no**. If there's something you don't want to do or something that you cannot do, then the best thing to do is to be honest and just say no. Don't prolong the situation, just say the word.

Saying no is not always easy, but it is an important life skill to learn. It can help you manage your time and commitments, and it can also help you set boundaries with other people. You may find yourself in situations where you feel under pressure to say yes. But it's important to remember that you have a right to say no. Even with friends and family, **you don't owe anyone anything**. It's OK to say no.

By being polite, and honest and offering alternatives, you can say no in a way that is respectful and helpful. Like all life skills, it takes practice, but with time and patience, you will get better at it.

> **Here are some tips for how to say no:**
> - **Be polite, but firm in your decision.** "I'm sorry, but I can't help you with that." Showing people that when you make a decision, you stick to it will help them respect your choices. Whilst they may be disappointed, they will understand that you have made up your mind.
> - **Be honest and explain your reasons for saying no.** "I'm sorry but I'm just not comfortable doing that." This can help the other person to understand where you are coming from and why you have made this decision.
> - **Offer an alternative solution.** "I can't do that, but maybe I can do this instead." If there is another way that you can help, let the person know. This shows that you are still willing to help, but in a way that works better for you.

CHAPTER 11:

KICKSTARTING YOUR CAREER

So, you've finished school or college and you're ready to take on the world. Congratulations! **The next step is to find a job that you love.** But with the job market being so competitive, it can be difficult to know where to start.

The one thing to remember is that if you persevere, you will get your opportunity, so don't give up!

> **Perseverance is failing 19 times and succeeding the 20th.**
>
> JULIE ANDREWS,
> ACTRESS

JOB HUNTING

Before you start job hunting, take some time to **figure out what you want to do**. What are your skills and interests? What type of work environment do you want to be in? Once you understand what you want, you can start looking for jobs that match your criteria.

There are many different ways to look for jobs. You can search online job boards, browse company websites, or go old-school and look through the classifieds section in your local newspaper or the windows of retail or hospitality establishments that state they are hiring.

Another great way to find jobs is by **networking**. Talk to your friends, family, and acquaintances and let them know that you are looking for work. They may know of someone who is hiring, or they may be able to put in a good word for you.

It's also a good idea to **attend job fairs and industry events**. This is a great way to meet potential employers and learn about different companies that are recruiting.

Another possibility, if you have a skill or an idea, is to become an entrepreneur by starting your own business. This can be a great option if you are creative and motivated.

Once you have found a few potential jobs that you are interested in, the next step is to apply for them.

APPLYING FOR A JOB

When you apply for a job, you will usually need to submit a resume and a cover letter. This is your chance to sell yourself to the employer and explain why you are the best person for the job.

CV OR RESUME

A resume is a document that outlines your skills, experience, and qualifications. It is important to tailor your resume to each job that you apply for, as this will show the employer that you have the relevant skills and experience for the role.

Your resume should be clear and concise, and it should highlight your skills, qualifications, and experience. If you have little or no work experience, don't worry, you can include any relevant volunteer work, internships, or extracurricular activities that you have participated in.

HOW TO WRITE A RESUME THAT CONVERTS

When writing a resume, make sure to:

- Summarise your key skills, qualities, and job titles. For example, if you worked in a café, you could introduce yourself as:

    A highly skilled, motivated, and reliable food service assistant, with excellent customer service skills and cash handling experience.

- Start with your **most recent job or experience and work backward**. Ensuring you include key details such as your job title, dates of employment, duties, and responsibilities.

- **Highlight your skills, qualities, and accomplishments**, ensuring you use keywords relevant to the job you are applying for. For example, if you are applying for a job as a barista, make sure to mention your experience making coffee and using different coffee machines.

- **Include transferable or soft skills** that may be relevant to the job you are applying for. For example, if you are applying for a customer service role, highlight your excellent communication and interpersonal skills.

- **Use simple language and action words** such as 'achieved', 'created', 'managed', or 'developed.'

- **Use clear formatting and include bullet points** rather than paragraphs so that it is easy to read.

- **Check your grammar and spelling.** Remember the person reading your resume is likely to spend less than 30 seconds looking at it before they decide to put it down or keep reading.

- Make it interesting and memorable, but you should **NEVER lie on your CV/resume**, or any other job application you make, as you will be found out. Employers carry out checks on identity, references, qualifications, and previous jobs or experience. It's not worth it—just be yourself, it's enough!

YOUR COVER LETTER

A cover letter is a document that accompanies your resume when you apply for a job. It is an opportunity to introduce yourself to the employer and explain why you are interested in the role and why you would be the best person for the job. Your cover letter should follow a simple format and **should be 1 page** in length.

Remember, this is a letter, so you should include your address and contact number on the right-hand side at the top, and the addressee's information on the left, just below yours.

Address the person you are writing to by name or 'Dear sir/madam,'. Just below this greeting, you should introduce yourself and the role you are applying for. 'Please find my application enclosed for the position of X'.

The body of the letter should **outline your relevant skills and experience**, highlighting how they make you the ideal candidate for the job. For example, if you are applying for an office role, you could mention your experience working in a fast-paced environment and your ability to juggle multiple tasks simultaneously.

Use specific examples to back up your claims. For example, if you are claiming to be an excellent communicator, you could mention a time when you had to diffuse a difficult customer service situation.

Once you have outlined your relevant skills and experience, **finish with a strong conclusion**, thanking the employer for their time and expressing your interest in meeting with them to discuss the role further.

If you are mailing your application, **print your resume and cover letter on high-quality paper** and send them to the person or organization directly. To email your application, include your resume and cover letter as attachments and address the email to the relevant contact person. In the email body, explain who you are and why you are interested in the role.

INTERVIEW TIPS FOR BEGINNERS

Congratulations, you've got to the next stage. The company liked your resume and cover letter and has asked you to come in for an interview. Here are some tips on how to make a great impression and ace the interview.

PREPARING FOR YOUR INTERVIEW

> **Failing to prepare is preparing to fail.**
>
> BENJAMIN GRAHAM,
> ECONOMIST, PROFESSOR & INVESTOR

Before the interview, there are several things you can do to ensure you are prepared.

- First, **research the company.** Have a look at their website and social media platforms to get an idea of their culture, values, and what they do. If you can talk intelligently about the company you are more likely to make a good impression and stand out from the crowd.

- Second, **research the role you are applying for.** This will help you understand what the company is looking for in a candidate and give you a better idea of how to sell yourself for the role.

- Third, **practice your answers to common interview questions**. This will help you to feel more confident on the day and give you a better chance of impressing the interviewer.

> **Some common interview questions are:**
> - What are your strengths?
> - What are your weaknesses?
> - Why are you interested in this role?
> - What experience do you have in this field?
> - Where do you see yourself in five years?
> - How do you think you'd fit in with the core values and company mission?

- **Practice your interview answers** with someone you know and ask them for some feedback. Try to be as specific as possible and use examples to back up your claims.

- Finally, **prepare some questions to ask at the end of the interview**. Think about what you would like to know about the job or the company. You could ask about development or promotional opportunities, or you could ask questions about the company's values and mission. This again shows that you are interested in the role and company, and helps you stand out from other candidates.

HOW TO NAIL YOUR INTERVIEW

It's interview day! Here are some final tips to help you make a great impression and ace the interview.

- **First, dress for success**. Make sure you are dressed appropriately for the role you are applying for. How formal is up to you but it's always better to be overdressed than underdressed.

- **Second, arrive 10 to 15 minutes early**. This will allow you to collect your thoughts and relax before the interview starts. Take a drink of water with you and make a note of the person's name you're meeting so you can ask for them and greet them personally.

- **Third, turn off your phone and leave it in your bag**. You don't want to be distracted by notifications during the interview.

- **Fourth, be confident, and positive and try to relax**. Greet the interviewer confidently, make eye contact, and remember to smile during the interview. You have nothing to fear. Maintain a positive attitude throughout, demonstrating a 'whatever it takes' attitude. When giving examples, always show your commitment!

LIFE SKILLS FOR YOUNG ADULTS

- **Finally, listen carefully, answer the questions honestly, and be yourself.** Keep your answers brief and use the preparation you did beforehand to guide you. The interviewer is looking for a genuine person who they can trust, so be honest, and sincere and let your personality shine through.

After the interview, it's a good idea to **send a thank-you note to the interviewer**. This shows that you are interested in the role and company and helps you to stand out from other candidates.

HOW TO GET PROMOTED FAST!

Congratulations, you got the job! Now the fun starts—it's time to start thinking about how to get promoted.

Getting promoted fast is all about getting noticed by your superiors and proving that you are an asset to the company.

Here are some tips to help you get promoted fast:

- **Learn your job quickly and do it well**. This sounds obvious, but it's important to focus on doing your best work every day. This will help you stand out from other employees and show that you are dedicated to your job.

- **Learn about the organization and the industry**. This will help you to understand how the company works and what is important to them. It will also give you a better idea of how you can contribute to the company's success.

- **Be proactive**, and take on additional responsibilities. This will show that you are willing to go above and beyond your job description and that you are capable of handling more responsibility. Take on new projects that challenge you and embrace changes—be a leader at learning new things and paving the way.

- **Develop a 'can-do' attitude**. Don't be put off if something looks difficult, **do it anyway** and if there's a problem, let your problem-solving skills shine!

- **Ask your boss for clear expectations**. Keep performing to the best of your ability and make your career ambitions known to your boss. Make the most of your supervision and performance reviews, by gaining feedback from your boss and expressing your wishes for new opportunities (such as training or work shadowing).

- **Show you're a leader** by acting as a leader and being heard! While it's important to be a team player, show you're a leader. Dress like a leader and lead whenever possible. When it comes to meeting targets and deadlines, rise to the occasion and encourage others in your team. At team meetings, always engage and contribute. Be innovative by trying new things, discussing new ideas, and encouraging others within your team to do the same.

- **Make your growth opportunities**, don't wait for others. You could take on new tasks or embrace online training in specific topics that will complement your current role. For example, if you're interested in becoming a team leader, look for learning opportunities in team leading.

- Always **take the initiative** and make it easy. Don't make things difficult. Take tricky situations and simplify them, then teach others how to do it too. For example, sometimes processes within a workplace are made more difficult than they should be, so if you know a better way, share it, model it, and teach it.

- Don't be afraid to **ask for a promotion**. If you've been working hard and there's no chance of any opportunities, then look for employment elsewhere.

While these tips don't guarantee a promotion, you can increase your chances of being noticed and achieving success in your career by building the right attitude and mindset.

So, what are you waiting for? Get started today and work towards your next promotion!

SELF-IMPROVEMENT AND EDUCATION

Self-improvement is a journey, not a destination. It's something you should be constantly striving for, regardless of where you are in life. Whether you're just starting in your career or you're a seasoned professional, there is always room for improvement.

SELF-IMPROVEMENT

Self-improvement takes many forms. It could be learning new skills, increasing your knowledge, or developing new attitudes and mindsets. Whatever form it takes, self-improvement is essential for furthering your career and achieving success.

One of the best ways to **improve yourself is through education**. You can make yourself more valuable to your organization and position yourself for future success by increasing your knowledge. There are many ways to educate yourself, including taking courses, attending seminars, and reading books and articles.

Educating yourself is all about adding to your toolbox of skills and knowledge so that you can be more effective in your job, career, and personal life. It's about taking the time to invest in yourself so that you can reap the rewards down the road.

By educating yourself you get to decide the direction of your life. You get to control your destiny. Set yourself some goals, surround yourself with people who will support your dreams, and never stop learning. Your career and personal life will thank you for it!

> The best teacher in life is experience.
>
> LEBRON JAMES,
> BASKETBALL PLAYER

And finally, while you can educate yourself in many ways, one way you can't is by taking life experience. This is something that comes with age and maturity. The best way to gain life experience is simply by living life and making mistakes. It's all part of the journey!

So don't wait, start your journey today! Good luck!

MONEY SKILLS FOR TEENS

A Beginner's Guide to Budgeting, Saving, and Investing

Everything a Teenager Should Know About Personal Finance

FERNE BOWE

INTRODUCTION

Congratulations! You're a teen, and the world is yours for the taking!

It's an exciting time, but it can also be daunting. With so much to learn and so many new experiences, it's easy to feel overwhelmed. But that's ok. It's perfectly normal to feel overwhelmed by the responsibility of growing up.

That's where this book comes in. To help you with one of the biggest responsibilities and challenges every young adult has to face: Money.

This book is here to help you understand the concept of money, what it is, how to earn and save it—and how to spend it wisely.

We'll cover all the basics, like how to open bank accounts, avoid scams, understand credit scores, budget wisely, and avoid debt. And we'll dig into more complex topics like how to get a mortgage, lease a car, and invest in the stock market.

We'll explain the facts and use real-life examples that make money matters easy to understand. Throughout the pages, you'll find valuable tips and tricks, interesting stats, and even some fun activities to put your knowledge into practice.

By the end of this book, you'll have all the financial knowledge you need to feel confident in navigating the world of money. Including:

- How to select and open a bank account
- An understanding of credit cards and how to establish a good credit score
- How to create a budgeting plan
- How to develop money-saving habits
- How to start investing in the stock market

And much more!

This book is designed to be your go-to guide for your financial journey into adulthood. To give you the solid foundations of money skills, knowledge, and experiences to help you make wise financial decisions throughout your life.

HOW TO USE THIS BOOK

This book is divided into five parts:

- Understanding Money
- Budgeting & Savvy Spending
- Borrowing, Debt, and Big Ticket Item Purchases
- Your Way to Wealth
- The Future of Money

Going through each, one by one will give you a good understanding of the world of money. You'll start with the basics and build your knowledge as you progress through the book. Feel free to jump around if there's something specific that interests you or if there's something you want to learn more about.

Finally, this book is intended to be the start of your financial journey. We'll point you in the right direction, but it's up to you to take action and make it happen. That means using what you learn, putting it into practice, and continuing to read and learn more about money and how it works. Remember, the more you know, the better decisions you will make!

Ready? Let's go!

Please note: The information in this book is general in nature and designed to be for information only. Whilst every effort has been made to ensure it is accurate it is for general educational purposes only and is not intended nor should it be taken as professional financial advice. It is important to consult with a qualified financial advisor before making any financial decisions. The author and publisher are not responsible for any actions taken based on the information presented in this book.

PART ONE:

UNDERSTANDING MONEY – THE BASICS

CHAPTER 1. MONEY (REALLY) MATTERS

Money makes the world go round.
Money talks.
Money doesn't grow on trees.
Money can't buy you happiness.

These are just some of the many sayings you may have heard about money. Some love it, some hate it, yet most of us don't know much about it.

Whether we like it or not, money is a massive part of our lives. It's how we get by day to day; it's a tool that can help us accomplish our goals and even shapes how we see ourselves. In this chapter, we will explore what money is, where it comes from, and why it's essential to be financially savvy early on in life.

What is money?

Most people think of money as paper bills or coins. And it's true—those are physical representations of money we use to exchange goods and services. But money is more than just pieces of paper or metal.

Money is a tool. It's what we use to buy the things we need (like food, clothing, and shelter) **and pay for services** (like getting a haircut). It's a way to exchange something of value between two people.

> *Think about it like this: When you give someone money for something they are selling, they aren't giving you that item because they care about you—they're exchanging it for something of equal value (money).*

Money comes in different forms, like coins, bills, credit cards, and digital payments. All of these types of money have different values. But no matter the form, money represents a promise of value.

Most countries have their own form of money. In the United States, it's dollars and cents. Other countries, like Canada, Mexico, and Japan, have different types of money with their own names and symbols.

But this wasn't always the case. Let's briefly explore life before money.

LIFE BEFORE MONEY

Before money, people used bartering or trading to get what they needed.

Bartering is the act of exchanging a physical good or service for another.

Instead of paying for something with coins or bills, someone would offer goods and services in exchange for other goods or services.

> *For example, if someone had extra apples they wanted to get rid of, they could trade them for something else, like a chicken or a pair of shoes.*

Bartering worked well for small items that had equal value, but it had some significant flaws.

For one, it was hard to compare the value of different items. If a person had a lot of apples but little else, they wouldn't be able to barter for more valuable items like clothing or tools.

Also, trading goods and services could only happen when two people were willing to make the same exchange. What if someone wanted to buy something but didn't have anything the seller wanted in return? That was an issue that bartering couldn't solve.

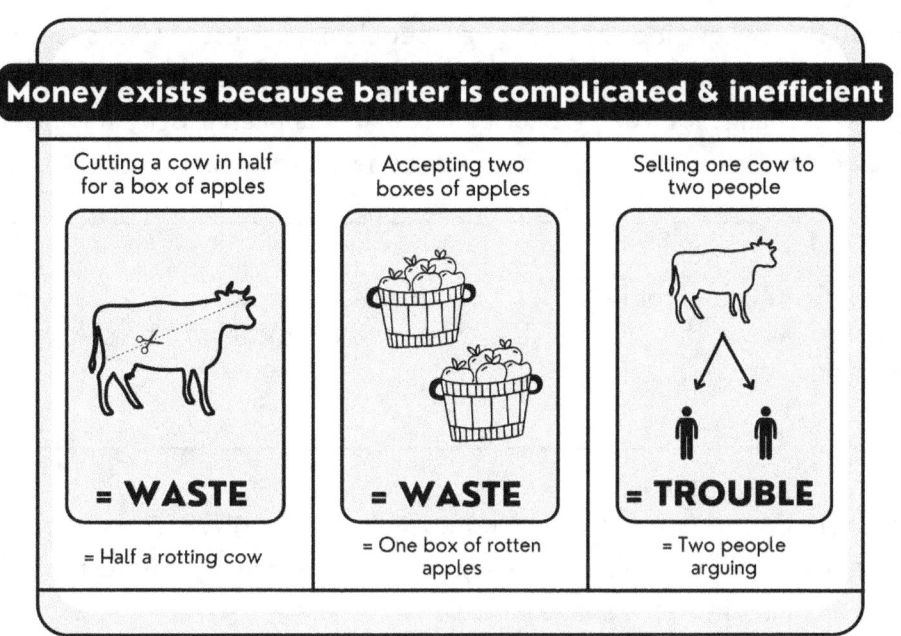

That's why money was created. It allowed people to easily trade for items of different value, no matter what they had to offer in return. It was also a way to store value, making saving up for bigger purchases easier.

A BRIEF HISTORY OF MONEY

Now that you understand bartering, why we use money makes more sense. People invented it so they could get what they needed without needing to barter. But it still took a while before people started using coins and notes.

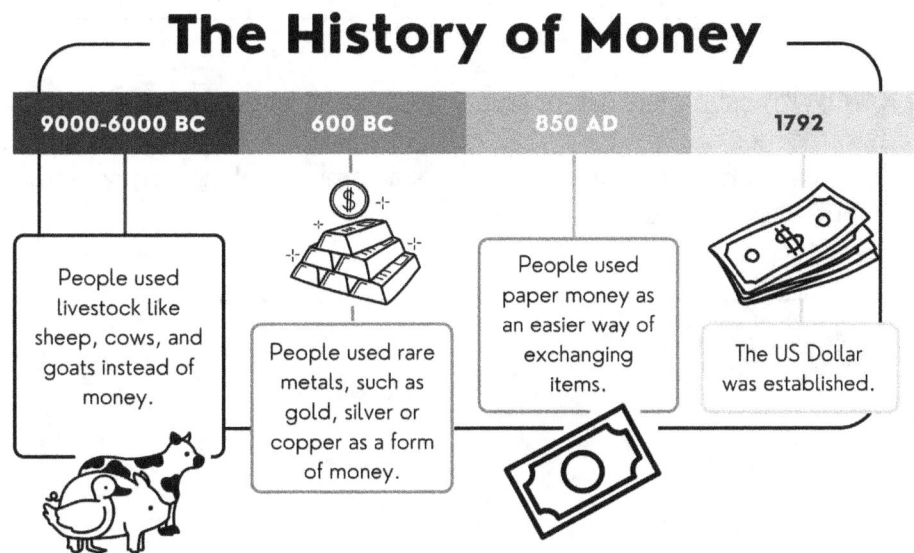

MONEY SKILLS FOR TEENS 111

- 9000 BC–6,000 BC. Believe it or not, long ago, people used livestock like sheep, cows, and goats instead of money. This may not seem like a great solution today (imagine carrying a cow down to the shops to exchange for your groceries!). Still, it was pretty logical in ancient times. These animals were portable and had a value that everyone agreed on.

> **DID YOU KNOW?** In ancient Rome, salt was used as a form of money. The word 'salary" comes from the Latin sal, meaning salt. The term "soldier" means "to be paid in salt," which was how soldiers were paid.

- 600 BC. Another common form of early money was gold or silver. These metals were rare and hard to find, making them valuable currency. Soon, these metals (and others, such as copper) were made into coins of various shapes and sizes.
- 850 AD. Paper money first appeared in China during the Song Dynasty (960–1279 AD). People used paper money as an easier way of exchanging items without having to carry around heavy coins or objects made of metal.
- 1792. The US government officially established the US dollar.

The first paper money in the United States was created in the 1800s, and it was backed by gold or silver. This meant that each dollar was worth a certain amount of gold or silver stored in the US Treasury.

Most countries no longer use gold or silver to back their money. Instead, money is supported by the laws and regulations of the government that created it.

> **DID YOU KNOW?** Most money isn't physical at all. In the United States, only a tiny portion of the money comprises physical cash. The majority of money today exists only as digital information (numbers on a computer screen). It's a reminder that money isn't just about coins and bills but numbers and transactions.

10 Key Money Terms

Savings — This is the money that you set aside for future use. Savings are a great way to secure your future and build financial security.

Budgeting — This is the plan you create to make sure that you spend your money in the most effective way possible. It helps you keep track of your income and expenses so that you can see where your money is going.

Taxes — Tax is money you pay to the government. It helps to pay for public services, such as roads and hospitals. Every person is taxed according to the amount of money they earn.

Investing — This is when you use your money to purchase something that may increase in value over time. Investing can be a great way to build wealth, but it's essential to understand the risks before you start investing.

Loans — Loans are money you borrow from a bank or other lender and have to repay with interest.

Interest —
Interest on money you save: When you save money in a bank account, the bank pays you interest as a reward for keeping your money with them.
Interest on money you borrow: If you borrow money from a bank, you have to pay interest on the amount you borrowed.

Debt — This is money you owe someone else, usually a bank or financial institution. This might be in the form of a loan, like a mortgage or a car loan, or something like credit card debt.

Stock — Stocks (or shares) are a type of investment where you buy shares in a company. When the company does well, the value usually increases, but when it does poorly, the value might decrease.

Credit — Credit is the ability to borrow money from a lender with the promise to pay it back in the future, usually with interest.

Risk — This is the possibility of losing money on something. High-risk investments have the potential for high returns but a greater chance of losing money, while low-risk investments typically offer lower returns but may be safer.

CHAPTER 2. BANKING 101

"In banking or finance, trust is the only thing you have to sell."—Patrick Dixon.

If money makes the world go round, financial institutions like banks allow this. They make it possible for people to safely store and manage their money.

Without banks, saving money, investing in the stock market, or borrowing money would be tough.

But as the quote above suggests, when it comes to banking and finance, the only thing lenders or institutions can offer is trust that they will handle you and your finances with respect, reliability, and honesty.

> **DID YOU KNOW?** Banks used to have a policy of complete secrecy.
>
> Until the 20th century, banks did not disclose information about their customers or their accounts, even to law enforcement. This policy of secrecy was known as "banker's discretion" and was considered essential for maintaining the trust of their customers. Today, banks must follow strict regulations and reporting requirements. However, the tradition of discretion and confidentiality is still essential to the banking industry.

BANK ACCOUNTS – WHAT ARE THEY? WHY DO YOU NEED ONE?

Imagine if you had to keep all of your money at home. Sure, you could keep it in a safe, under your mattress, or in suitcases. But that would be a lot of work, and it's unsafe. What if there was a flood, fire, or someone broke into your home? Then you'd be out of all of your money!

That's why a bank account can be a great option. A bank account is like an online safe to store your money. It's much safer than keeping it at home!

There are other reasons to have a bank account:

- **Convenience:** A bank account makes it easier and more convenient to manage your finances, pay bills, save for the future, and access cash when needed.

- **Accessibility**: Bank accounts are available 24/7, meaning you can access your money whenever needed.

- **Interest income:** You can earn interest on your money if you save it in a savings account. This means that, over time, your money grows.

- **Added security**: Banks help to keep your money safe and secure, protected against theft, loss, or damage.

- **Credit building**: A bank account is one of the first steps to establishing and building a good credit history.

Having a bank account is integral to taking charge of your finances. Now that you know the basics, let's look at how to use one!

DIFFERENT TYPES OF ACCOUNTS

When selecting a bank account, different types of accounts are available, depending on your needs. Here are a few of the most common types:

- **Checking account**: A checking account is an excellent option if you need to access your money quickly and frequently. This type of account is mainly used for everyday transactions, like paying bills or buying things with a debit card.

- **Savings account**: A savings account is where you can put your money and earn interest. The interest is a small amount of money that the bank pays you for keeping your money with them. Savings accounts are great for saving up for short-term goals, like a new bike or a trip to the amusement park.

- **Investment account**: An investment account (also known as a brokerage account) is an ideal choice to invest your money and grow your wealth over the long term. This type of account usually offers a variety of investments, such as stocks, bonds, and mutual funds. However, you should know that investments involve risk, so always research before investing.

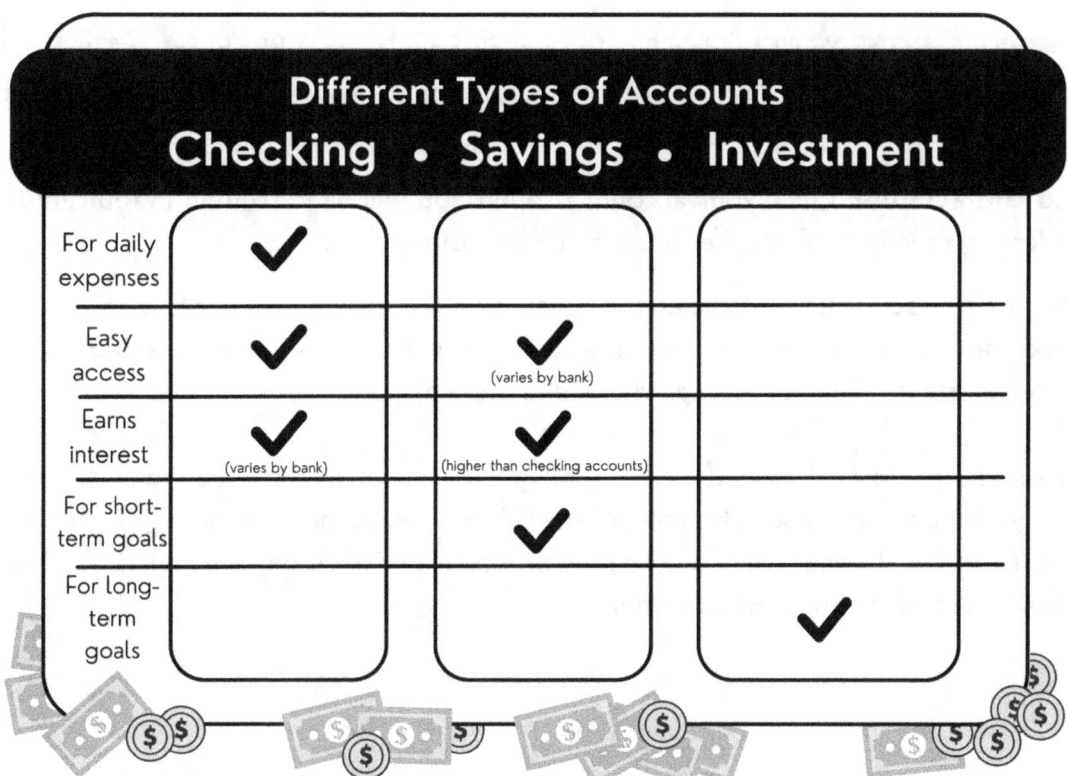

Different Types of Accounts
Checking • Savings • Investment

	Checking	Savings	Investment
For daily expenses	✓		
Easy access	✓	✓ (varies by bank)	
Earns interest	✓ (varies by bank)	✓ (higher than checking accounts)	
For short-term goals		✓	
For long-term goals			✓

OPENING A BANK ACCOUNT IN SIX EASY STEPS

Opening a bank account can be a great way to save money and access various financial services. To open a bank account, follow these six easy steps:

1. **Compare accounts**: Before choosing an account, find one that meets your needs. Consider factors like minimum deposits, account fees, possible interest rates, and features like online banking, debit cards, and mobile applications. Some banks might even offer special promotions or discounts for students.

2. **Gather required documents**: To open a bank account, you must provide a valid form of identification, such as a driver's license, passport, or birth certificate. If you're under 18, you might need an adult to help verify your identity and provide proof of your address. You should check with the bank to see what documents they require.

3. **Choose a bank**: Once you've compared accounts and gathered the necessary documents, it's time to choose one. You can look for banks with branches or ATMs near your home or school. You might also consider banks with mobile applications, good customer reviews, or rewards programs.

4. **Open the account**: You'll need to fill out an application to open the account. This can typically be done online or in person. Make sure you double-check your information before submitting the application.

5. **Fund the account**: Once your account is open, you will need to fund it. You can do this by transferring money from another account or depositing cash.

6. **Activate the account**: If you open the account online, the bank will usually send you an email or text message with a link to activate your account. Once you have activated your account, you can access it online or through the bank's mobile app.

Following these steps should make it easy to open a bank account. Once you're all set up, you can safely store your money and take advantage of the other services the bank offers. But before you do, there are a few other things you'll need to know to manage your money effectively. One important thing to keep track of is your bank statement.

BANK STATEMENTS

Your bank statement lists all transactions made on your account, including deposits, withdrawals, payments, etc.

Bank statements used to be mailed out to customers monthly or quarterly, but now most banks offer digital statements that can be viewed online. Reviewing your bank statement regularly is a good habit to ensure the transactions are accurate and to keep track of your spending.

STATEMENT FROM JANUARY 1-15, 2023

ACCOUNT 123456789

DATE	DEPOSITS	WITHDRAWALS	BALANCE
JAN02	1000.00		
JAN05		100.00	900.00
JAN10		215.00	685.00
JAN12	157.50		842.50
JAN14	500.50		1343.00
TOTAL	1658.00	315.00	1343.00

Here's a quick guide to reviewing your statement:

1. **Check the balance**: The first thing to check is your account balance. This is the amount of money you have in your account. Ensure it matches what you expect and that you have enough money to cover upcoming payments.

2. **Review transactions**: Go through each transaction in your statement to ensure accuracy. If you see a transaction you don't recognize, it could be a mistake or an instance of fraud. Contact your bank as soon as possible if you suspect any errors.

3. **Check for fees**: Make sure you understand the costs associated with your account. Some standard fees include overdraft fees, monthly maintenance fees, and fees for using ATMs outside your bank's network. Contact your bank for more information if you need clarification on a fee.

4. **Monitor account activity**: Regularly reviewing your bank statement is an excellent way to monitor your spending. Seeing your transactions in one place can help you stick to a budget and identify areas where you can reduce **spending**.

By following these steps, you can ensure your bank account is in good standing, and your finances are on track.

UNDERSTANDING TRANSACTIONS

When reviewing the activity on your account, it's helpful to understand the different types of payments on your account.

- **Direct Debits:** A direct debit is an agreement between you and a company to automatically deduct a certain amount from your bank account each month. This type of payment is commonly used for bills such as utility bills, phone bills, and insurance premiums. With direct debits, you won't have to worry about missing a payment or incurring late fees because the payments are automatically made for you.

- **Standing Orders:** A standing order is similar to a direct debit, but it is usually used to transfer a fixed amount each month rather than a variable amount. *For example, you might set up a standing order to pay your rent or monthly gym membership each month.*

- **Recurring Payments:** Recurring payments are similar to direct debits and standing orders, but they're made through cards like credit and debit cards, and the transactions will appear in your statement as "recurring" or "subscription." *For example, let's say you subscribe to a video streaming service like Netflix. Netflix will automatically charge your debit or credit card for the subscription fee every month. You don't have to do anything; it happens automatically.*

- **Bank Transfers:** A bank transfer is a payment you make from one bank account to another. Bank transfers can be made online, over the phone, or at a bank branch. You will need the recipient's bank account information, including their account number and sort code, to make a bank transfer. Bank transfers are typically processed within a few working days.

- **Card Payments:** A card payment is a payment made using a debit or credit card. Card payments can be made in person, online, or over the phone. Card payments are processed almost instantly and are a convenient way to pay for goods and services. When you make a card payment, the money is deducted from your bank account (if you use a debit card) or from your credit card limit (if you use a credit card).

It's also important to look out for any charges or fees that you don't recognize. This could be an indication of fraudulent activity on your account. If you see any suspicious transactions, contact your bank immediately.

Accessing your Money

ATM
Most banks have ATMs you can use to withdraw cash from your account. Some ATMs are only for customers of the bank, while others are part of a network that customers of different banks can use.

Debit Card
Most bank accounts come with a debit card that can be used to withdraw cash from ATMs or make purchases at merchants that accept debit cards.

Online Banking
Most banks offer online banking services that allow you to view your account information and make transactions online. You can also use online banking to transfer money between your bank accounts or to pay bills.

Mobile Banking
Many banks offer mobile banking apps you can download to your smartphone. These apps allow you to access your account information and make transactions on the go.

In-Person Banking
Some banks have branches where you can go to speak with a customer representative in person. You can also deposit cash or checks at these branches.

ACCESSING YOUR MONEY

Once you've set up your bank account and are equipped with the skills and knowledge to manage it effectively, you'll need to know how to access your money. There are several ways to access your money, depending on your needs and the services offered by your bank. Here are a few common options:

- **ATM:** Most banks have ATMs that you can use to withdraw cash from your account. Some ATMs are only for bank customers, while others are part of a network that can be used by customers of different banks.

- **Debit card:** Most bank accounts come with a debit card that can be used to withdraw cash from ATMs or make purchases at merchants that accept debit cards.

- **Online banking:** Most banks offer online banking services allowing you to view your account information and transact online. You can also use online banking to transfer money between your bank accounts or to pay bills.

- **Mobile banking:** Many banks offer mobile banking apps you can download. These apps allow you to access your account information and make transactions on the go.

- **In-person banking:** Some banks have branches where you can speak with a customer service representative. You can also deposit cash or checks at these branches.

By understanding the different ways to access your money, you can choose the best methods for you and your lifestyle.

> **DID YOU KNOW?** The first ATM (automated teller machine) was installed in London in 1967!

CHAPTER 3. CREDIT REPORTS – WHY YOUR CREDIT SCORE MATTERS!

In this chapter, we'll be talking about credit reports.

Credit reports may not be the most exciting thing in the world—in fact, they can seem pretty dull and unimportant at first glance. But they're actually super important and will play a big role in your financial life as you get older.

BUT FIRST UP, WHAT IS CREDIT?

Credit refers to the ability to borrow money or receive goods or services now and pay for them later. Individuals, businesses, or financial institutions, such as banks and credit card companies, can extend credit.

When you use credit, you are borrowing money that you will have to pay back later, usually with interest.

> *For example, when you use a credit card to make a purchase, you are borrowing money from the credit card company, and you will have to pay back the borrowed amount plus any interest charges.*

Credit can also be used to purchase big-ticket items such as cars, home appliances, or even a home. This is called installment credit and is a loan that's paid back over a period of time, usually with interest.

Credit can be helpful in many ways. It allows people to buy things they need or want without paying for them all at once. But it's essential to use credit responsibly and make payments on time; otherwise, it can lead to debt and negatively impact your credit score.

> **DID YOU KNOW?** The first credit reporting agencies were established in the late 19th century. Before credit reporting agencies were invented, banks relied on personal relationships and their own records to determine a borrower's creditworthiness.

WHAT IS A CREDIT REPORT?

A credit report is a document prepared by a credit reporting agency that shows your credit history. It's like a report card for your finances, showing how well you've handled credit in the past. This information is used by lenders, landlords, and other people or organizations to decide whether or not to give you credit or to approve you for a loan or rental property.

Every time you apply for a credit card, loan, or any other type of credit, the lender will check your credit report to see how responsible you've been with credit in the past. Your credit report will show information such as:

- Your credit accounts, including credit cards, loans, and mortgages
- How much credit you have been given
- How much credit you are currently using
- How promptly you have paid your bills
- Any late payments or defaults on your credit accounts
- Any bankruptcies or legal judgments against you

CREDIT REPORTS VS. CREDIT SCORES – WHAT'S THE DIFFERENCE?

Your credit report and credit score are related but not the same thing.

Your credit report is a detailed document that shows your credit history.

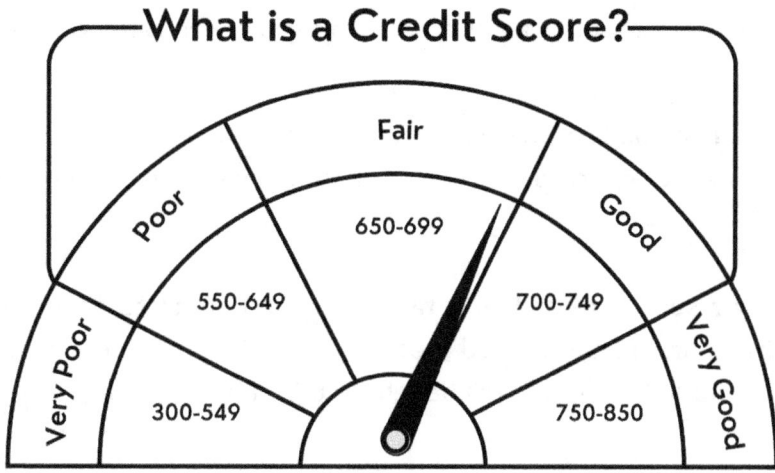

Your credit score, on the other hand, is a numerical value that is calculated based on the information in your credit report. It's a snapshot of your creditworthiness, and it's used by lenders to decide whether or not to approve you for credit. Credit scores are generally between 300 and 850. The higher your score, the better your creditworthiness.

. . . .

WHY A GOOD CREDIT SCORE MATTERS & WHY YOU SHOULD CARE!

Even though you may not have the need for credit in the near future, it's important to start thinking about your credit score now because the choices you make with your money today will impact your credit score.

Here are a few reasons why having a good credit score matters:

- **Access to credit:** A good credit score will make it easier to get approved for credit in the future. This includes credit cards, car loans, student loans, and mortgages. When you have a good credit score, lenders see you as a lower risk, and they are more likely to approve you for credit.

- **Lower interest rates:** When you have a good credit score, you'll be offered lower interest rates on loans and credit cards. This means you'll save money on interest charges over time.

- **Better rental options:** Landlords often check credit reports when you apply to rent a property. A good credit score can make you more likely to be approved for a rental.

- **Job opportunities:** Some employers check credit reports as part of the hiring process. A good credit score can help you get the job you want.

- **Insurance:** A good credit score can also help you get lower rates on insurance, such as car insurance.

- **Building good habits:** Building good credit takes time; the earlier you start, the better. Learning how to manage your credit responsibly now is essential so you'll be prepared when you need it in the future.

Think of it like planting a seed in a garden. It takes time and effort to grow, but the end result is a beautiful and healthy plant. Building a good credit score is similar. It takes time and effort, but the result is a solid financial foundation that will benefit you in the long run.

BUT WHAT DOES IT MEAN IN REALITY?

Let's say you want to buy a car. You've saved up enough money for a down payment and are ready to start looking for car loans.

If you have a good credit score—say around 700 or above—lenders will likely see you as a low-risk borrower. They'll be more willing to lend you money, and you'll probably qualify for a lower interest rate on your loan. This means you'll pay less in interest over the life of the loan, and you'll be able to afford a more expensive car.

On the other hand, if your credit score is low—let's say around 600 or below—lenders will see you as a high-risk borrower. They'll be less likely to lend you money, and you'll likely be offered a higher interest rate on your loan. This means you'll pay more in interest over the life of the loan, and you may not be able to afford the car you want.

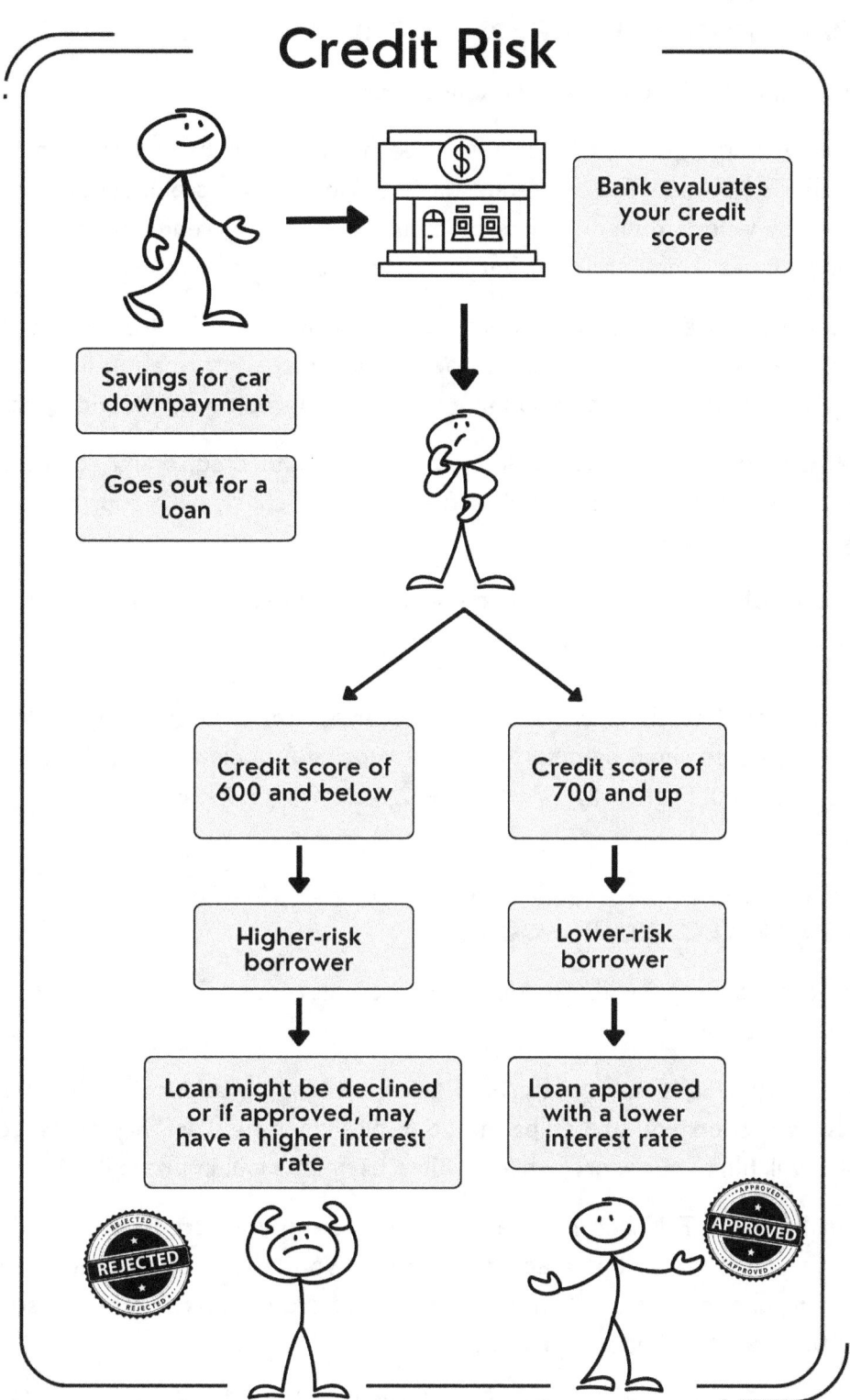

HOW YOU CAN CHECK YOUR CREDIT SCORE

There are a few ways you can check your credit score:

1. **Credit reporting agencies:** The US's three major credit reporting agencies are Equifax, Experian, and TransUnion. You can request a free copy of your credit report from each agency once a year by visiting their websites or calling them. Your credit report will show you the agency's information on file for you, but it will not include your credit score.

2. **Online credit score providers**: Several online providers offer free credit score checking. These providers will give you a credit score based on the information in your credit report. Some popular online providers include Credit Karma, Credit Sesame, and Quizzle.

3. **Banks and credit card companies**: Some banks and credit card companies offer their customers free access to their credit scores. You can check with your bank or credit card company if they provide this service.

4. **Credit counseling services**: Some credit counseling services will provide you with your credit score for free as part of their services.

It's important to note that the credit score you receive from different sources may vary slightly. This is because it is determined by different credit scoring models and may have different ranges. However, the score should generally be close enough to give you an idea of where you stand.

FACTORS THAT AFFECT YOUR SCORE

Your credit score is based on the information in your credit report. The five most significant factors that affect your credit are:

1. Payment history: This is the most crucial factor, making up about 35% of your credit score. It reflects how good you are at paying your bills on time. Late payments, collections, and bankruptcy will hurt your score, while on-time payments will improve it.

2. **Credit utilization:** This factor makes up about 30% of your credit score and refers to how much credit you're using compared to how much you have available. The more you use (*for example, using a lot of your credit card limit*) the lower your score. In comparison, using less of your available credit will help improve it.

3. **Length of credit history:** This makes up about 15% of your credit score and reflects the age of your credit accounts and how long you've been using credit. The longer your credit history, the better—as long as you have a good track record of paying on time.

4. **Credit mix:** This factor makes up about 10% of your credit score and refers to the different types of credit you have, such as credit cards, loans, and mortgages. A mix of credit types can be helpful for your score—as long as you're making payments on time.

5. **New credit:** This factor makes up about 10% of your credit score and refers to how many new credit applications you've made recently. Every time you apply for new credit, it can affect your credit score, so it's best to limit the number of new applications you make.

By understanding these factors, you can work to improve your credit score.

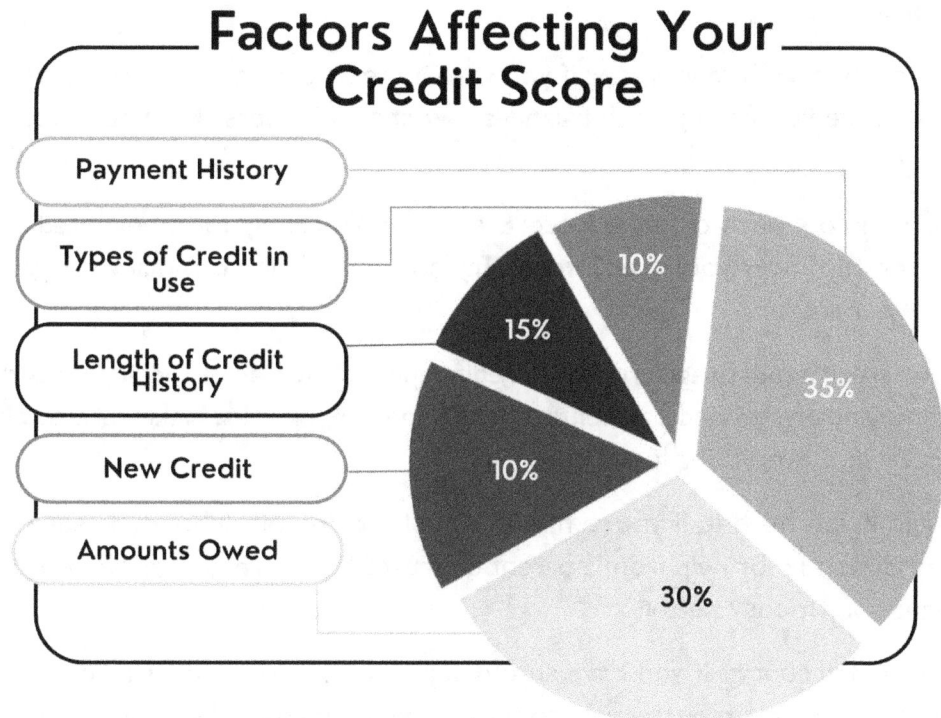

DID YOU KNOW? Individuals and businesses aren't the only ones to borrow money. Governments also borrow money to fund essential projects or infrastructure improvements. In fact, as of February 2023, the U.S. national debt was over 31 trillion dollars!

HOW YOU CAN MAINTAIN A GOOD CREDIT SCORE OR IMPROVE YOUR CREDIT SCORE

Knowing the basics of how credit works can help you manage it properly. There are no shortcuts to improving your credit score, just good financial behavior.

Here are some general tips for maintaining a good score or improving your score:

1. Pay your bills on time: This is the most important thing you can do to keep your credit score healthy. Make sure you pay all of your bills by their due date so that you don't fall behind and get hit with late fees.

2. Keep your credit card balances low: If you have a credit card, try not to use up too much of your available credit. Keeping your balances low shows lenders that you're responsible with your money.

3. Don't apply for too much credit at once: Every time you apply for a new credit card or loan, it can temporarily lower your credit score. Try not to apply for too many things at once, or it could hurt your score.

4. Check your credit report regularly: Your credit report shows all of the accounts that are open in your name and any missed payments or other negative marks. Make sure to check it every year to make sure everything looks right.

5. Ask for help if you need it: If you're having trouble paying off debts or keeping up with bills, don't be afraid to ask for help from a parent or trusted adult. They might be able to advise you on managing your money better.

6. Don't close old accounts: If you have an old account you no longer use, don't rush to close it! Closing an account can hurt your score because it shortens the length of time that you've had credit.

7. Be patient: Building good credit takes time! Don't worry if things aren't perfect immediately—just keep making good choices, and your score will improve over time.

It's important to note that there's no instant way to improve your credit profile. It takes time and effort to do so. However, by following these tips and being responsible with credit, you can improve your credit profile over time.

CHAPTER 4. JOBS & MONEY

> **DID YOU KNOW?** The average person spends 90,000 hours working in their lifetime!

Work is changing fast, and it's becoming more common for people to change jobs multiple times throughout their careers. The rise of the gig economy, remote work, and the increasing demand for specialized skills are some of the factors that are contributing to this trend.

The average person today will have 11-15 jobs during their lifetime. This means they must adapt to new roles and responsibilities, learn new skills, and build new professional networks.

That's why it's essential to be adaptable, open to new opportunities, and always willing to learn.

This chapter is designed to give you a solid foundation for understanding the world of jobs and money to prepare you for the ever-changing job market. It will help you be more informed and confident about your finances and better prepared for the world of work when you are ready to join the workforce. Whether you're thinking about your first job or already working and looking to improve your finances, this chapter will provide you with the information you need to make smart decisions about your money and be ready for the opportunities that come your way.

Before we delve into the world of work, let's quickly look through some key terms you'll be hearing:

Different Types of Employment Status

Employed	A person who works for a company or organization and receives a salary or wage in exchange for their services. E.g. a waiter at a restaurant or an attorney at a law firm.
Self-employed	A person who runs their own business and is responsible for managing all aspects of it, including finances, marketing, and operations.
Full-time	An employee who works a set number of hours per week, typically 35-40 hours, and is eligible for benefits such as health insurance and paid time off.
Part-time	A job that typically requires an employee to work fewer hours per week, usually less than 35 hours.
Temporary	A job that is offered for a specific period of time, usually to cover for a leave of absence, seasonal work or special projects.
Freelance	A type of self-employment that allows a person to work independently and choose their own clients and projects.

- **Employed:** When a person is working for an employer, typically on a regular schedule and receiving a salary or wages. This could be anything from being a waiter at a restaurant to an attorney at a law firm.

- **Self-employed:** When people work for themselves, typically as independent contractors or freelancers. They are responsible for their own taxes and benefits.

- **Full-time:** A job that typically requires an employee to work at least 35–40 hours per week.

- **Part-time:** A job that typically requires an employee to work fewer hours per week, usually less than 35 hours.

- **Temporary:** A job offered for a specific period, usually to cover a leave of absence, seasonal work, or special projects.

- **Freelance:** A type of self-employment that allows people to work independently and choose their clients and projects.

Each type of employment has pros and cons, and understanding them is helpful before deciding what type of work is best for you.

EMPLOYED VS. SELF-EMPLOYED

Whether you work for yourself or someone else is a personal decision that depends on your needs, preferences, and circumstances. Some people prefer the stability and benefits of being an employee. Whilst others enjoy the freedom and earning potential of being self-employed. Both types of employment have unique challenges and rewards, and it's wise to consider your values, skills, and goals when deciding.

Here are some pros and cons to consider:

EMPLOYED

Pros:

- Consistent income: As an employee, you will typically receive a regular salary or hourly wage.
- Benefits: Many employers offer health insurance, retirement plans, paid time off, and more.
- Job security: Being an employee means you have a contract with your employer, which provides some level of job security.
- Professional development: Employers often provide training and development opportunities for their employees to improve their skills and advance in their careers.
- Structure: Employers usually have established systems and processes that employees can rely on.

Cons:

- Limited autonomy: As an employee, you will likely have to follow a set of guidelines and procedures set by your employer.
- Limited earning potential: Your earning potential may be capped by your employer's salary structure or budget.
- Lack of flexibility: Employers usually expect employees to be available during set working hours.

What's Right For You?

	Employed	Self-Employed
PROS 	• Regular salary and benefits, such as health insurance and retirement plans • Opportunities for advancement and career growth • Structured work environment and support from colleagues • Job security and stability • Less responsibility for business operations and taxes	• Greater control over work schedule and projects • Ability to pursue passions and interests • Potential for higher income and tax deductions • Greater flexibility in work location and environment • Opportunity to build a business and work with a variety of clients
CONS 	• Less control over work schedule and projects • Limited opportunity to pursue passions and interests • Potential for limited income growth • Limited flexibility in work location and environment • Potential for office politics and conflict with colleagues.	• Uncertain income and potential for financial stress • Responsibility for all aspects of business operations • Lack of benefits, such as health insurance and retirement plans • Limited opportunities for advancement or career growth

SELF-EMPLOYED

Pros:

- Autonomy: As a self-employed person, you have more control over your work schedule, clients, and projects.

- Unlimited earning potential: Your earning potential is not limited by an employer's salary structure or budget.

- Flexibility: You can work the hours that suit you.

- Variety: You can take on various clients and projects, making your work more diverse and exciting.

Cons:

- Uncertain income: As a self-employed person, your income may be inconsistent and depend on the availability of clients and projects.

- No benefits: As a self-employed person, you are responsible for your own benefits, such as health insurance and retirement savings.

- Job insecurity: You have to constantly look for new clients and projects to maintain a steady income.

- No structure: Self-employed people have to create their own systems and processes, which can be time-consuming and overwhelming.

It's important to weigh the pros and cons of each type of employment before making a decision.

EMPLOYABILITY AND EARNING POTENTIAL

You might have heard people talk about your earning potential. Earning potential refers to the amount of money you can make in your career based on your education, skills, experience, and other factors. It is an estimate of what you might earn in the future and is influenced by several variables. Some of the critical factors that can impact your earning potential include:

1. Education: A higher level of education can often lead to higher-paying jobs, as many employers are looking for workers with specialized skills and knowledge.

2. Work experience: Having work experience in your field or related fields can help increase your earning potential. This is because you have demonstrated your ability to perform well on the job and have developed skills and expertise that are valuable to employers.

3. Industry: The industry you work in can also impact your earning potential. Some industries, such as technology, finance, and medicine, tend to offer higher salaries than others.

4. Location: The cost of living and the average salaries in a particular area can also impact your earning potential. For example, workers in cities with a high cost of living may need to earn more to cover their expenses.

5. Skills and talents: Having unique skills or talents can also increase your earning potential. They can help you stand out from other job applicants and command a higher salary.

It's important to note that these are just a few factors that can impact earning potential.

It's also important to recognize that earning potential is not the only measure of success or happiness. In fact, money is just one of many vital aspects of a happy and fulfilling life. Many other factors contribute to a person's overall well-being and a sense of purpose, including relationships, health, hobbies and interests, community involvement, and personal growth and development.

While a high-earning job can help you achieve your financial goals, it doesn't guarantee happiness or financial stability. Having a good work-life balance, living in a low-cost area, and having a solid support network can all play a role in helping you achieve financial stability and security.

Ultimately, it's important to find a balance that works for you, considering your values, priorities, and financial goals and needs.

EVERYTHING YOU NEED TO KNOW ABOUT PAYCHECKS

Congratulations, you've gotten your first paycheck! This is an exciting milestone in your journey toward financial independence. But before you go out and spend all your hard-earned money, it's important to understand what's included in your paycheck.

Paycheck

Jane's Business
123 Main Street
Nowhere, USA 00000

Week of April 2-6, 2022
Joe Employee
123-45-6789

Gross Pay $500
Deductions

1. Federal Tax .... -68.00
2. State Tax .... -64.00
3. Social Security .... -31.00
4. Medicare .... -7.25

Net ———————————————— $329.75

WHAT IS A PAYCHECK AND WHY IS IT IMPORTANT?

A paycheck is a document showing the amount of money you've earned for your work. Your paycheck shows how much money you earned from your job and how much was taken out for taxes, health insurance, retirement plans, and other deductions.

It is also called a salary slip, pay stub or payslip.

As an employee, it's essential to understand and review your paycheck and ensure the information is correct, including your gross pay, deductions, and net pay. If you notice any errors, contact your employer and have them corrected.

CALCULATING YOUR PAY - GROSS VS. NET

Your paycheck will typically include your gross and net pay.

Gross pay is the total money you've earned before taxes and deductions.

Net pay is how much money you take home. This is the amount of money you have left after all deductions and taxes have been removed. This is the money you will have available to use for expenses, savings, and investments.

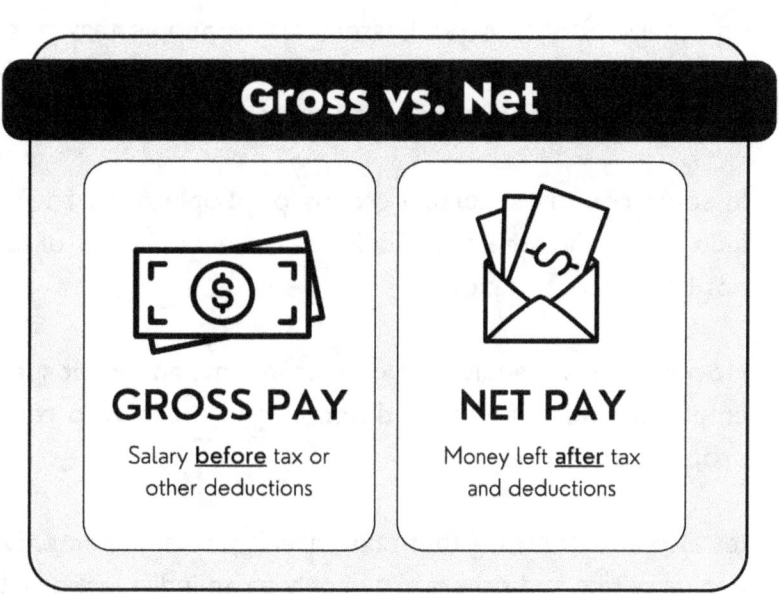

TAX – WHERE DID ALL THE MONEY GO?

Taxes can be a confusing and sometimes frustrating part of earning money. Seeing a large portion of your paycheck go towards taxes can be disheartening. Still, it's important to remember that taxes are a necessary part of our society. They help fund essential services such as schools, roads, and health care.

When you earn money, a percentage is withheld from your paycheck to go towards federal and state income taxes and other taxes such as Social Security and Medicare. The amount withheld depends on your income level, filing status, and any deductions or credits you may qualify for.

WHO PAYS TAXES?

Not everyone pays taxes. Tax laws vary from country to country, but taxes are usually based on a person's income and assets. Some people may not have to pay taxes because they do not earn enough money to reach the minimum income threshold, while others may be eligible for tax exemptions or credits that reduce their tax liability.

In some countries, certain groups of people don't have to pay taxes, such as students, disabled individuals, and veterans. Additionally, certain types of income, such as gifts and inheritance, may not be subject to taxes.

However, most people who earn an income and meet specific criteria must pay taxes. This includes employed and self-employed people and those who receive money from investments and rental properties.

It's also worth noting that taxes aren't just on income. Different types of taxes, such as sales tax, property tax, and others, may apply to an individual or a business.

CHAPTER 5. KEEPING IT PRIVATE – FRAUDS AND SCAMS

Fraud and scams are unfortunately common in today's world. These crimes occur when someone uses deceit or trickery to take money or personal information from unsuspecting individuals.

Fraud can come in many forms, from online scams to phone scams. It can target anyone, regardless of age, income, or education level. It's important to be aware of the different types of fraud and scams and to take steps to protect yourself and your personal information from fraud.

In this chapter, we'll cover fraud and scams, how they work, and what you should look out for. We'll also discuss how to protect yourself and your personal information from fraud and scams and what to do if you suspect you've been a victim.

WHAT ARE FRAUD AND SCAMS, AND WHY DO PEOPLE DO IT?

Fraud and scams are criminal activities that involve deceiving or tricking people into taking their money or personal information. Fraudsters and scammers use a variety of tactics to trick people, such as using fake websites, emails, phone calls, or social media messages to steal personal information or money.

People do it because they think they can get away with it and make money without doing any real work. Unfortunately, fraudsters often target vulnerable people who are desperate for cash or looking for an easy way out of their problems.

There are many different types of fraud and scams. It's essential to be aware of these scams and take steps to protect yourself from them.

> **DID YOU KNOW?** According to the Federal Trade Commission (FTC), individuals in the US lost $5.8 billion to fraud in 2021.

Examples of online scams include:

- **The Nigerian Prince Scam**

    The Nigerian Prince scam is a type of fraud where someone sends you an email claiming to be a wealthy prince from Nigeria. The email says that the prince needs your help to transfer his money out of the country and promises to give you a large portion of the money if you help him. However, once you agree to help, the scammers will ask for personal information or money to cover "fees" or "taxes" related to the transfer. In reality, there is no prince and no money—it's all just a scam to trick people into giving away their hard-earned money.

    This scam is also called an "advance-fee scam" because the scammers ask for money upfront.

- **The Imposter Scam**

    The Imposter scam is similar to the Nigerian Prince scam, but instead of someone claiming to be an actual prince, they pretend to be someone you know and trust, like a friend or family member. They might create a fake social media account or email address and contact you, saying they're in trouble and need money urgently. They'll ask you to wire money or give them your credit card information, but it's all a lie—the person pretending to be your friend or family member is a scammer trying to steal your money.

You might think you'll never fall for a scam, but it's important to remember that scammers are super smart. They are becoming more sophisticated in their tactics and are constantly coming up with new ways to trick people. They may use convincing language, official-looking documents, and even fake websites and social media accounts to make their scams seem real.

WHAT STEPS CAN YOU TAKE TO AVOID BECOMING A VICTIM OF FRAUD?

Now that you have a better understanding of the tactics scammers use to trick people into giving them money or sensitive information, let's look at some of the steps you can take to avoid becoming a victim of fraud:

1. **Keep your personal information private:** Don't share your personal information, such as full name, address, phone number, email, or social security number, with anyone you don't know or trust.

2. **Be cautious when using public Wi-Fi:** Public Wi-Fi is often unsecured and easily hacked. Avoid making financial transactions or entering sensitive information while using public Wi-Fi.

3. **Use strong passwords:** Create strong passwords that include letters, numbers, and special characters for your online accounts. Avoid reusing passwords across multiple accounts.

4. **Don't click on suspicious links:** If you receive an email or message with a suspicious link, do not click on it. It could be a phishing scam designed to steal your personal information.

5. **Double-check before giving out personal information:** Always double-check the identity of the person asking for your personal data through another means of communication before giving it out.

6. **Monitor your bank accounts:** Regularly check your bank accounts for any unusual activity.

7. **Don't send money to strangers:** Never wire money to someone you don't know or trust, especially if they urgently ask for it.

8. Be wary of offers that seem too good to be true: Scammers often use offers that seem too good to be true, such as winning the lottery! Unfortunately, if it sounds too good to be true, it probably is.

9. Report suspicious activity: If you suspect someone is trying to scam you, report it to the authorities immediately.

10. Educate yourself about different types of fraud: Stay informed about different types of fraud so that you can recognize them when they occur and take appropriate action to protect yourself.

Following these suggestions can significantly reduce your risk of falling victim to fraud or scams. Remember to always be cautious, do your research, and trust your instincts. By staying informed and vigilant, you can better protect yourself and your finances from fraud and scams.

Frauds & Scams

There are many different types of fraud and scams, some examples include:

Phishing Scams
These are a type of cyber attack where scammers attempt to get hold of sensitive information such as usernames, passwords, and credit card details. This is often done through fraudulent emails or websites that appear to be legitimate.

Investment Scams
These scams involve fraudsters who create fake businesses that trick people into giving them money by promising big returns. But in reality, these people just take the money and run.

Lottery Scams
These scams involve fraudsters who tell people they've won a large sum of money, but in order to claim the prize, they need personal information or bank account details to process the payment.

Work-from-home Scams
These scams involve fraudsters who promise people the opportunity to make money from home, but in reality, the job is non-existent, or the employer is not real. They may ask for personal information or money as part of the application.

Romance Scams
These scams involve fraudsters who create fake online profiles and pretend to be interested in a romantic relationship, in order to gain trust and steal money or personal information from the victim.

Charity Scams
These scams involve fraudsters who pretend to be a charity and ask for donations to help a cause, but in reality, they keep the money for themselves.

Online Shopping Scams
Scammers create fake websites that look like real online stores, but when people make a purchase, they don't receive the item and lose their money.

Identity Theft Scams
Scammers steal personal information, such as a person's name, address, or social security number, and uses it to open credit cards or take out loans in that name.

WHAT TO DO IF YOU THINK YOU'VE BEEN SCAMMED?

If you've fallen victim to a scam, it's important to remember that it's not your fault. Scammers are experts at finding new ways to trick people, and it's not uncommon to be scammed. Unfortunately, you are not the first person it has happened to, so don't be too hard on yourself. Instead, focus on the steps to report the scam and recover what you can.

If you suspect that you have fallen victim to a scam, there are a few steps you should take immediately:

1. **Don't send any more money to the scammer:** This may sound obvious, but once you realize you have been scammed, stop all financial transactions with the scammer. Scammers can be very persuasive and may try to convince you to make additional payments.

2. **Contact your bank:** Tell them what happened and ask them to freeze your account or cancel any unauthorized transactions.

3. **Report the fraud:** Contact relevant authorities, such as the US Federal Trade Commission (FTC) or Action Fraud in the UK. They will help you report the incident and provide guidance on how to proceed.

4. **Gather evidence:** Collect any documentation, emails, or messages related to the scam. This will be useful when you file a report or make a claim.

5. **Don't pay for recovery:** If a scammer tells you to pay them to recover your money, don't do it. Scammers often ask for payment to trick you into giving them more of your money.

6. **Take care of your emotional well-being:** Scams can be traumatic, and taking the time to process the experience and care for yourself is important.

7. **Learn from it:** As painful and unpleasant being scammed is, try your best to learn from what happened to keep yourself safe in the future.

Unfortunately, not every scam can be stopped or recovered from. But remember that it's not your fault you've been scammed, and try to learn from the experience to avoid future scams.

PART TWO:

BUDGETING AND SAVVY SPENDING

CHAPTER 6. BUDGETING – MAKING A PLAN (AND STICKING TO IT)

In this chapter, we'll dive into the world of spending habits and budgeting. We'll start by looking at different spender personalities, so you can understand your own spending habits and how to make them work for you. We'll also cover the importance of creating a budget and how to make one that works for you. We'll talk about the difference between needs and wants and how to ensure you spend your money on what truly matters. Finally, we'll introduce the 50/30/20 rule, a simple way to ensure you save enough for your future. By the end of this chapter, you'll better understand how to manage your money and make it work for you.

WHAT KIND OF SPENDER ARE YOU?

Everyone has their own unique way of spending and managing their money. Understanding your own spending personality can help you make better financial decisions.

Here are a few examples of spending personalities:

Spending Personalities

The Impulse Spender: This type of spender tends to make impulsive and unplanned purchases, often without thinking about the consequences.

The FOMO Spender: This type of spender often spends money to keep up with friends or to avoid missing out on social events and experiences.

The Emotional Spender: This type of spender tends to use money as a way to cope with emotions, such as stress or anxiety.

The Bargain Hunter: This type of spender enjoys the thrill of finding a good deal and will often go to great lengths to save money on purchases.

The Hoarder: This type of spender has a hard time letting go of money and will often save more than they spend.

- **The impulse spender:** This type of spender tends to make impulsive and unplanned purchases, often without thinking about the consequences.

- **The FOMO spender:** This type of spender often spends money to keep up with friends or to avoid missing out on social events and experiences.

- **The emotional spender:** This type of spender tends to use money as a way to cope with emotions, such as stress or anxiety.

- **The bargain hunter:** This type of spender enjoys finding a good deal and often goes to great lengths to save money on purchases.

- **The hoarder:** This type of spender has difficulty letting go of money and will often save more than they spend.

By understanding your spending personality, you can make more conscious and deliberate spending decisions and ensure that your spending habits align with your financial goals.

THE IMPULSE SPENDER

The impulse spender tends to make impulsive purchases without thinking about the financial consequences. They might see something they like and buy it without considering whether they can afford it or need it. They often have difficulty resisting sales and discounts and may struggle to stick to a budget. However, this spender personality can also be spontaneous and fun-loving and may enjoy the thrill of the purchase.

THE FOMO SPENDER

The FOMO (fear of missing out) spender is someone who spends money because they don't want to miss out on experiences or opportunities. They feel a sense of pressure to keep up with others, whether it's the latest fashion trends, gadgets, or social events. They are always looking for new experiences and tend to be impulsive when spending. They may also have trouble saying no to friends and family regarding social activities involving spending money. This type of spending can lead to financial stress and difficulty sticking to a budget, as they may not be considering the long-term financial consequences of their spending decisions.

THE EMOTIONAL SPENDER

The emotional spender is someone who uses shopping and spending as a way to cope with their emotions. They may turn to shopping as a form of stress relief or use it as a way to celebrate or reward themselves. They may not be aware that their spending is out of control or connected to their emotions. They may also have difficulty saying no to themselves or others or find themselves constantly buying things they don't need. This type of spending can lead to financial problems and debt if not addressed. Emotional spenders need to learn how to manage their emotions and create a budget to help them stay on track.

THE BARGAIN HUNTER

The bargain hunter loves finding a good deal and always looks for discounts and sales. They enjoy the thrill of the hunt and seek ways to stretch their money further. They often have a keen eye for detail and can spot a good deal from a mile away. They are skilled at comparison shopping and can usually find the same item for a much lower price than others might pay. However, they may also have a tendency to overspend on things they don't really need just because they are a good deal.

It's crucial for bargain hunters to set a budget, stick to it, and make sure they only spend money on things they truly need and value.

THE HOARDER

The hoarder is a type of spender who has difficulty letting go of their possessions, whether physical items or money. They may have trouble spending money on things they need or want and may hold onto items even if they no longer have any use for them. They often feel secure in having a lot of money or possessions and may struggle to part with them. This type of spending behavior can lead to financial stress and clutter in their home or life. Hoarders need to understand their behavior and work on developing healthier spending habits, such as setting a budget and learning to prioritize their needs and wants.

Of course, there are many other spending personality types, and you may identify with more than one. The important thing is to understand your own spending habits and how they affect your financial goals. Once you know your spending personality, you can work on creating a budget that works for you and your lifestyle.

AN INTRODUCTION TO BUDGETING

Budgeting is the simplest way to take control of your money. A budget is a financial plan that considers all the money you will make over a certain period and how much you're likely to spend. You make the plan, and then you stick to it.

What is the basic aim of budgeting? To try and control your spending. The ultimate goal? To spend less money than you make.

This may sound simple. How do you, after all, spend money you don't have? But many people do this each month, relying on credit cards, loans, or overdrafts to allow them to spend money they haven't yet earned.

Think of budgeting like driving a car—you need to know where you're headed and how much gas you have in the tank to make it to your destination safely and efficiently. Just like you need to plan your route and monitor your fuel levels, you also need to plan your income and expenses to ensure you're on the right track financially.

Remember, budgeting is about controlling your money instead of your money controlling you.

> **DID YOU KNOW?** Budgeting is good for your health. By taking control of your finances and setting clear goals for your spending, budgeting can reduce stress and increase feelings of security and well-being. In fact, studies have shown that people who regularly practice budgeting are more likely to have higher levels of life satisfaction and a more positive outlook on their financial future.

NEEDS VS. WANTS...

You might want that new laptop, but do you really need it?

Understanding the difference between needs and wants is an essential part of budgeting.

"Needs" are essential items or services that are required for survival, such as food, shelter, and clothing.

"Wants" are things that are desired or desirable but not essential. They are often luxuries or things that would make life more comfortable or convenient but that are not necessary for survival, such as a new laptop or a vacation.

Being able to distinguish between needs and wants can help you make more informed financial decisions and prioritize where to allocate your money.

> *For example, having a fancy car or designer clothes may be a want, but having a reliable means of transportation to get to work or school is a need.*

MONEY SKILLS FOR TEENS

HOW TO BUDGET IN 5 SIMPLE STEPS

Creating a budget can be overwhelming, but it's really quite simple. It just takes a bit of effort to make sure you know exactly how much you're earning and how much you're spending. Think about it like a game plan for your money, and it's not as intimidating as it seems.

Here are five simple steps to help you get started.

1. **Calculate your income:** This is the first step in creating a budget. You need to know how much money you have coming in every month to make a plan for how to spend it. This includes all sources of income, including your salary or any allowance you may receive and any additional income you might earn through side hustles or investments.

2. **Calculate your spending:** In this step, you'll need to take a close look at how much money you're currently spending. This includes two types of spending:

    - Your regular expenses or needs. These are the things you need to pay for to survive, like a place to live, transportation, communication, and food. These are the essentials that you can't live without.

    - Your discretionary spending or wants, such as dining out, shopping, and entertainment. These expenses are things you choose to spend money on and can live without.

    You'll want to track your spending for at least a month to get a good sense of where your money is going.

3. **Set goals:** Now that you know how much money you have coming in and going out, it's time to set some financial goals. This can be saving for a vacation, buying a car, or a down payment on a house. Whatever your goals, make sure they are specific, measurable, and achievable.

4. **Make a plan:** With your income and spending calculated and your goals set, you can now plan how to reach those goals. This plan should include specific steps for reducing unnecessary expenses, increasing income, and ensuring you're putting enough money into savings to reach your goals.

5. **Track your spending and adjust:** Finally, it's crucial to track your spending and make adjustments as necessary. Review your budget regularly and look for areas to reduce expenses or increase your income. Be flexible and adjust your budget as needed to ensure you're on track to reach your financial goals. Remember, a budget is not a one-time thing; it's an ongoing process.

THE 50/30/20 RULE OF BUDGETING

The 50/30/20 rule of budgeting is a simple and effective way to budget your money. It suggests that you divide your after-tax income into three categories:

- 50% for things you need (essential items)
- 30% for things you want (non-essential items)
- 20% for savings or paying off debts

This rule can be helpful because it provides a clear guideline for how to allocate your money, and it's easy to remember.

Let's break it down:

- **50% of your income should be allocated to essential expenses**, like rent, food, and transportation. These are the things you can't avoid that are essential to your survival.

- **30% of your income should be allocated to wants** like eating out, shopping, and going out with friends. These are the non-essential expenses that you can cut back on if you need to save money.

- **20% of your income should be allocated to savings and paying off any debt**. This includes saving for emergencies, investing for the future, and paying off credit card debt.

By following this rule, you can be sure you're allocating enough money for your necessities while allowing yourself some room for fun and saving for the future. It's a simple and effective way to budget your money, ensuring your expenses are in balance.

Activity Time! Budgeting Case Study

Background: Jo is a 19-year-old student who is determined to make the most of her time at college.

INCOME
She earns $15/hour at a local part-time job, working Saturdays, earning a total of $450 per month. On top of this, she receives $400 in in financial aid from her college.

EXPENSES
Jo has a number of regular expenses to cover each month. These include rent ($350), food ($150), transport ($100) and online subscriptions ($50). In addition, Jo visits the cinema regularly, spending $50 per month on tickets and snacks. Finally, she has to pay for her textbooks, stationery and other course materials, which come to $100 per month.

How much does Jo spend each month?

Is she spending more than she has coming in?

YES   NO

Which items are wants and which are needs?

Wants: Needs:

How might Jo reduce her monthly expenditure?

ESSENTIAL SKILLS EVERY TEEN SHOULD KNOW

CHAPTER 7. SPENDING – HOW TO GET MORE FOR LESS!

When it comes to spending your hard-earned money, it's important to be smart about it. Just because you have cash in your pocket doesn't mean you should spend it all at once.

Being smart about your spending is about getting the most for your money and ensuring your dollars go as far as possible. It's about being mindful of your purchases and ensuring you get the best deal. Think of it like a game where the goal is to stretch your money further and make it work harder for you.

In this chapter, we'll look at ways to be a savvy spender and make your money go the extra mile. From finding deals and discounts to learning how to negotiate, we'll cover it all so you can get more for your money.

VALUE FOR MONEY

Value can be applied to just about anything, but value for money means getting the best quality or service for the price you pay. It's about making sure that you're not overpaying for something and that you're getting the most bang for your buck.

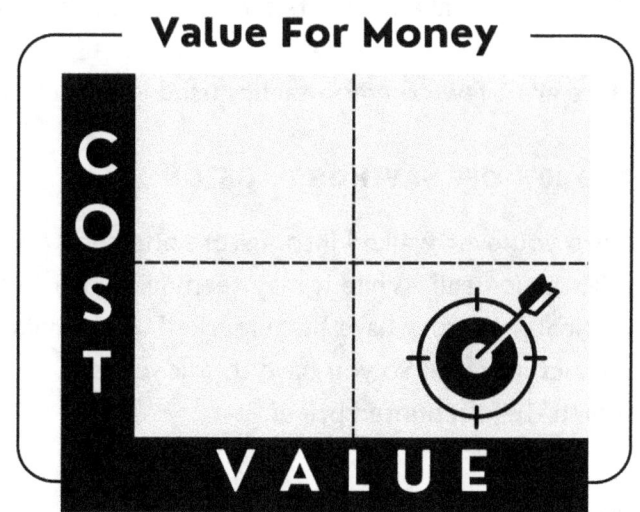

> *For example, if you want to buy a new pair of shoes, you might find one that is very cheap but not very durable, meaning it will wear out quickly and you'll have to buy another pair soon. On the other hand, you could find a more expensive pair made with higher-quality materials that will last longer. While the more expensive pair may cost more upfront, it will save you money in the long run because you won't have to replace them as often.*

Understanding the concept of value for money can help you make smart financial decisions and ensure you're getting the most for your money.

WHAT MAKES SOMETHING GOOD VALUE OR A GREAT DEAL?

When something is considered to be good value or a great deal, it means that it offers a high level of quality or benefit in relation to its cost.

> *For example, if you buy a phone with many features and it functions well, but is not too expensive, it would be considered a great deal. Similarly, if you buy a shirt made of high-quality material that lasts a long time, but is not too expensive compared to other shirts with similar quality, then it would be considered good value for money.*

It's important to note that good value or a great deal can mean different things to different people depending on their needs and preferences. For example, you may find great value in a product that lasts a long time. At the same time, another person may consider a product that is cheaper in price to be a better value.

MARKETING TRICKS AND HOW TO AVOID THEM

Be aware of marketing tricks and tactics used to get you to buy something you don't need. Ads are designed to make products attractive, but they can often be misleading.

Here are a few common tactics used in advertising to be aware of:

THE 40% OFF SAVINGS ILLUSION

Have you ever walked into a store and seen a sign that says "40% off" and felt like you just found a fantastic deal? While it may seem like you're getting a significant discount, the reality is that the original price may have been marked up to make it seem like you're getting a bigger discount than you actually are. So you have to ask yourself, is the 40% saving really a saving? Is the product even worth the discounted price?

THE LIMITED-TIME OFFER

A limited-time offer is a marketing strategy businesses use to create a sense of urgency and encourage customers to make a purchase quickly. It usually involves offering a discount or promotion that is only available for a short period, such as 24 hours or one week. The idea behind these offers is to make customers feel a sense of FOMO (the fear of missing out) and get them to make rushed decisions without taking the time to do their research.

THE "BUNDLING" TRICK

Also known as "buy one, get one" deals, this strategy encourages you to buy a bundle of products at a discounted price. Bundling items together can save you money, but businesses often use bundling to increase sales of slower-moving products or services by pairing them with more popular items. While the bundle price may be lower than buying each item separately, it's important to consider whether you need all the products or services included in the bundle.

THE FIRST MONTH FREE DEAL

This is a common tactic used in subscription services. You are offered the first month free. After the free trial period ends, you are automatically charged for subsequent months without realizing it. Although some countries have strict rules about this, it is still a common trick used to get people to sign up for services without fully understanding the terms and conditions or how to cancel.

CELEBRITY ENDORSEMENTS

Companies often hire celebrities to promote their products in the hopes that customers will associate their products with the celebrities' positive attributes. Celebrity endorsement may make a product seem more desirable, but it doesn't necessarily mean it is the best value or most suitable choice for you. It's important to remember that they are being paid for their endorsement and may not actually use or believe in the product themselves. Do your own research.

> **DID YOU KNOW?** The colors used in product packaging and advertising can significantly impact purchasing decisions. Studies have shown that consumers associate different colors with different emotions and personalities. Companies will often choose colors for their products based on the feelings they want to evoke. For example, red is often used to represent excitement and urgency, while blue evokes feelings of calm and trustworthiness.

HOW TO AVOID THESE MARKETING TRICKS

- **Be an informed consumer**—Take time to research products, compare prices, and read reviews before purchasing.

- **Look for value rather than discounts**—Don't be fooled by offers of huge savings or discounts. Instead, focus on getting the most value for your money.

- **Ignore limited-time offers**—If it's a good deal, it won't disappear overnight. If you're unsure about a product, take your time to make an informed decision.

- **Read the fine print**—Ensure you understand precisely what you're getting and check for additional fees or hidden costs before purchasing anything.

- **Don't be afraid to walk away**—If an offer doesn't seem worth it, don't be scared to walk away. There will always be other deals and opportunities to save money.

By following these steps and understanding how marketing tactics work, you can avoid getting tricked into buying something you don't need or spending more than necessary. Remember, there's more to being smart with your money than just getting discounts—it's about making wise decisions.

HOW TO GET MORE FOR LESS

If value for money is about making your money go further, there are some simple tips you can follow to ensure you're getting the most out of your purchases.

COMPARE PRICES

Before making a purchase, research and compare prices from different retailers to ensure you're getting the best deal.

- **Use price comparison websites** to easily compare prices from multiple sellers.

- Consider the total cost of an item, including shipping, taxes, and any additional fees.

LOOK FOR DISCOUNTS AND COUPONS

Keep an eye out for discounts, coupons, and promotional deals that can help you save money on your purchases. If you see a box with "Enter Voucher Code" on a checkout page, take the time to search for a discount code or coupon that can be applied to your purchase.

- **Sign up for email newsletters** and alerts from your favorite retailers to receive exclusive discounts and coupons.
- **Check online coupon websites** like RetailMeNot, Coupons.com, and Groupon for deals and discounts.
- **Follow your favorite brands** and stores on social media for special promotions and sales.
- **Add a browser plug-in** like Honey to get the latest discounts.
- Check for student discounts.
- Join loyalty or rewards programs to earn points or cash back on purchases.

CONSIDER SECOND-HAND OR NEARLY NEW

Second-hand or nearly new items often come at a much lower price than brand-new items, meaning you can save money without sacrificing quality.

- **Check online marketplaces** such as Craigslist, Facebook Marketplace, or eBay for gently used items at a lower cost.
- **Visit thrift stores or charity shops** for clothing and household items.
- **Attend garage sales** or markets for unique finds at a discounted price.
- Look for refurbished or reconditioned electronics, which may have been previously used but have been restored to like-new condition.
- Look for open-box or floor-model deals at retail stores, which may have been previously used for display but are still in good condition and sold at a discounted price.

> **DID YOU KNOW?** In addition to the cost-saving benefits, buying second-hand items is also a great way to reduce waste and be more environmentally friendly.

INVEST IN QUALITY

"Buy once, buy well"—While it can be tempting to buy cheaper items, investing in products of higher quality can actually save you money in the long run, as they last longer and don't need to be replaced as often.

One way to do this is to consider an item's "cost per use" rather than just the initial price tag. A more expensive item that lasts for years and gets used frequently may be better value than a cheaper item that needs to be replaced often.

> For example, you might consider spending more money to buy a pair of shoes that will last longer than a cheaper, lower-quality pair. Instead of buying a new pair of shoes with the lower-quality option every few months, you can invest in higher-quality shoes that may only need to be replaced every couple of years. The cost per use of the higher-quality shoes over the long term is much less than the lower-quality option.

CONSIDER DIFFERENT BRANDS AND PRODUCTS

Do your research and compare quality and prices across different brands. Just because a brand is expensive doesn't mean it's the best quality.

So-called "premium brands" often use marketing and advertising tactics to justify their higher prices when you may find the same quality with generic or store-brand products at a lower price.

BUY IN BULK

Buying in bulk is a great way to save money if you know you'll use all the items. Look for stores offering discounts on bulk purchases and buy what you need in larger quantities to get more bang for your buck.

HOW TO REDUCE YOUR MONTHLY SPENDING

If you follow the advice and tips above, you're well on your way to getting more for less. But what about reducing your monthly spending even further? Here are some ways you can do just that.

1. **Cut out subscriptions you don't use:** Think of the streaming services, magazines, or apps you pay for each month. If you're not using them, cancel them. It's like cutting out the fat from your budget.

2. **Make your coffee and lunch:** Instead of buying expensive lattes or takeout, bring your coffee and lunch to school or work. You'll save a lot of money in the long run, and it's like putting money back in your pocket.

3. **Use public transportation or carpool:** Instead of driving or taking an Uber or Lyft everywhere, consider taking the bus or train. Or, if you're going to the same place as a friend,

consider carpooling. Not only will you save money on gas and transportation, but you'll also help the environment.

4. **Shop with a list:** Before you go shopping, make a list of what you need and stick to it. Impulse buying can be a budget killer, so think of your list like a game plan for your shopping.

5. **Look for free activities:** Instead of spending money on entertainment, look for free activities like going to a park, visiting a museum, or hiking. It's like finding money in your pocket that you forgot was there.

6. **Do it yourself:** Instead of hiring someone to fix things around the house or care for your car, learn to do it yourself. Search on YouTube for tutorials or ask someone handy to teach you. Over a lifetime, this can save you a lot of money and be a great way to learn new skills.

> *DID YOU KNOW?* Saving money can be done without cutting back. One way to save money without reducing spending is by using rewards programs such as cashback sites, loyalty programs, and credit card points. By taking advantage of these opportunities, you can maximize the value of your purchases while also putting some extra savings into your pocket!

The above are some simple tips to help you reduce your monthly spending, but perhaps the most important thing you can do is to adopt a mindful and money-savvy mindset.

WHAT IS A MONEY-SAVVY MINDSET?

Adopting a money-savvy mindset means being mindful of your spending and finding ways to save money without sacrificing the things you love and enjoy. It's about being creative and resourceful with your money and finding ways to stretch it further. This can include cutting back on unnecessary expenses, looking for deals and discounts, and thinking about the long-term implications of every purchase.

It's not about being cheap or living a minimalist lifestyle but rather about being smart with your money. Simply asking yourself, "Do I really need this?" before buying something can make a huge difference.

> For example, instead of buying pre-packaged meals, you could cook your own meals at home with ingredients you buy in bulk. Instead of going out to eat every weekend, you could plan a dinner with friends. Instead of buying new clothes every season, you could learn to sew and make clothes or shop at thrift stores.

By being mindful of your spending and finding creative ways to save money, you can enjoy life without breaking the bank. Start small and look for ways to save money gradually—little steps will eventually add up! It is all about being conscious of your spending habits, so you can enjoy what you love while managing your finances wisely. Good luck!

PART THREE:

BORROWING, DEBT, AND BIG-TICKET ITEM PURCHASES

CHAPTER 8. INTRODUCTION TO BORROWING MONEY AND DEBT

"Too many people spend money they haven't earned to buy things they don't want to impress people they don't like." — Will Rogers.

Borrowing and debt are a part of life that allows people to fund their goals and dreams. Without it, many of us couldn't afford things like a home, a car, or a college education. But it's important to understand how borrowing and debt work and how to use them responsibly.

You may think that these topics don't apply to you yet, but the truth is that understanding how borrowing and debt work is important for your financial well-being. As the Will Rogers quote above suggests, going into debt for things you need is one thing, but going into debt for something you don't need can eventually make you poorer.

It's about having a healthy attitude toward debt, minimizing the amount, and knowing the difference between good and bad debt.

In this chapter, we'll be exploring the different types of debt, the pros and cons of borrowing money, and how to make smart financial decisions when taking on debt. You'll learn the difference between good debt and bad debt and how to avoid falling into the trap of taking on too much debt. By the end of this chapter, you'll better understand how to use borrowing and debt responsibly to support your financial goals.

WHAT IS DEBT?

Debt is when you borrow money and agree to pay it back over a period of time, usually with interest (extra money) added on top.

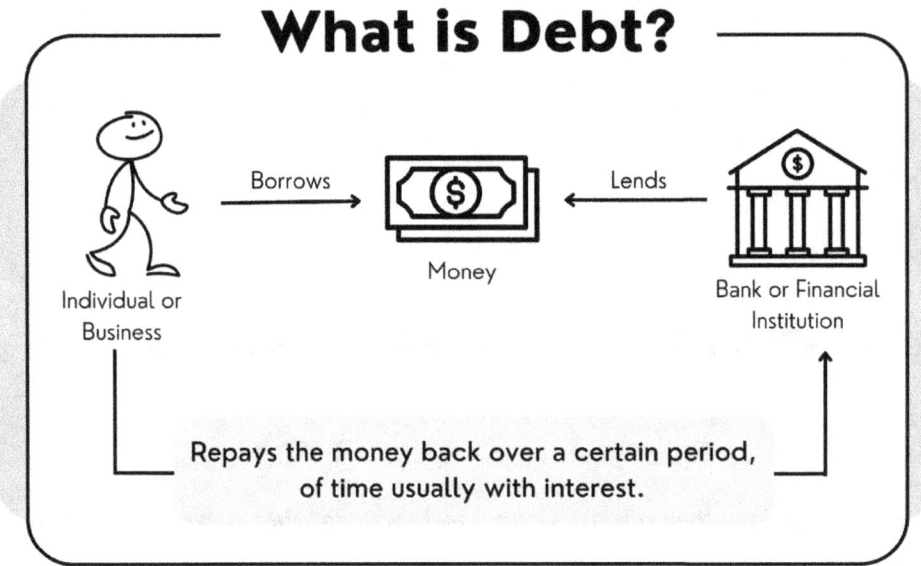

This can be for big things like buying a house or going to college or more minor things like using a credit card. It's a way for individuals or businesses to get the money they need to buy items. Still, it comes with the responsibility of repaying the borrowed amount back with interest over a period of time.

> *For example, let's say you want to buy a car but don't have enough money saved up. You can borrow money from a bank and agree to pay it back with interest. This means that you'll end up paying more than the original amount you borrowed, but it allows you to get the car you need now instead of waiting until you have enough money saved.*
>
> *The amount of time to repay the loan, and the interest rate, are determined by the agreement between you and the bank.*

> **DID YOU KNOW?** Debt has been a part of human civilization for thousands of years. In ancient civilizations such as Mesopotamia and Babylon, people used clay tablets to record loans and repayments.

DEBT VS. CREDIT

It's easy to confuse debt and credit, and the difference between them is subtle.

Debt is the amount of money you owe to someone. It can be a loan, mortgage, credit card balance, or other types of borrowing.

On the other hand, credit is the ability to borrow money or access financing.

Here are two examples:

- *Debt:* Imagine you borrow $1000 from your parents to buy a new computer. You promise to repay them the $1000 plus interest over a certain period. Your debt is $1000.

- *Credit:* If you have a credit card with a $1000 limit, your credit is $1000.

The difference between debt and credit is that **debt is money you owe to someone** specifically, like a loan from a bank or a friend, while **credit is an agreement with a lender to borrow money up to a specific limit**, like a credit card.

WHO PROVIDES DEBT AND WHY?

Debt is typically provided by financial institutions such as banks, credit unions, and online lenders.

Financial institutions are in the business of making money, and lending is one way they do it. They essentially provide a service—offering individuals and companies money that they need—and the lenders profit from the interest rates paid on each loan.

WHAT ARE INTEREST RATES (OR APR) AND HOW DOES IT WORK?

When you borrow money, you usually have to pay back more than you borrowed because of interest charges and other fees.

The interest rate is the percentage a lender charges on the amount borrowed.

> *For example, if you borrow $1,000 with an interest rate of 5%, you must pay back $1,050 ($1,000 + 5% interest).*

The APR (annual percentage rate) is the total cost of borrowing money over one year, expressed as a percentage. This includes the interest rate charged on the amount borrowed and any additional fees or charges associated with the loan.

> *For example, if you take out a $1,000 loan with an APR of 10%, you would end up paying back $1,100 ($1,000 + 10% interest) over one year.*

The higher the APR, the more expensive it is to borrow money.

Interest rates can vary depending on the type of loan or credit product. They can also be affected by your credit score, the amount you borrow, and the loan term.

A lower interest rate (or APR) is generally better because it means you pay less in interest over the life of the loan.

DIFFERENT TYPES OF DEBT

Debt can take many forms. Some common types of debt include secured, unsecured, revolving, nonrevolving, and mortgages. Understanding the differences between these types of debt can help you make informed decisions about borrowing money and managing your finances.

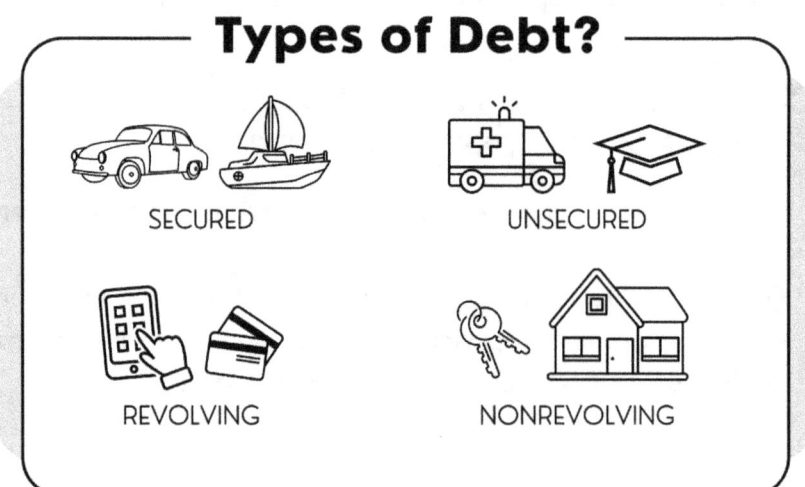

SECURED DEBT

This type of debt is backed by something specific (known as "collateral"), such as a car or a house. This means that if you can't repay the borrowed money, the bank or lender can take the item you used as collateral to make up for the money you owe.

> *For example, let's say you jump into a brand-new Audi convertible and drive off the dealership lot. You have just taken out a secured debt by taking a car loan. Although you have the keys in your hands and the wind in your hair, you don't own the car. The lender does, and the vehicle you purchased is the collateral. The lender can take the car if you don't repay the loan on time.*
>
> *Similarly, if you take out a mortgage to purchase a home, the home itself is the collateral and can be taken by the lender if you fail to make the mortgage payments.*

This type of debt is often less risky for lenders because they have something they can take if you don't pay them back. As a result, secured debts usually have lower interest rates and more favorable terms than unsecured debt.

UNSECURED DEBT

This type of debt is not backed by collateral, which means if you can't pay back the money you borrowed, the lender has nothing specific they can take from you to make up for what you owe. Instead, they may take legal action against you or send debt collectors to try and get their money back.

Examples of unsecured debt include personal loans, credit card debt, and medical bills.

These debts are usually riskier for lenders, so they often come with higher interest rates.

REVOLVING DEBT

This type of debt has no set repayment schedule and allows you to borrow money up to a specific limit and then pay it back over time.

The key feature of revolving debt is that the available credit replenishes as you make payments. You can continue borrowing and paying off the balance as long as you stay within your credit limit. A typical example of revolving debt is a credit card. You can use your card to make purchases up to your credit limit and then pay off the balance at your own pace.

> For example, if you have a credit card with a limit of $10,000 and spend $500, your available credit is reset to $9,500. As you pay off your balance, your available credit increases, and you can continue to borrow and spend up to your limit.

The danger with this type of debt is that it can lead to many debt and financial difficulties if you don't manage it carefully.

Revolving debt allows you to repeatedly borrow money, which can give the illusion that you have unlimited funds. But if the balance is not paid in full each month, you get charged interest, making it more challenging to pay off the debt. This can lead to a cycle of borrowing and repayment that becomes difficult to break out of.

To avoid this, it's vital to use revolving credit responsibly and **only borrow what you can afford to repay.**

NON-REVOLVING DEBT

This type of debt has a set repayment schedule, with a specific end date for when the loan must be paid back in full. Unlike revolving debt, you cannot continue to borrow once the loan is repaid.

> For example, if you take out a personal loan to pay for a home renovation project, you will receive a lump sum of money and then make fixed payments until the loan is paid off.

The advantage of non-revolving debt is that it gives you a clear timeline for when the loan will be paid off and helps you plan your finances more effectively. However, it may also come with higher interest rates compared to revolving debt and may not offer the flexibility to access additional funds if needed.

MORTGAGES

This type of debt is a loan used to buy a home. You borrow a large sum of money and pay it back over a long time, typically 15–30 years. The property is collateral for the loan, meaning that the bank can take the property to recoup their losses if you don't pay the mortgage.

> For example, let's say you take out a mortgage of $200,000 to buy a home and agree to make payments over 30 years at a fixed interest rate. Each month, you pay the bank to pay off the principal amount you borrowed ($200,000) and the interest on the loan. As you make payments, the amount you owe decreases. Eventually, after 30 years, you have paid off your mortgage and own the house outright.

GOOD DEBT VS. BAD DEBT

Not all debt is created equal, and it's essential to understand the difference between good debt and bad debt.

Good debt is debt that is taken on for investments that helps you build wealth or generate income in the future.

Some examples of good debt include:

- **A student loan to pay for college education**—This is considered good debt because it can help you get a better job and earn more money in the long run.

- **A mortgage loan**—This is money borrowed from a bank to buy a home. This is also considered good debt, as the price of houses tends to go up in value over time, so the home could eventually be sold for a profit.

Bad debt is any type of debt that does not increase your financial well-being and may harm your financial situation. Some examples of bad debt include:

- **High-interest credit card balances used to purchase non-essential items like clothing**—This is considered bad debt because the purchases are unlikely to increase in value over time.

- **A loan to buy a car that loses value**—This is considered bad debt because the car will likely lose value over time.

The key takeaway is that it's important to understand the difference between good and bad debt and how to use credit responsibly.

Good debt can help you build wealth and gain financial freedom, while bad debt can lead to financial stress and difficulties.

Pros & Cons of Using Debt

PROS

1. Provides funds to make large purchases, such as a home or car.
2. Can be used to invest in a business or education that can lead to higher earning potential in the future.
3. Debt can help manage cash flow during difficult times, such as job loss or medical emergencies.

CONS

1. Too much debt with high interest can make it really hard to keep up with the payments, causing stress and financial problems.
2. Taking on too much debt, can limit your ability to do things you want in the future because you'll have less money available.
3. Not paying your bills on time can hurt your credit score, which makes it harder to borrow money in the future.
4. If you don't pay your bills on time you could lose the item you bought on credit, like a house or car.

WHEN IS DEBT HELPFUL, AND WHEN CAN IT BE A PROBLEM?

Debt can be useful when used to make investments that will ultimately increase your earning potential or improve your overall financial situation, such as taking out a student loan to pay for education or a mortgage loan to buy a house.

However, debt can also be a problem when it is used to purchase unnecessary items or when you cannot make the payments on time, leading to high-interest rates and penalties. This can ultimately cause financial strain and make it challenging to achieve your financial goals.

Additionally, taking on too much debt can make it difficult to handle unexpected financial emergencies.

WHAT SIMPLE STEPS CAN YOU TAKE TO ENSURE YOU'RE USING DEBT RESPONSIBLY AND AVOIDING FINANCIAL TROUBLE?

Some steps you can take include:

- **Avoid taking on** (too much) **debt**.
- Ensure you understand the terms and conditions of any loan or credit before taking it out.
- **Only borrow what you can afford to pay back**.
- Keep track of your payments and due dates, and always pay on time.
- Be mindful of your credit score and maintain a good credit history.
- Be aware of the potential risks and consequences of not being able to make payments.
- Consider seeking advice from a financial professional if you're struggling with debt.
- Be aware of the interest rate, which can significantly affect how much you pay over time.
- Try to pay off debt with the highest interest rate first.

It's important to remember that debt can be a helpful tool when used responsibly, but it can also be very dangerous if not managed properly.

WHAT CAN YOU DO TO GET OUT OF DEBT?

If you're in debt and can't make your payments or have large amounts of debt, there are a few steps you can take.

1. **Speak to the lenders:** See if they can offer you a different repayment plan or if there are any options for consolidating your debt. Most lenders will work with you to find a solution that works for both of you. This could include extending the loan term, lowering the interest rate, or consolidating multiple loans.

2. **Make a budget:** This will help you see where your money is going and where you can make cuts.

3. **Prioritize your debts:** Pay off the debts with the highest interest rates first, as they will cost you more in the long run.

4. **Create a payment plan:** Break down your payments into manageable chunks and make sure you pay at least the minimum amount due each month.

5. **Look for ways to increase your income:** This could be through a part-time job, side hustle, or asking for a raise at your current job.

6. **Seek help if needed:** Several organizations and government programs can help you with debt relief, such as credit counseling services and debt management plans.

7. **Avoid new debt:** Once you're on the road to paying off your existing debts, avoid taking on new debt, which can make it harder to get out of the hole.

Getting out of debt can take time and effort, but you can do it with a plan and determination.

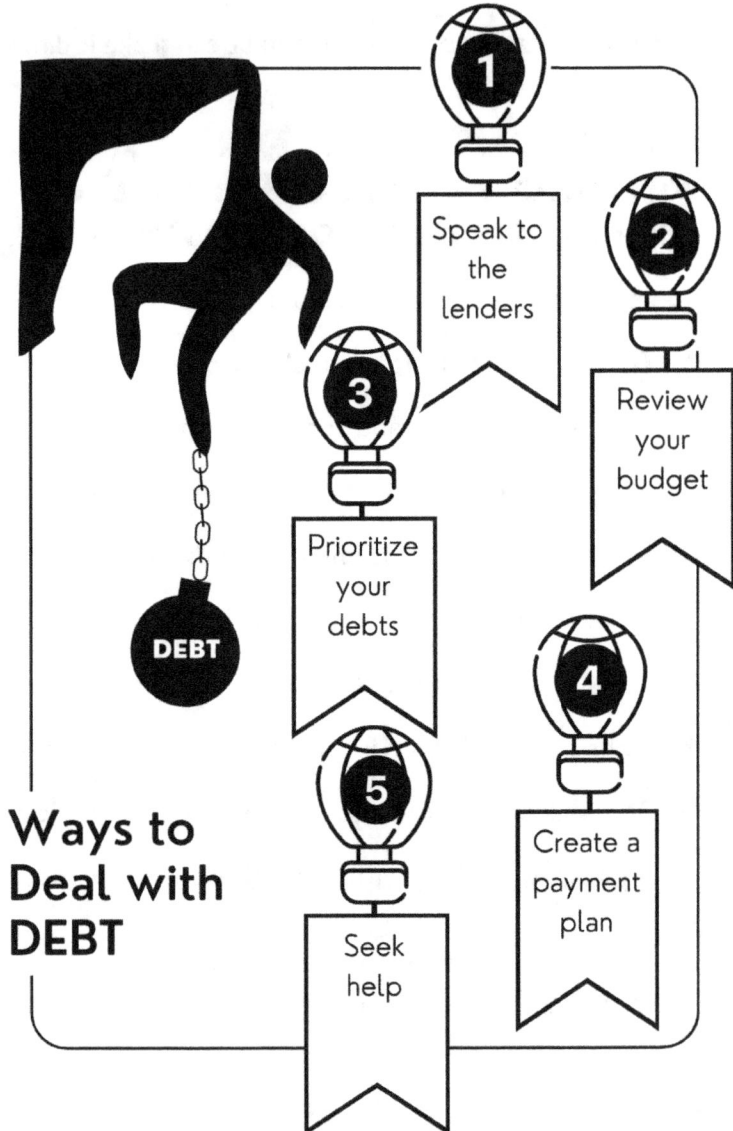

Ways to Deal with DEBT

CHAPTER 9. BIG-TICKET ITEM PURCHASES

A big-ticket item usually refers to large, expensive things that cost more than a single paycheck, such as a home, car, expensive furniture, appliances, gadgets, or computers. These purchases often require careful planning and saving to afford them.

As a teen, you may not be considering buying a house or car right now. Still, it's helpful to start thinking about how you can financially prepare for these big purchases in the future.

In this chapter, we'll be talking about the process of saving up for and buying big-ticket items. We'll cover things like setting a budget, saving for a down payment, understanding mortgages, and some of the associated ongoing costs to consider before you make a large purchase.

THINGS TO CONSIDER WHEN YOU'RE PLANNING A BIG-TICKET PURCHASE

It can seem daunting when it comes to big-ticket purchases, like buying a house or car. But with a bit of planning and preparation, it doesn't have to be.

Before you start, research the item you are interested in buying. This will help you figure out what's within your budget and what features you can get for your money. You might also find it helpful to seek advice from friends and family about the choices they made. They can probably provide some valuable insights about their experiences and potential pitfalls.

Once you have a good idea of what you're looking for, it's time to start thinking about how you will pay for it.

One option is to save up and buy it outright. This can be a great choice if you have the discipline and financial means to save. But for many people, this isn't an option.

Another option is to borrow money. This can be through a mortgage for a house or a car loan for a vehicle. But it's important to know the costs associated with borrowing, including the interest rate and any fees. It's also important to consider if the loan repayments will be manageable for you in the long term.

It's also essential to consider the ongoing costs of the item, such as property taxes, insurance, and maintenance. This will give you a more accurate picture of the total cost of ownership and help you determine if it's a financially sound decision.

Let's have a look at each of these in turn.

BUYING OUTRIGHT VS. BORROWING MONEY

There are two main options when buying big-ticket items: **buying outright** or **borrowing money**.

Buying outright has the benefit of not paying interest on a loan, meaning you'll save money in the long run. It also gives you full ownership of the item and eliminates the risk of defaulting on a loan. However, it also means that you'll need to have the full amount of money saved up, which may not be possible for some people. This might be similar to saving all your allowance for months to buy a new video game console.

On the other hand, borrowing money allows you to purchase the item immediately and spread the cost over some time. This can be helpful if you don't have all the money saved up yet, but it also means you'll have to pay interest on the loan, which can add up over time.

It's important to weigh each option's pros and cons and consider your financial situation before deciding. And always remember to think about the long-term aspects of the purchase, not just the short-term ones.

UPFRONT COSTS VS. ONGOING COSTS

When buying big-ticket items, it's vital to consider both upfront costs and ongoing costs.

Upfront costs are the expenses you pay when you first purchase the item, such as a down payment or closing costs. **Ongoing costs are the expenses you pay after the purchase**, such as insurance, maintenance, and repairs.

For example, suppose you purchase a car for $20,000. In that case, the upfront costs could include the car's price, a sales tax of 7%, a registration fee of $50, and an extra $1000 for additional features. Ongoing costs might include insurance premiums of $100 per month, regular maintenance costs of $50, and gas expenses of $200 per month.

When considering a big-ticket purchase, it's crucial to consider both the upfront and ongoing costs and how they will impact your budget over time.

FINANCIAL PLANNING FOR BIG-TICKET ITEMS

A financial plan is a roadmap for saving and managing your money to reach a specific financial goal, such as making a large purchase. Implementing a financial plan for a big purchase involves several steps.

1. **Determine your goal:** Be specific about what you want to purchase and when you want to buy it.

2. **Assess your current financial situation:** Look at your income, expenses, savings, and any existing debts.

3. **Make a budget:** Create a budget that takes into account your goal, current financial situation, and any other financial commitments you have.

4. **Start saving:** Make sure you are setting aside enough money each month to reach your goal.

5. **Look for ways to increase your income:** Consider taking on a part-time job or finding ways to make extra money.

6. **Consider different funding options:** You may be able to buy the item outright, or you may need to borrow money through a loan or mortgage.

7. **Compare costs:** Be aware of any upfront and ongoing costs and ensure you get the best value for your money.

By following these steps, you will be able to create a plan that will help you save up for and purchase your big-ticket item. It's important to remember that saving up for a big purchase will take time, but with a plan, you can reach your goal.

Now let's look at some specific examples.

CHAPTER 10. AN INTRODUCTION TO CAR OWNERSHIP

Owning your first car is an exciting milestone for any young adult. But buying a vehicle is not just about picking out the color and model you like; it is a big financial commitment.

Whether saving up to buy one outright or looking into financing options, it's important to understand the different ways to purchase a car and the ongoing costs of owning one.

In this chapter, we'll explore how the finance side of things work.

HOW TO PAY FOR YOUR FIRST CAR

If you're thinking about buying a car, there are a few things you need to consider.

One of the most important is how you're going to finance it. There are a few options, such as buying outright, financing, and leasing. Each has pros and cons, so it's important to understand what they are before deciding.

- **Buying outright:** If you have enough money, buying a car outright can be a great option. This way, you own the vehicle outright and don't have to worry about making monthly payments. However, this can also be a significant financial burden if you don't have huge savings.
- **Financing:** Another option is to finance a car. This means taking out a loan from a bank or other lender to pay for the vehicle. This allows you to spread the cost over several years, making it more manageable. However, you'll need to pay interest on the loan, which can add to the cost of the car.
- **Leasing:** A third option is to lease a car. This means paying a monthly fee to use a car for a set period. At the end of the lease, you can buy or return the car. Leasing can be a good option if you don't want to commit to buying a car outright or if you want to drive a newer car. However, you will have mileage and wear-and-tear limits and may not be able to customize the vehicle.

ONGOING COSTS

Owning your first car is exciting, but it's important to remember that purchasing a vehicle is just the start. You'll need to budget for many ongoing costs associated with car ownership. Here are a few examples of ongoing costs to keep in mind.

- **Fuel costs:** You must pay for gasoline, diesel, or electricity to power your car. The cost will depend on the fuel price in your area and how many miles you drive.

- **Insurance:** Most countries require drivers to have car insurance. The insurance cost will depend on factors such as your age, driving record, and the make and model of your car.

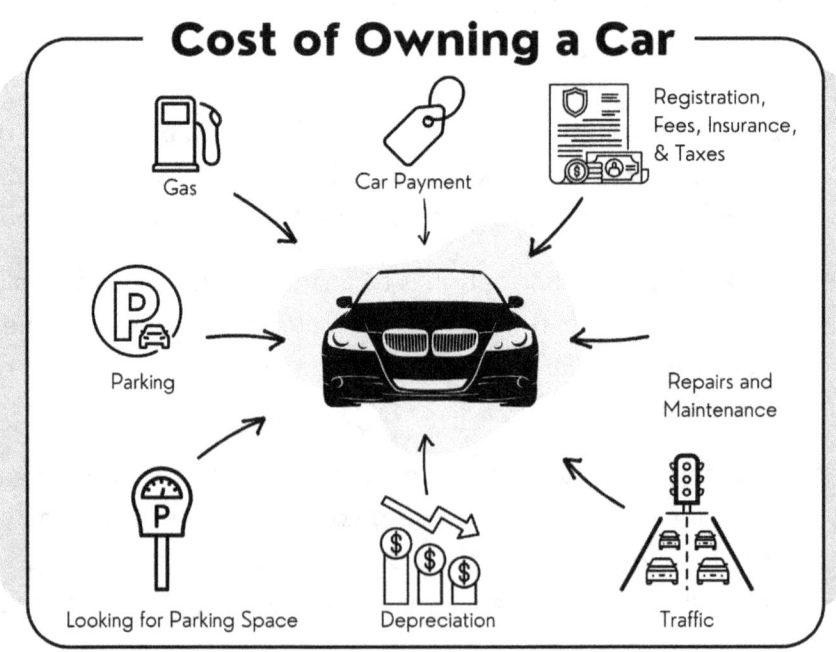

- **Maintenance and repairs:** Cars require regular maintenance, such as oil changes, tire rotations, and brake pad replacement. They may also need repairs if something goes wrong. The cost of maintenance and repairs will depend on the car's age, make, model, and how often you drive it.

- **Tires:** Tires need to be changed periodically. The cost will depend on the type of tires and how often you drive.

- **Registration and licensing:** You'll need to pay for registration and licensing for your car, the cost of which can vary depending on where you live.

- **Depreciation:** The value of your car will decrease over time. This is known as depreciation and could affect the resale value of your vehicle, meaning you can't sell it for as much as you paid for it.

- **Parking:** If you don't have a driveway or garage, you may need to pay for parking.

> **DID YOU KNOW?** According to AAA, the average cost of owning a car in the US is $10,728 per year. This includes car payments, maintenance, fuel, insurance, and depreciation.

CHAPTER 11. AN INTRODUCTION TO HOME OWNERSHIP

Buying a home is one of the biggest financial decisions you'll ever make. It's a significant investment that can give you a sense of stability and security. But before you start searching for your dream house, it's important to understand how to finance buying a home and what to expect in terms of ongoing costs.

Most people don't have enough money to buy a house outright, so they get a mortgage.

A mortgage is a loan from a bank or other financial institution to buy a home. To get a mortgage, you'll need to put down an initial deposit—usually around 10–20% of the purchase price. This is known as your "down payment." Then, you'll pay back the rest of the loan every month for 15-30 years until it's all paid off.

There are several different types of mortgages available, such as fixed-rate mortgages and adjustable-rate mortgages.

A fixed-rate mortgage is a loan where the interest rate stays the same for the entire duration of the loan. This means your monthly payments will remain the same, no matter what happens in the economy. This can be helpful as it makes budgeting for your mortgage payments easier.

On the other hand, an adjustable-rate mortgage (ARM) has an interest rate that can change over time. This means your monthly payments might increase or decrease depending on the economy. This type of mortgage can be riskier because you don't know how much your payments will be in the future. But it also can have a lower interest rate at the beginning of the loan, which can be helpful for people who cannot initially afford higher payments.

Choosing which type of mortgage is right for you depends on how much money you have saved up, how good your credit score is, and your plans for the future.

> **DID YOU KNOW?** According to recent data, the average age of first-time homebuyers in the United States is 36.

HOW MUCH MORTGAGE CAN YOU AFFORD?

When trying to figure out how much mortgage you can afford, there are a few things to keep in mind.

First, mortgage lenders usually look at your income and debts to determine how much you can borrow. They'll typically use a debt-to-income ratio (DTI), which compares your monthly income to your monthly debt payments. This measures how much of your income goes towards paying off your debts, such as credit card payments and car loans. The lower your DTI, the more likely you are to be approved for a mortgage and the more you can borrow.

> *For example, if you earn $5,000 a month and have $1,000 in monthly debt payments, your DTI is 20%. This means that 20% of your income goes towards debt payments. Most lenders typically want your DTI to be at or below 43%.*

The second factor is your gross income, which is your total income before taxes and other deductions. Mortgage lenders usually look at a multiple of your income to determine how much you can borrow.

> *For example, if you make $50,000 a year and the lender uses a multiple of 4, you may be able to borrow up to $200,000.*

The third factor is the down payment, or the money you pay as a deposit. It's usually a percentage of the purchase price—typically at least 5–20%. The bigger the down payment, the smaller the mortgage loan you'll need, which usually results in lower monthly payments.

> *For example, if you're looking to buy a house for $300,000 and can afford to put down 20% or $60,000 as a down payment, you'll need to borrow $240,000. This will lower your monthly mortgage payment.*

A larger down payment can also make getting approved for a mortgage easier and can help you get a better interest rate.

HOW LONG ARE MORTGAGES FOR?

When you take out a mortgage to buy a home, the loan is typically spread over 15 to 30 years. This is known as the term of the mortgage. The longer the term, the lower your monthly payments will be, but you'll end up paying more in interest over the life of the loan.

If you decide to move before paying off your mortgage, you have a few options. One is to sell the home and use the money to pay off the remaining balance on the loan. Another option is to refinance the mortgage, which means you get a new loan with a different interest rate or loan term.

You can also consider renting out your home and becoming a landlord. The rent would go towards paying the mortgage and other expenses. Remember that this also brings additional responsibilities, such as finding tenants, managing the property, and dealing with maintenance issues.

ONGOING COSTS OF HOME OWNERSHIP

Owning a home can be an excellent investment, but it comes with ongoing costs. These include:

- **Property taxes**—You'll have to pay taxes on your property every year. The amount you pay depends on how much your home is worth and the tax rate where you live.

- **Homeowners insurance**—This kind of insurance protects your home and belongings if something terrible happens, like a natural disaster or theft. Usually, banks require you to have it if you have a mortgage.

- **Maintenance and repairs**—As a homeowner, it's up to you to ensure your house stays in good condition. This means fixing things that break like leaky pipes, painting walls, or replacing the roof when it gets old.

- **Utilities**—When you own a house, you pay for things like electricity, gas, water, and the internet. Make sure to budget for these expenses so you don't get surprised by high bills!

It's essential to keep these ongoing costs in mind when you're budgeting for a home purchase. Setting aside money each month for unexpected repairs is also a good idea. After all, you never know what's going to happen.

PART FOUR:

YOUR WAY TO WEALTH

CHAPTER 12. SAVING – YOUR RAINY DAY FUND

Saving money is integral to learning to be responsible with your finances, regardless of age. It's like building a fortress around your future—the more you save, the stronger and more secure it will be!

Saving can take many forms from setting aside a certain amount each month to investing in stocks or bonds. It's all about having the discipline to put money away for a rainy day and not spending it on something you don't need right now.

> **DID YOU KNOW?** The concept of "saving for a rainy day" originated in India. It was common practice to set aside grains during times of plenty to use during drought or famine.

SAVING VS. INVESTING

Saving and investing are ways to grow your money, but they work in different ways.

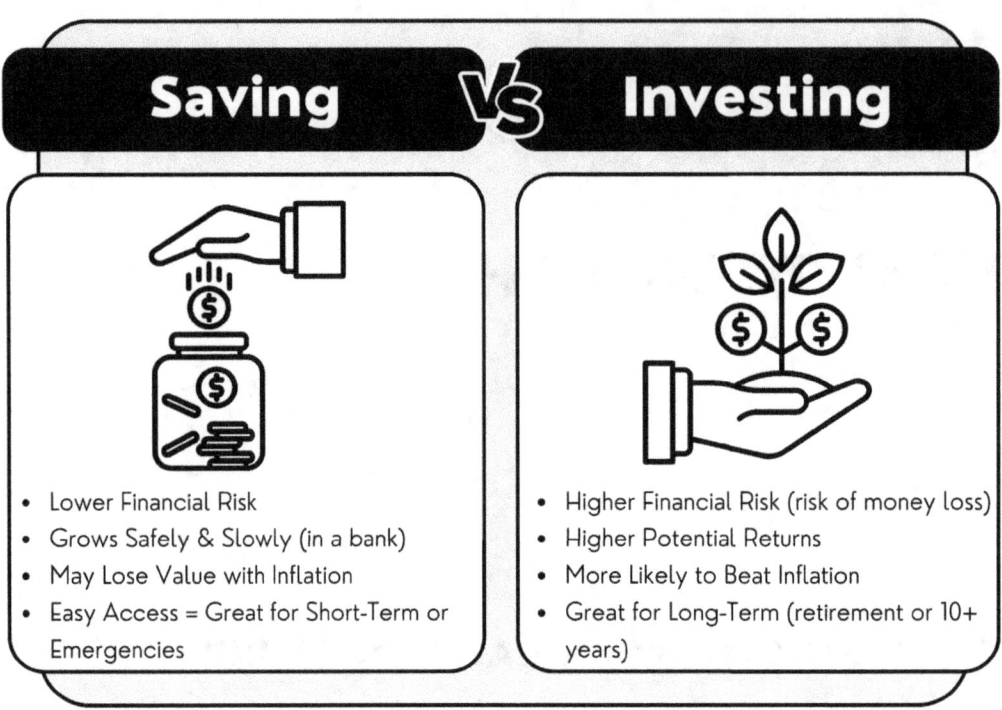

Saving money is when you put aside a portion of your income for future use, usually into a savings account at a bank. You're setting it aside for a specific goal or rainy day. This money will grow slowly, and it's generally considered a lower-risk option. In addition, the money is easily accessible when you need it. *For example, you might save money for a car down payment or emergency fund.*

Investing, on the other hand, is like planting a seed in the ground. When you invest, you're putting your money into something like stocks, bonds, or real estate with the expectation that it will grow in value over time. It's generally considered a higher-risk option but can also create greater returns.

While saving helps you to put money aside for short-term goals and emergencies, investing is about growing your money over the long term—but you need to be comfortable with the higher risk involved.

WHY IT PAYS TO START SAVING YOUNG

It's never too early to start thinking about saving. The earlier you start, the better—for several reasons.

THE POWER OF COMPOUND INTEREST

The earlier you start saving, the more time your money has to grow. This is because of the power of compound interest.

Compound interest is where the interest earned is added to the original amount of money. Then future interest is earned on top of that. This means that the longer you save your money, the more interest it will make, and the more your money will grow.

> *Imagine you put $100 into a savings account that earns 10% interest per year. After one year, you would have $110. But if you left that $110 in the account for another year, it would earn 10% interest again, bringing the total to $121. The longer you leave your money in the account, the more it will grow.*

Here's another example:

> *Let's say two individuals, Jane and Mike, want to save for retirement. Jane starts saving at age 21 and manages to save a total of $24,000 by the time she is 41, at which point she stops saving. Mike doesn't start saving until age 47 and manages to save $24,000 until he retires at 67.*
>
> *Assuming an annual interest rate of 8%, Jane's investment of $24,000 will have grown to $471,358 by the time she retires at 67.*
>
> *On the other hand, Mike started later, so his investment of $24,000 has had less time to grow and is only worth $59,295 by the time he retires at 67.*

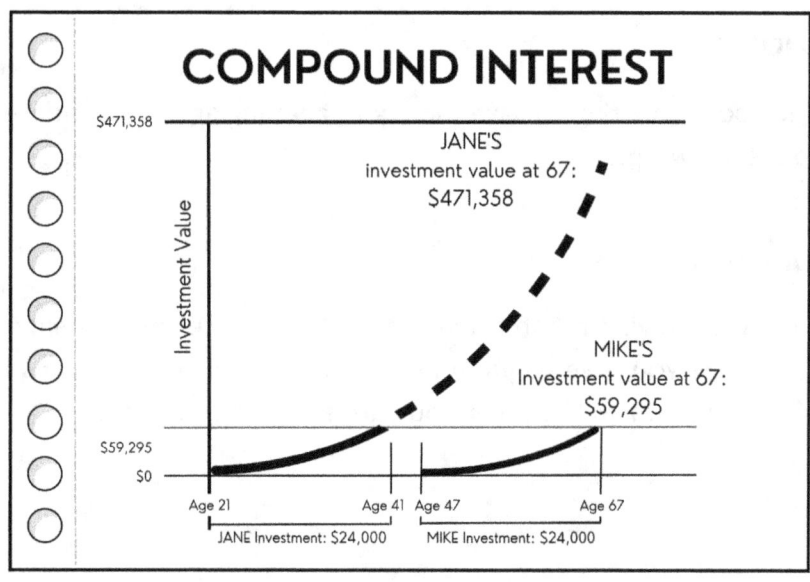

Time is one of the most significant advantages when saving and investing. The longer your money has to compound, the more it can grow over time—even with a small amount of savings each month!

STARTING YOUNG HELPS DEVELOP GOOD FINANCIAL HABITS

Another reason why it pays to start saving young is that it helps you develop good financial habits. The more you save and budget your money, the more you will understand how to make your money work for you. It's like learning a new skill—the more you practice, the better you get.

- *For example, if you start saving $50 a month from age 16, you will have $3,600 saved by the time you are 21 ($50 x 12 months x 6 years). That's a lot of money that could be used for a down payment on a car or an emergency fund.*

STARTING YOUNG PREPARES YOU FOR UNEXPECTED EVENTS

Additionally, if you start saving young, you'll be more prepared for unexpected expenses or big life events like college, buying a house, or starting a family. It's like planning a trip—the more you plan, the better prepared you are.

Saving may not be the most exciting thing, but it's an important step toward financial independence and security. It will give you the freedom to make choices and pursue opportunities that might otherwise be out of reach.

HOW TO SAVE MONEY

As we have explored above, starting to save money at a young age is essential—but how do you actually do it? Here are a few tips:

1. MAKE SAVING A HABIT

First, just focus on making saving a habit and gradually increase your savings once it becomes comfortable. Don't feel like you have to jump in with enormous contributions right away. Setting aside just $5 or $10 each month will help get you started on the right track.

2. HAVE GOALS AND TRACK YOUR PROGRESS

Having clear goals will help you stay motivated when it comes to saving. Making sure you track your progress along the way will make those goals seem more achievable and keep you on track toward reaching them.

> *For example, you might set a goal of saving $1,000 for college by the time you turn 18. You can then break this down into smaller goals and track your progress each month to see how much closer you are to achieving it.*

3. HAVE MULTIPLE ACCOUNTS

Having multiple savings accounts can help you better manage your money. You could have a short-term savings account to save for things like holidays and a long-term savings account to save for things like college or buying your first car. You can usually set up multiple savings accounts at your bank, but you may want to shop around for the highest interest rates.

4. AUTOMATE YOUR SAVINGS

Setting up an automatic transfer from your primary checking account into your savings accounts each month is a great way to ensure you don't forget about putting money into savings. Automating your savings also helps you save more because it removes the temptation of spending that money before it goes into your savings account.

5. LOOK FOR WAYS TO EARN EXTRA MONEY

Look for part-time jobs or freelance work that you can do during your free time, or even consider starting your own small business. The extra income can go straight into your savings account, helping you reach your goals faster.

6. LOOK FOR DEALS AND DISCOUNTS

Saving money doesn't always mean putting money away. It can also mean finding ways to cut back on your spending.

When you're shopping for anything, always be on the lookout for deals and discounts. By taking advantage of sales and coupons, you can save money on your purchases and put more into your savings account. You can also look into free trials, samples, and freebies or buy used items.

> **DID YOU KNOW?** Small, everyday expenses can add up to significant savings over time. For example, skipping a $5 latte every workday for a year would save you $1,300!

7. LEARN TO BUDGET AND PRIORITIZE EXPENSES

Creating a budget will help you understand how much money you have coming in and going out each month. Prioritizing your expenses and cutting back on unnecessary spending can free up more money for your savings.

> *For example, instead of buying a new video game every month, you could save that money towards a bigger purchase, like a laptop or a new bike.*

8. START SMALL AND GROW YOUR SAVINGS

Remember, starting small is better than not starting at all. Even if you can only save a little bit each month, that's better than nothing. Over time, as you get used to saving and building the habit, you can gradually increase the amount you save each month.

By having a plan and sticking to it, you can start building a healthy financial future from a young age with just small steps each day.

SIMPLE SAVINGS METHODS

Now that you have a good idea of how to save money, let's explore some of the methods to put that into practice.

THE ENVELOPE METHOD

The envelope system is a simple method of budgeting that involves physically dividing your cash into different envelopes labeled with various expenses, such as "groceries" or "entertainment." When the money in an envelope runs out, you know you need to stop spending on that category for the rest of the month.

This system can also be adapted for online banking and budgeting apps. Instead of using physical envelopes, you would create virtual "envelopes" or categories within the app and assign a certain amount of money to each.

> *For example, you could set a budget for "shopping" and "eating out" and transfer the appropriate amount into those categories at the beginning of each month. When the funds in a category run low, it serves as a reminder to cut back on spending in that area.*

THE SAVE FIRST METHOD

The Save First Method is another simple savings method that can help you build a habit of saving. The basic idea behind this method is to save a certain percentage of your income **before** spending it on other things. This can be a set percentage, such as 10% or 20%, or a flexible percentage based on your income and expenses.

Even though you may not yet have a full-time job, you can still apply this method to your allowance or part-time job income.

> *For example, let's say you get a part-time job and earn $500 a month. Under the 50/30/20 system, you would allocate $250 for necessities like housing, food, and transportation, $150 for wants like shopping, entertainment, and dining out, and $100 for savings.*

Another way to apply the save first method is to set up an automatic transfer from your main checking account into your savings accounts each month. This way, your savings will be taken care of before you even have a chance to spend it.

It's important to note that the Save First Method is adaptable, and you can adjust the percentages to suit your financial situation. The most important thing is to prioritize saving and build it into your regular budget.

These strategies are great for getting into the habit of saving money and ensuring that you have a healthy financial future. Whether setting up multiple savings accounts, automating your transfers, or putting aside some cash as soon as you get it, there are many easy ways to start saving today!

SAVINGS AND TAX

This is not a book about taxes, but it's helpful to understand tax regarding savings.

When you save money, sometimes the government will take a small percentage of that money in taxes. This is called "tax on savings." It's similar to paying taxes on the money you earn from a job.

There are different types of savings accounts, some of which are "tax-efficient," meaning that you don't have to pay as much tax on the money you save in them. In fact, some savings accounts are called "tax-free savings accounts" because you don't have to pay any tax on the interest you earn from them.

It's important to remember that taxes can be complex and differ by country. You should talk to a tax professional or financial advisor if you have any tax questions or if are unsure how taxes work with your savings and investments.

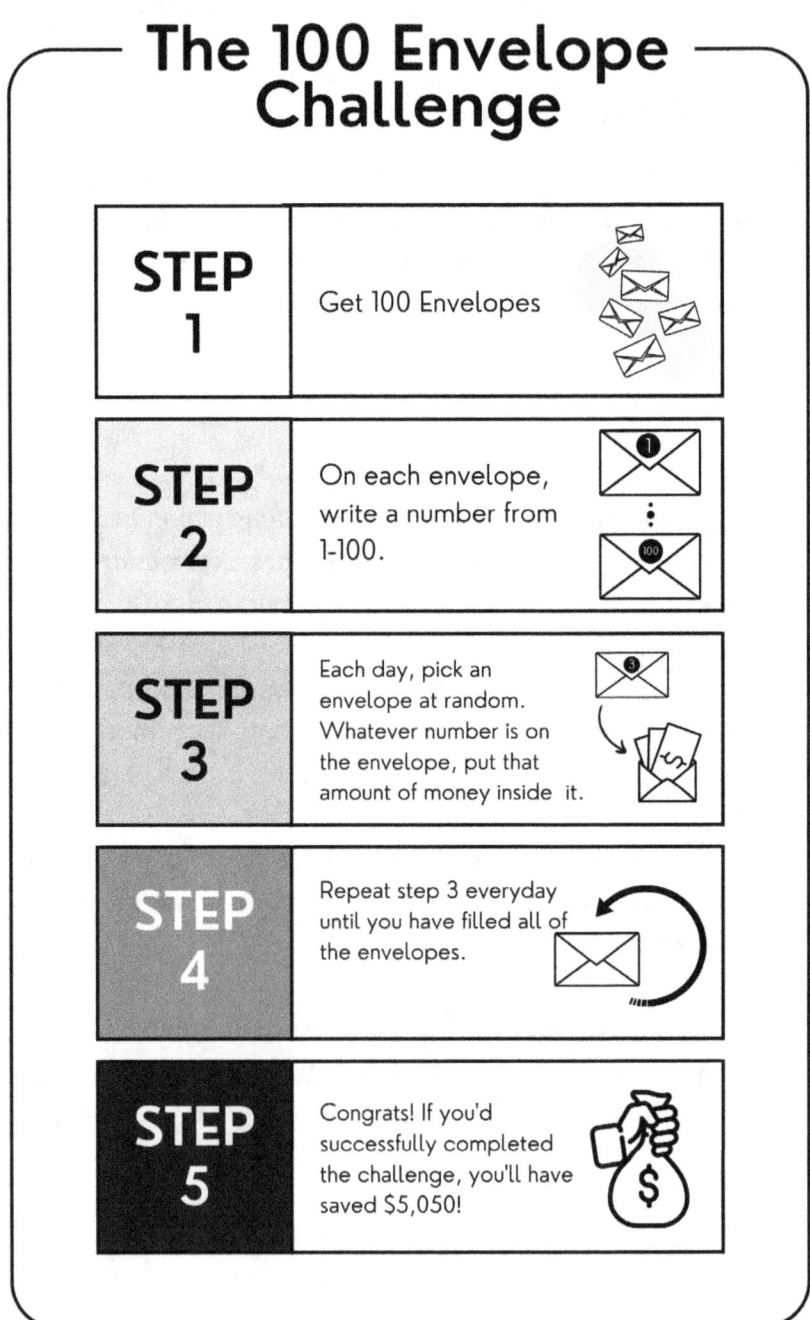

CHAPTER 13. INVESTING – BUILDING WEALTH

Investing can seem mysterious and daunting, but it's a lot simpler than it appears.

Imagine your money is like a seed you plant in fertile soil. That seed can grow into a healthy and strong tree with the right amount of water, sunshine, and care.

Investing works in a similar way! Putting your money into different types of high-quality investments can help it grow and become more valuable over time.

Like a garden, you can make many different types of investments, each with its own risk level and potential reward. Some investments, like stocks or businesses, have the potential to snowball, but they also come with a higher level of risk.

Other investments, like bonds or savings accounts, offer a more stable and reliable return but with lower growth potential. When investing, the key is to find the right balance between risk and reward to help your money grow in a way that works best for you.

In this chapter, we'll be exploring the world of investing. We'll look at the different types of investments available to grow your money. We'll review the pros and cons of each and help you understand the risk vs. reward aspect of investing. Finally, we'll talk about the importance of having a long-term horizon when it comes to investing and the difference between short-term and long-term investments.

But first up, what exactly is investing?

Investing is putting your money into something with the hope of making more money in the future.

When you invest your money, you are buying a piece of something, like a company (stocks), real estate (property), or a loan to a company or government (bonds). These investments can generate income or grow in value so you can sell them later for a profit.

The idea behind investing is to put your money to work, instead of letting it sit in a savings account. But while you can make money by investing, you can also lose money if the investment doesn't perform well. This is why educating yourself and understanding the different types of investments and their associated risks is crucial.

DIFFERENT TYPES OF INVESTMENTS

When you start to build out your financial portfolio, there are many different types of investments available to you. Each comes with pros, cons, risks, rewards, and time horizon. Let's have a look at some of them:

STOCKS

When you buy stocks, you essentially buy a small piece of ownership in a company. *For example, if a company has 100 shares and you buy one share, you own 1% of that company.* Companies sell shares of their stock on the stock market to raise money and to give people a chance to own a piece of the company.

When you buy a share of stock, you have the potential to make money in two ways.

1. Capital appreciation: If the company does well and its stock price increases, you can sell your shares for a profit.
2. Dividends: If the company is profitable, you may also receive a portion of the company's profits in the form of dividends, which are payments made to shareholders.

However, there is also a risk involved with buying stocks. **If the company does poorly, its stock price might decrease, and you could lose money.** That's why it's essential to research and make informed decisions before buying stocks.

Pros: High potential for growth and an excellent way to participate in a company's growth.

Cons: The stock market can go up and down. There's always the risk that a company could go bankrupt, and your investment could be lost.

Time horizon: Long-term (five years or more).

> **DID YOU KNOW?** The world's first stock market was established in Amsterdam in 1602 by the Dutch East India Company. The company issued shares to investors, making it one of the earliest examples of a publicly traded company.

BONDS

When you purchase a bond, you essentially lend funds to a company or government. In return, they promise to pay you back the amount you lent, plus interest, over an agreed-upon time. The company or government uses your money to finance its operations or pay for big projects.

Think of buying a bond like lending your friend some money. They promise to pay you back the amount you lent, plus a little extra for letting them use your money. Just like with your friend, when you buy a bond, there's a risk that the company or government won't be able to pay you back. In general, however, bonds are considered less risky than stocks.

When the bond reaches the end of its term, the company or government will pay you back the amount you lent. The interest you receive from a bond is usually paid to you in regular payments. The interest you receive is based on the interest rate agreed upon when you bought the bond.

> *For example, let's say you purchased a $1,000, 10-year bond with a 5% annual interest rate. In this case, you would receive $50 per year in interest payments until the bond reaches maturity in 10 years. At that point, you would receive your original $1,000 investment back.*

Generally, bonds can be a good investment choice for people looking for a relatively stable and predictable source of income. However, it's important to remember that bond prices can still go down, and there's always some risk involved.

Pros: Bonds are generally considered a lower-risk investment than stocks and can provide a steady income stream.

Cons: The returns on bonds are usually lower than those of stocks, and there's a risk that the borrower could default on the loan.

Time horizon: Medium-term (1 to 10 years).

Different Types of Investments

Investment Type	Description	Risk	Reward
Stocks	Stocks are a way to own a small piece of a company and potentially make money if the company does well.	High	High
Bonds	Bonds are investment options where your money is invested with a government or company, and they promise to pay you back with interest.	Low	Low
Funds	Funds are a way to invest money in a group of companies or assets, sometimes managed by professionals or passively following an index.	Medium	Medium
Property	Real estate investing refers to buying and owning property, such as apartments, with the goal of generating income or appreciation.	Depends on Portfolio	High
Alt. Assets	Alternative assets are investments in assets other than stocks, bonds, and real estate. These include metals, energy, & even cryptocurrency.	High	?

FUNDS

A fund is a type of investment that pools money from many different investors to buy a variety of different assets, such as stocks, bonds, or real estate. When you invest in a fund, you own a small piece of the entire portfolio of assets instead of just one individual stock or bond. This can be an excellent way to diversify your investments, spreading your money across different types of assets to reduce risk.

There are two main types of funds: actively managed funds and passively managed funds.

1. Actively Managed Funds

Actively managed funds are managed by a professional fund manager who makes investment decisions on behalf of the fund's investors based on their judgment and expertise. The fund manager selects the assets to include in the fund and continually monitors the portfolio's performance to make necessary changes.

Pros: Potential for higher returns, as the fund manager uses their expertise and research to make investment decisions on behalf of the fund's investors. Additionally, actively managed funds can be more flexible. The fund manager can adjust the investments in response to market conditions.

Cons: Higher fees, as the fund manager's salary and research expenses are reflected in the fund's expense ratio. Additionally, actively managed funds may underperform passive funds over the long term due to the higher fees and the difficulty of consistently outperforming the market.

Time horizon: Can be short-term or long-term, depending on the fund manager.

2. Passively Managed Funds

Passively managed funds, also known as index funds or ETFs, track a specific market index, sector, or region. The idea behind these funds is to provide investors with a low-cost, diversified way to invest in the stock market. Instead of trying to beat the market through active stock picking and frequent trading, passively managed funds simply aim to match the performance of the underlying index.

> *For example, an S&P 500 index fund invests in all 500 companies included in the S&P 500, in proportion to their weighting in the index. If the S&P 500 index goes up, the fund is also expected to increase. Similarly, if the S&P 500 index goes down, the fund would be expected to go down.*

Passively managed funds have become increasingly popular in recent years due to their lower costs and simplicity than actively managed funds. They are often considered a good option for long-term investment, especially for novice investors who are just starting to build their portfolios.

Pros: Passive funds are easy to buy and sell, provide diversification, and have low fees.

Cons: The performance of ETFs and index funds are tied to the underlying assets, so there's always a risk that those assets could decline in value.

Time horizon: Can be short-term or long-term, depending on the fund.

> **DID YOU KNOW?** Studies have shown that passive funds tend to outperform managed funds over the long term due to lower fees and expenses.

PROPERTY

Real estate investing refers to buying and owning property, such as apartments, office buildings, and retail spaces, to generate income or sell and profit if the price increases. Like funds, real estate investing allows you to diversify your investments and spread your money across different assets.

One way to invest in real estate is to directly buy a property, such as a rental or vacation home. Another way is to invest in a real estate investment trust (REIT), a type of fund that invests in income-generating properties. REITs can be publicly traded, like stocks, or privately held.

The main advantage of real estate investing is the potential for steady income from rent and the potential for an increase in the value of the property over time.

Pros: Property has the potential to provide a stable source of income and can go up in value over time.

Cons: Property investments can be expensive and require much maintenance. In addition, there's always the risk that property prices could fall. They can also be difficult to sell. Additionally, vacant rental properties can soon wipe out any potential profits.

Time horizon: Long-term (five years or more).

BUSINESSES

When you invest in a small business, you essentially become a part owner of the company and share in its potential profits and losses. You can invest in a small business by putting money into a startup, buying into an established business, or even setting up your own business.

Investing in a startup can be risky, as many fail within the first few years of operation. However, if you believe in the business idea and the people behind it, you could potentially reap substantial rewards if the business is booming.

Buying into an established business can offer a lower-risk option, as the company has already proven its ability to survive and generate profits. However, the potential for reward may also be lower, as the company may already be close to its growth potential.

Starting your own business can also be a form of investing, as you put your time, energy, and money into building a company from the ground up. This can be a high-risk, high-reward option, as you have complete control over the success or failure of the business.

Pros: The potential for high returns, being your own boss, and having control over your investment.

Cons: Business investments can be risky, and there's always the possibility that the business could fail.

Time horizon: Long-term (five years or more).

> **DID YOU KNOW?** Steve Jobs (the co-founder of Apple) paid his first employees at Apple with stock options, which meant they could purchase Apple shares at a discounted price. Those early employees, including a secretary and a graphic designer, did well to accept his offer, becoming millionaires when the company went public years later.

ALTERNATIVE ASSETS

Alternative asset investing refers to investments in assets other than stocks, bonds, and real estate. These include commodities such as precious metals or energy, hedge funds, private equity, and cryptocurrency.

When you invest in alternative assets, you own a small piece of the asset, similar to investing in a stock or bond. The asset's value can fluctuate based on market conditions and the specific asset's performance.

Investing in alternative assets can be a way to diversify your investments, reducing risk by spreading your money across different types of assets. However, alternative assets can also be riskier and more volatile than traditional investments, and there is often a lack of information available about the performance and prospects of these investments.

Cryptocurrency, for example, is a relatively new and rapidly evolving asset class that has seen significant price swings in recent years. Investing in cryptocurrency can offer the potential for high returns but also involves a high degree of risk and uncertainty.

When considering alternative asset investments, it's essential to understand the potential risks and rewards, as well as your personal investment goals and risk tolerance. It is also helpful to consult a financial advisor to determine whether alternative assets are appropriate for your investment portfolio.

Pros: Alternative asset investing allows investors to invest in unique and innovative assets that offer diversification with the potential for higher returns.

Cons: Higher risk than traditional investments due to lack of regulation, information, and stability in some alternative markets. Additionally, it can be difficult to accurately value and understand these assets.

Time horizon: Short-term to medium-term (one to five years).

> **DID YOU KNOW?** A British IT worker accidentally threw away a hard drive containing 7,500 Bitcoins in 2013. Today those lost coins are worth over $175 million! Ouch!!!

One approach to potentially reduce risk is to create a diversified portfolio that includes a mix of different types of investments to spread your investments across different assets. This helps to minimize the impact of any losses and may provide a better chance of generating a positive return over the long term.

THE IMPORTANCE OF DIVERSIFICATION

Diversification is a key principle of investing that involves spreading your money across various assets to reduce risk.

Investing in a diverse range of assets can help minimize the impact of any one investment that may not perform well. When one investment performs poorly, if you are well diversified, another investment will likely perform better, which helps to balance out your overall returns.

> *For example, imagine an investor with all their money invested in just one stock. If that stock performs badly, their entire portfolio will drop in value. On the other hand, the impact might be reduced if that same investor had diversified their investments across a range of stocks, bonds, real estate, and alternative assets.*

Diversification can also help reduce your portfolio's overall volatility, which can be beneficial in uncertain market conditions. Investing in various assets helps ensure that you are not overexposed to any one market or sector, which helps minimize the risk of loss.

VOLATILITY AND HAVING A LONG-TERM HORIZON

Volatility refers to the ups and downs in the value of an investment over time. In other words, it's a measure of how much the price of an investment fluctuates. Some investments, such as stocks, can be very volatile and experience big swings in price. In contrast, others, such as bonds, tend to be less volatile.

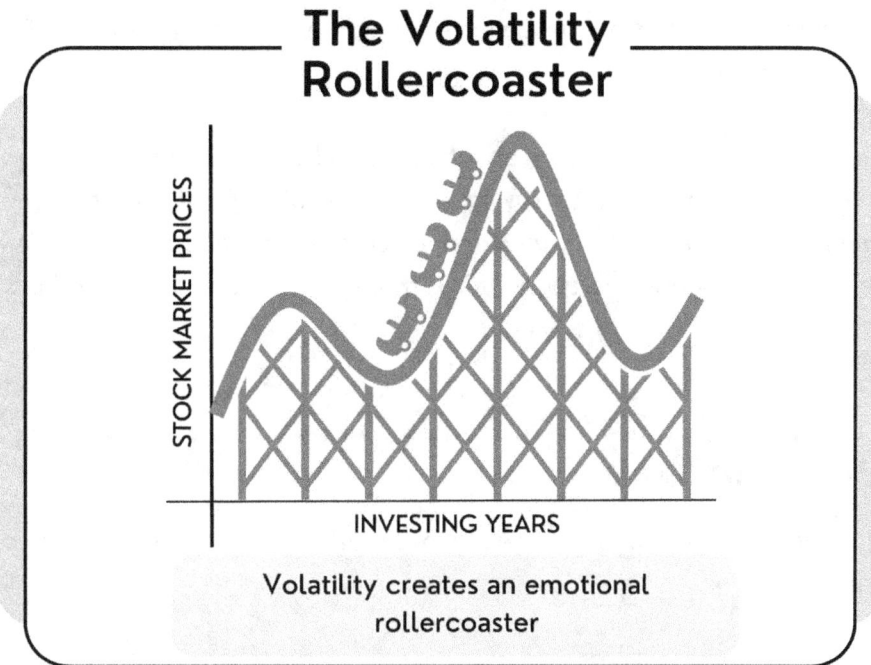

A long-term approach to investing can help you weather the ups and downs of volatility. By investing long-term, you can give your investments time to grow and recover from any short-term losses. This is why many investors choose to invest in a diversified portfolio of assets, with a mix of stocks, bonds, and other investments, and hold onto their investments for several years or even decades.

> *For example, if you invested $10,000 in the S&P 500 index at the end of 1999, you would have seen the value of your investment fall dramatically during the crash in 2000 and 2001. However, if you had held onto your investment and not sold, your investment would have grown to more than $40,000 by the end of 2019, despite the ups and downs in the market along the way.*

This demonstrates the power of having a long-term perspective and not being scared off by short-term drops.

UNDERSTANDING RISK

Risk tolerance refers to an individual's willingness and ability to accept the possibility of losses in exchange for the potential for higher returns when investing. It's important because it helps determine what types of investments suit a particular individual and what level of risk they can handle.

Everyone's risk tolerance is different, and it's influenced by several factors, including age, financial situation, investment experience, and personal goals. Some people are comfortable taking on high levels of risk and are willing to tolerate short-term losses to potentially achieve higher returns in the long term. Others prefer more conservative investments, with a lower risk of loss but also a lower potential for growth.

> *For example, a young person with a long time horizon and a high-risk tolerance might be comfortable investing a significant portion of their savings into a portfolio of high-risk, high-reward assets, such as stocks and real estate. In contrast, an older person close to retirement with a lower risk tolerance might prefer a more balanced portfolio with a mix of stocks and bonds and cash and other low-risk assets.*

WHY IT PAYS TO START EARLY

We have already looked at compounding interest in the previous chapter, but it is so important that it's worth revisiting.

Compounding is the process by which an investment earns returns, not just on the original investment but also on the returns earned over time. It is a powerful way to grow wealth over the long term.

The importance of starting early cannot be overstated. The earlier you start investing, the more time you have for your investment to compound and grow.

> *For example, if, at 20 years of age, you were to invest $100 per month into a stock portfolio that earns an average of 7% per year, after 40 years, you would have invested a total of $48,000, but your portfolio would be worth nearly $240,000.*
>
> *Now consider if you wait until you are 40 to start investing, but you save $200/month. After 20 years, despite investing the same amount of money ($48,000), your total investments be worth just under $100,000.*

That's a huge difference—and that's the power of compounding. The bottom line is that starting early and taking advantage of the power of compounding can significantly impact your financial future.

It is never too early to start thinking about your investments and how you can grow your wealth over time.

GET STARTED IN SIX SIMPLE STEPS:

Starting to invest can seem overwhelming, but it can be broken down into six simple steps. By following these steps, you can start investing and building wealth over time.

STEP 1: DETERMINE YOUR INVESTMENT GOALS

The first step to investing is to determine your investment goals. What do you want to achieve through investing? Your investment goals will guide your decision-making process and help you choose the right investments.

> *For example, let's say you are a 10th grader who wants to save up for college. Your investment goal might be to have enough money to cover tuition and fees by the time you start college. In this case, you might focus on investments designed to grow your money over the medium term, such as stocks or funds.*
>
> *As another example, let's say you are saving for a short-term goal, like a trip to Europe. Your investment goal might be to have enough money saved up to pay for your trip in the next year. In this case, you might focus on less volatile investments that are less likely to lose value, such as bonds or a high-interest savings account.*

It's important to determine your investment goals before you start investing because it will help you make decisions that align with your financial goals and what you want to achieve.

STEP 2: ASSESS YOUR RISK TOLERANCE

The second step is to assess your risk tolerance. How comfortable are you with the idea of losing money? Some people are willing to take on more risk to pursue higher returns, while others prefer a more conservative approach. Understanding your risk tolerance will help you choose investments that align with your comfort level.

> *For example, if you have a low-risk tolerance, you may prefer investments that are more stable and predictable, such as bonds or index funds. On the other hand, if you have a higher risk tolerance, you may be more interested in investments with the potential for higher returns but also carry a greater risk, such as stocks or real estate.*

Here are a few ways to assess your risk tolerance.

- **Consider your personal financial situation:** If you have a large emergency fund, a stable income, and no immediate need for your investment capital, you may be able to tolerate more risk. On the other hand, if you have a lot of debt, a single income, and an immediate need for the money you're investing, you may prefer to be more conservative.

- **Think about your personality:** Some people are naturally more risk averse, while others are comfortable taking on more risk. Consider your personal comfort level with risk when making investment decisions.

- **Use online tools:** There are many online tools available to help you determine your risk tolerance. They are not perfect, but they can give you a good idea of your risk tolerance.

STEP 3: EDUCATE YOURSELF ON THE DIFFERENT TYPES OF INVESTMENTS

The third step is to educate yourself on the different types of investments available. This can include stocks, bonds, mutual funds, exchange-traded funds (ETFs), real estate, and more. Take the time to understand the risks and rewards associated with each type of investment and consider which types may align with your goals and risk tolerance.

> **DID YOU KNOW?** A $100 investment in the S&P500 in 1990 was worth $2,148 in 2022. That's a 2,048% increase or a 9.79% yearly return.

STEP 4: OPEN A BROKERAGE ACCOUNT

The fourth step is to open a brokerage account. This is an account that allows you to buy and sell investments. There are various kinds of brokerage accounts available, including conventional brokerage accounts, robo-advisory services, and self-managed accounts.

Here are some things to consider when choosing a brokerage.

- **Fees:** Some brokerages charge fees for trading or for maintaining your account. Be sure to compare the fees charged by different brokerages and choose one that suits your budget. However, remember that cheaper doesn't always equal better.

- **Ease of use:** Consider how easy it is to use the brokerage's website or mobile app. You may want to look for a brokerage that offers helpful educational resources and tools to help you make informed investment decisions.

- **Investment options:** Make sure the brokerage offers the type of investments you're interested in, such as stocks, bonds, mutual funds, etc.

- **Customer service:** Look for a brokerage with good customer service so you can get help and support when you need it.

Once you've chosen a brokerage, you must provide personal and financial information to open an account. You'll also need to link the account to a bank account so that you can deposit money into the account and make trades.

STEP 5: START INVESTING

Once you've completed the first four steps of your investment journey, it's finally time to start investing! This is where you put your knowledge and preparation into action and start building your portfolio.

Depending on your investment goals and risk tolerance, you can do this in a few different ways.

Here are some options to consider.

- **Start small:** Starting small can help you gain confidence and experience in investing. It can also help you avoid making big mistakes that could impact your financial situation.

- **Invest in mutual funds or exchange-traded funds (ETFs):** If you're looking for a more hands-off approach, you can invest in mutual funds or ETFs. These are pools of investments managed by professional fund managers, providing a level of diversification that can help reduce risk.

- **Start with a robo-advisor:** If you're new to investing and want a low-cost, automated option, consider starting with a robo-advisor. These services use algorithms to manage your investments for you. They can be a great way to get started if you're not yet comfortable making investment decisions on your own.

- **Buy individual stocks or bonds:** Once you feel confident in choosing specific assets, you can purchase individual stocks or bonds directly through your brokerage account. This can give you more control over your investments, but it also comes with greater risk and requires more research and monitoring.

- **Consider dollar-cost averaging:** This is a strategy where you regularly invest a fixed amount of money over a long period of time rather than investing a lump sum all at once. This can help reduce the risk of investing in volatile markets, as you buy more units when prices are low and fewer units when prices are high.

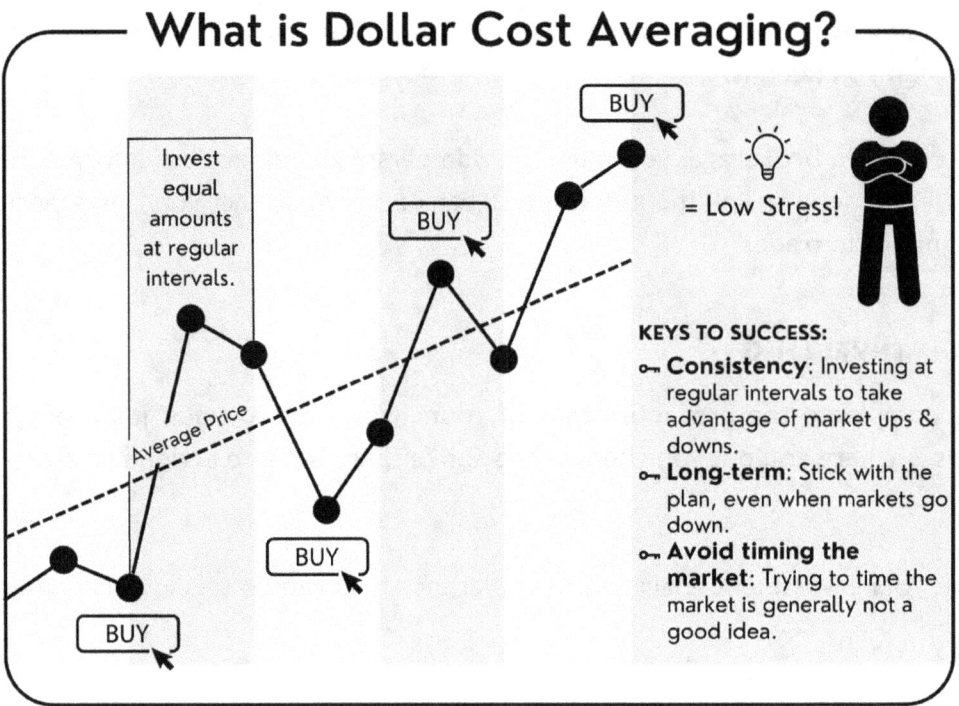

STEP 6: AUTOMATE YOUR INVESTING

Once you've started investing, you might consider automating your investments. Automating your investing involves setting up a regular schedule for investing a set amount of money into your brokerage account. This can be done on a monthly, bi-monthly, or quarterly basis. The idea behind automating your investments is to take the emotion out of investing and make it a habit. By investing small amounts of money regularly, you can reduce the impact of market volatility and benefit from the power of compounding over time.

Automating your investments is easy and can be done through your brokerage account. You can specify the amount you want to invest, the frequency of your investment, and the investment vehicle you want your money to go into. This can help you stay disciplined in your investing and ensure that you are consistently putting money towards your financial goals.

Regardless of your chosen approach, the key is to start investing early and to remain disciplined about your investment plan. Remember that investing is a long-term game. It's important to stick to your goals and stay the course, even during market ups and downs.

In conclusion, these six steps will help you get started with investing. Investing can be a powerful tool for building wealth over time, but it's essential to be patient and disciplined in your approach.

PART FIVE:

THE FUTURE OF MONEY

Money has come a long way since the days of bartering goods and services. Although we still have cash, checks, and credit cards, we increasingly rely on digital payment forms.

In recent years, there has been a growing trend towards a cashless society, with people using apps on their smartphones or other digital devices to pay for goods and services. This shift is driven mainly by advances in technology and the growing popularity of online and mobile banking.

In this chapter, we will explore how money is changing and what it means for young people like you. We will look at how our relationship with money is becoming more digital as we move from land-based banking to the internet, and then to app-based banking.

We will also examine the potential consequences of this shift as money becomes more like digits on a screen than something you hold in your hand. With instant gratification just a tap away, it's helpful to understand how this can impact spending habits and financial well-being.

CHAPTER 14. FROM CASH TO CASHLESS

In recent years, society has been moving towards a cashless economy.

In this new cashless economy we are more and more reliant on digital forms of payment such as credit cards, debit cards, and mobile payment apps like Apple Pay and Venmo. This shift towards a cashless society has been driven by technological advancements and the convenience of digital payments for consumers and businesses.

> **DID YOU KNOW?** The move to a cashless society could lead to the extinction of coins and banknotes? This means that future generations might not even know what physical money looks like!

WHAT THIS MEANS FOR YOU

On the positive side, shifting towards a cashless society offers many conveniences.

With electronic payment methods like debit and credit cards, mobile wallets, and online banking, it's easier to make purchases and keep track of your spending with mobile banking apps. Transactions can be processed quickly and securely, and you don't need to carry cash. In addition, cashless transactions are often more convenient and faster than traditional methods, as you can make purchases with just a tap of your phone or a click of a button.

However, there are also some potential downsides. For one, relying solely on digital payments may make you more vulnerable to identity theft and fraud. Additionally, not having readily available cash can make it harder to stick to a budget, as you may be more likely to overspend when using electronic payment methods.

> *For example, overspending can be easier when you don't physically see the money leaving your pocket or bank account.*

When money becomes just digits on a screen, there can be a disconnect between the value of your spending and the physical items you're buying. This is because you no longer have a tangible representation of your spending money, like physical cash or coins. When you can't physically see the money leaving your account, losing track of your spending and overspending can be easier. This is particularly true in a world of instant gratification, where you can make purchases with a tap on a screen or a swipe of your phone.

INSTANT GRATIFICATION

On the one hand, the ability to purchase items with a simple tap on a screen has made it easier for people to get what they want when they want it.

> *For example, if you're hungry and want a quick snack, you can order food through a delivery app and have it arrive at your door in just a few minutes.*

This convenience can be especially appealing for younger people who have grown up with technology and are used to instant access to information and goods.

However, this instant gratification, or the ability to have what you want right now, can be a dangerous trap. When you can buy something with a few clicks or a tap, it can be harder to control your spending. Additionally, the temptation to buy now and pay later can lead to overspending and debt. This is especially true when combined with targeted advertising and the influence of social media, which can create a constant urge to buy things you don't necessarily need.

It's important to be aware of instant gratification's potential risks and drawbacks of instant gratification and to practice good money management habits to avoid overspending and debt.

FINTECH AND THE FUTURE OF PERSONAL FINANCE

Fintech, or financial technology, has a major impact on how we manage our money and the financial services industry. The latest advancements in fintech are making it easier for people to save, invest, and manage their money by offering new and innovative financial products and services. There are many examples of fintech products and services.

- **Mobile banking apps:** These apps allow you to access your bank account from your smartphone or tablet, making it easy to view your account balances, transfer money, and pay bills.

- **Digital wallets:** Digital wallets, such as Apple Pay and Google Pay, allow you to store your credit and debit card information securely in one place, making it easier to make payments with your phone.

- **Robo-advisors:** Robo-advisors are online investment management services that use algorithms to create and manage portfolios based on your financial goals and risk tolerance.

- **P2P lending:** P2P lending platforms like LendingClub and Prosper allow you to lend money directly to individuals or small businesses, bypassing traditional banks.

- **Cryptocurrencies:** Cryptocurrencies like Bitcoin and Ethereum are digital currencies that use encryption techniques to secure transactions. While still relatively new and highly volatile, cryptocurrencies have the potential to change traditional finance by offering a decentralized and borderless alternative to traditional money.

These new products and services are not only making it easier for people to manage their money, but they are also providing more accessible and affordable financial services to people who may have been previously excluded from the traditional financial system. Overall, fintech is making it easier for people to take control of their finances and build wealth for the future.

How to Avoid Overspending

Setting a budget and sticking to it
Having a clear idea of how much you can afford to spend each month can help you resist the urge to splurge on unnecessary purchases.

Waiting before making a purchase
Before making a purchase, take a step back and ask yourself if you really need the item. Try waiting 24 hours.

Unsubscribing from marketing emails
Marketing emails and advertisements can be tempting, but unsubscribing can help reduce the temptation to spend.

Turning off push notifications
Push notifications from shopping apps can be especially tempting. Consider turning off push notifications.

Deleting shopping apps altogether
Removing shopping apps on your mobile device helps reduce the temptation to scroll, tap & purchase.

Finding alternative ways to spend your time
Instead of shopping, find alternative activities that bring you joy, such as exercise, reading, or spending time with friends and family.

Using cash
Try to use cash instead of a debit or credit card. Using cash can make it easier to stick to a budget and help you avoid overspending.

FINANCE IN THE FUTURE

It's difficult to predict what the future of finance will look like, but there are a few trends that suggest the industry will continue to become increasingly digital and more focused on meeting the needs of consumers.

One trend is the rise of open banking, which will give consumers more control over their financial data and make it easier to compare and switch between financial products and services. This could result in a more competitive and innovative financial services industry, with new startups and established players offering more personalized and user-friendly products and services.

Another trend is the growth of financial wellness and budgeting tools, which use technology to help people better understand their spending habits and make informed financial decisions. This could lead to a future where people are more financially literate and in control of their money, reducing the need for financial intermediaries like banks.

Artificial intelligence and machine learning are also expected to play a bigger role in finance, helping to automate and streamline processes, reduce risk, and improve the customer experience. This could lead to the development of new financial products and services that are more accessible and affordable, especially for people who have traditionally been underserved by the financial system.

Overall, the future of finance is likely to be shaped by technology and the changing needs of consumers. The focus will be on making finance more accessible, affordable, and user-friendly, to empower people to take control of their financial futures.

It's going to be an exciting journey. Just as the iPhone changed how we interact with technology, it's possible fintech may change how we interact with money.

LET'S GET STARTED!!!

While money isn't everything, it does play a big role in our lives. Having the skills to manage it effectively can greatly impact our well-being and future success. By reading this book, you've taken an important step towards becoming financially literate and empowered to make informed decisions about your money.

Through the different chapters in this book, you've learned about the basics of money, from earning it to saving it and spending it wisely. You now know what a budget is, how interest works, and how to avoid scams. You understand credit scoring and why having a good score can help you in the future.

Congratulations on being empowered with the knowledge you need to be smart with your hard-earned money! Just like building a solid foundation is crucial for any structure to stand the test of time, reading this book has laid the foundation for your finances.

You've taken an important first step toward achieving long-term financial success. Now it's time to put what you have learned into practice. Start budgeting today, keep an eye out for great deals, save in advance for those big purchases, and protect yourself from online scams and frauds.

Most importantly, never stop learning, and don't be afraid to ask for help if you're unsure about something. Knowledge is power, but having the support of friends and family can be invaluable!

With the right attitude and determination, you'll soon have a healthy relationship with money and a secure financial future.

Good luck!

DIGITAL LIFE SKILLS FOR TEENS

The Essential Digital Survival Guide

How to Communicate, Behave, Stay Safe and Find Balance in an Online World

FERNE BOWE

INTRODUCTION

What kinds of skills do you think are most important and useful for people today? There are the basics, like reading, writing, and mental arithmetic—these skills remain as crucial as ever. But, alongside these old favorites, a whole new set of skills has emerged that are fundamental for thriving in the modern environment. They're called digital skills.

WHAT ARE DIGITAL SKILLS?

The term "digital skills" refers to the skills that people use online (when connected to the Internet) or when using their electronic devices (cell phones, laptops, tablets, etc.). It covers everything from learning the rules of online etiquette to knowing how to search effectively and understanding how to stay safe and secure online. These skills have become central to daily life over the past few decades, and are likely to become even more important in the future.

If you think about how often you reach for your computer or a device to look up or check in on your friends, and how much of your schoolwork and leisure time involves using an electronic screen, you'll begin to understand how vital these skills are.

A TOOLKIT FOR THE MODERN WORLD

The reasons to develop your digital skills are many and varied. From using software to submit your homework on time to accessing your money, life is easier when you know how to work with technology. But staying safe online, avoiding scams, navigating different online spaces, and getting the most out of the Internet when searching or shopping takes practice. No one is born knowing this stuff!

This book is your guide to essential digital skills that will stay with you for life. It covers:

- The history of digital communication
- How to stay safe online

- Etiquette in online spaces
- Developing strong communication skills
- Techniques for finding exactly what you need online
- Tips for secure online shopping
- Strategies for balancing your online and offline lives

HOW TO USE THIS BOOK

This book is designed to be flexible, so you can use it however works best for you. Whether that means reading it cover-to-cover or dipping in and out as topics become relevant, it's up to you. Keep it around when you spend time online, in case you want to check or reference something. You might also find it helpful to share some of the ideas with your parents, other trusted adults, and your friends.

By the end of the book, you'll have a good understanding of a wide range of digital skills and how and when to use them. You'll be able to send an email without stress, find exactly what you're looking for in a sea of search results, and spot fake news like a pro. You'll also find valuable tips on how to stay healthy mentally and physically in an increasingly digital world, plus some bonus ideas about useful life skills, such as budgeting.

Let's get to it! Your voyage of digital discovery starts here.

CHAPTER 1:

THE DIGITAL EVOLUTION: HOW TECHNOLOGY TRANSFORMED OUR LIVES

Can you imagine a world without computers? It's hard to picture, right? But believe it or not, there was a time before Alexa could play you a song, before Google was the go-to resource for research, and when you had to wait until the end of a film to learn an actor's name.

Now, these things are everyday essentials. But while it can feel like computers and mobile devices have been around forever, their rapid advancement is relatively recent. Let's rewind and see how it all started.

A BRIEF HISTORY OF COMPUTING

It's not possible to cover every advance in computing here, but this timeline should help you get a general idea of the developments over the years.

PRE-1800S: HUMAN COMPUTERS

The word "computer" comes from the Latin word "putare," meaning "to think" and "to prune." Add "com," meaning "together," and you get "computare," meaning "to calculate."

Humans did all the calculations in the olden days, and the word "computer" referred to mathematicians.

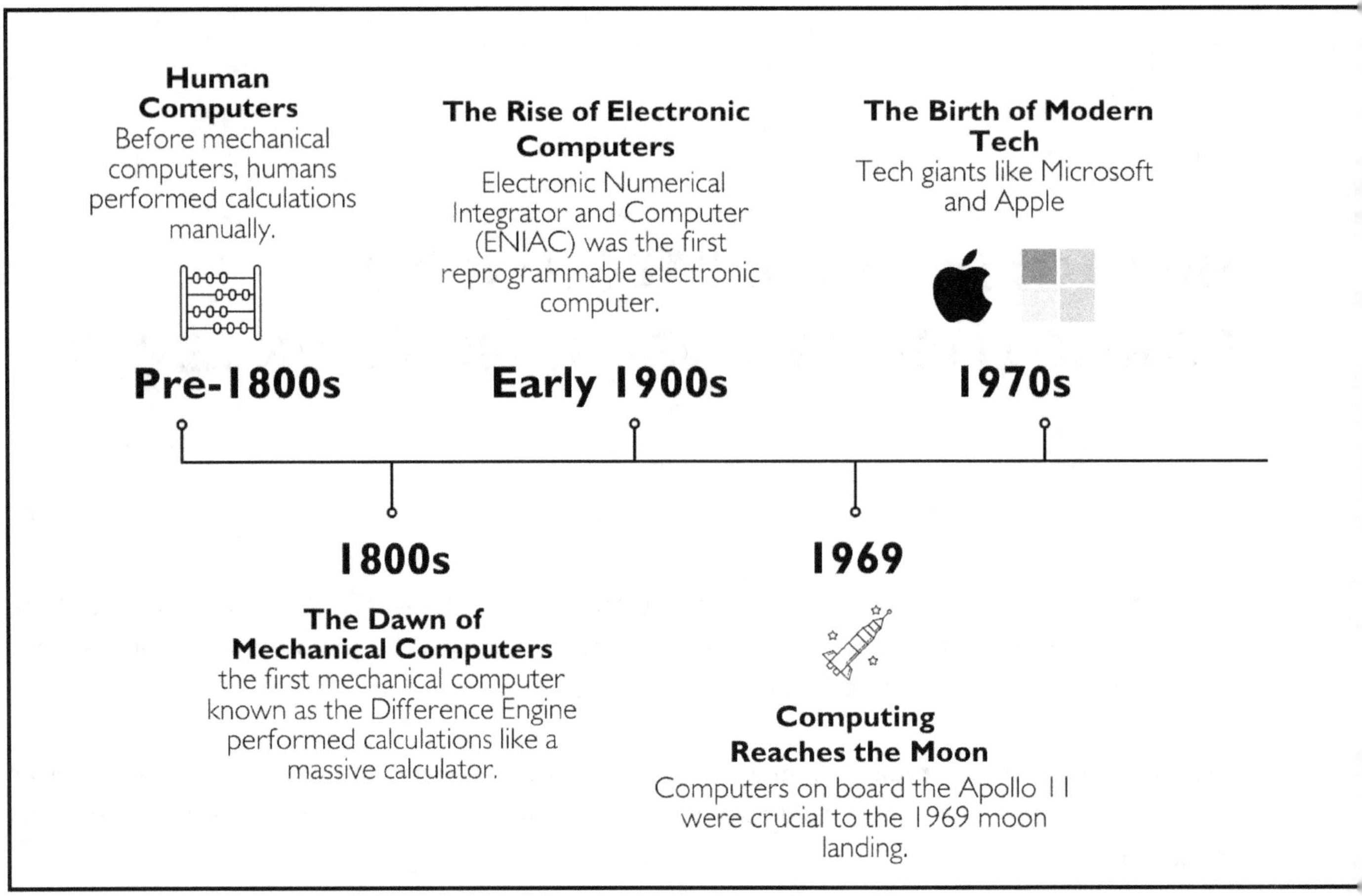

Human Computers
Before mechanical computers, humans performed calculations manually.

Pre-1800s

The Rise of Electronic Computers
Electronic Numerical Integrator and Computer (ENIAC) was the first reprogrammable electronic computer.

Early 1900s

The Birth of Modern Tech
Tech giants like Microsoft and Apple

1970s

1800s

The Dawn of Mechanical Computers
the first mechanical computer known as the Difference Engine performed calculations like a massive calculator.

1969

Computing Reaches the Moon
Computers on board the Apollo 11 were crucial to the 1969 moon landing.

THE 1800S: THE DAWN OF MECHANICAL COMPUTERS

In the 1820s, long before electricity or the invention of the telephone, British inventor Charles Babbage designed the first mechanical computer. Known as the Difference Engine, this steam-powered device performed calculations like a massive calculator.

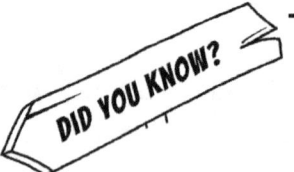

Out of a global population of around 8 billion, 85% (or 7 billion) use smartphones.

91% of Americans own smartphones, up from 35% in 2011.

93% of American adults use the Internet, a significant increase from 52% in 2000.

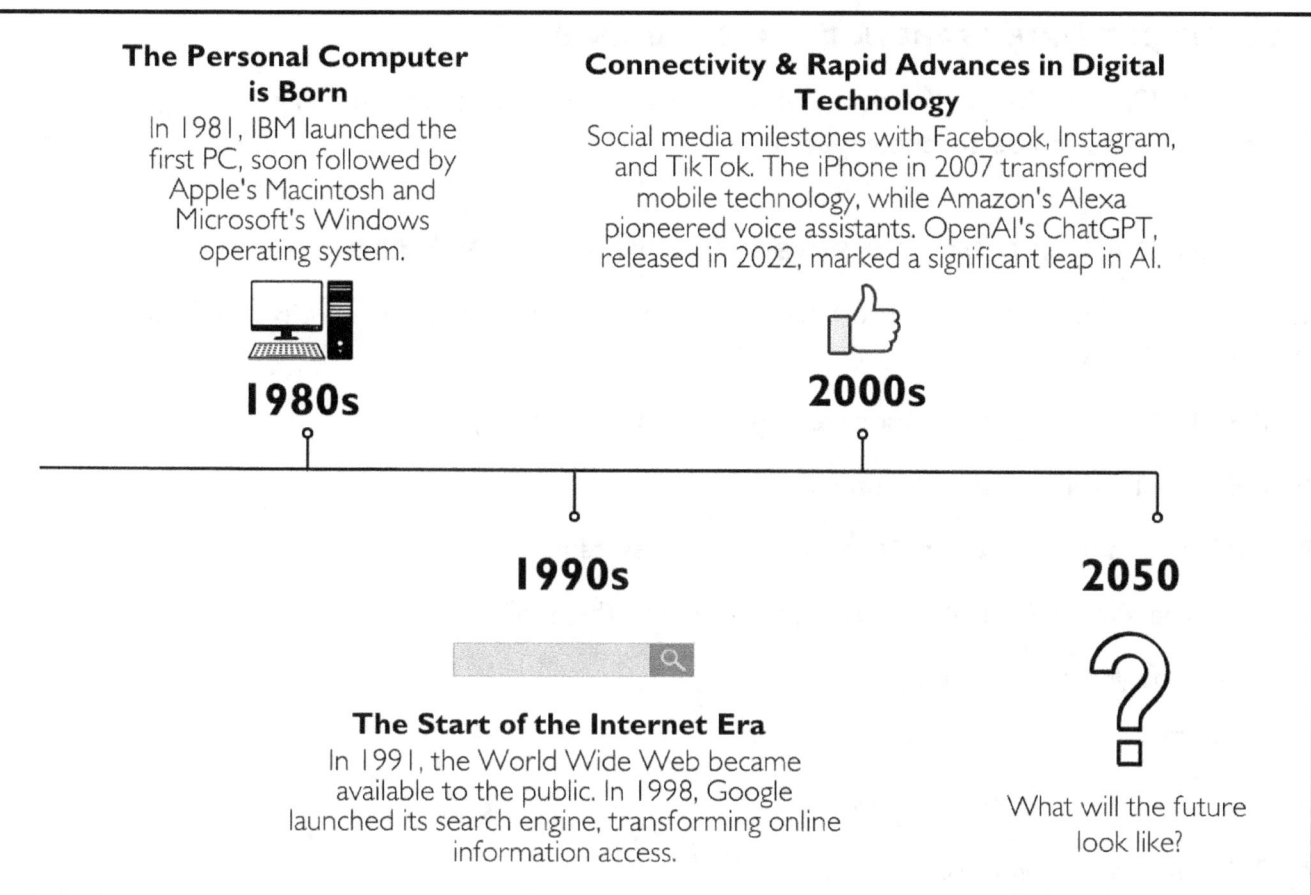

EARLY 1900S: THE RISE OF ELECTRONIC COMPUTERS

Fast forward a century and meet the Electronic Numerical Integrator and Computer (ENIAC). Completed in 1945 for the US Army, this giant was the first reprogrammable electronic computer. It was as big as a house and weighed 30 tons!

To put that into perspective, 30 tons is about the weight of six African elephants!

1969: COMPUTING REACHES THE MOON

The year 1969 was a monumental one for technology. The Apollo Guidance Computer on board Apollo 11 was integral to the 1969 moon landing, despite having less computing power than a modern smartphone.

THE 1970S: THE BIRTH OF THE MODERN TECH GIANTS

The late 1970s saw the rise of companies like Apple and Microsoft, marking the beginning of widespread home and personal computing.

FROM THE 1980S TO TODAY: THE PERSONAL COMPUTER REVOLUTION

In the 1980s, computers started to become a part of everyday life. Here's a (very) brief look at some of the big events:

- 1981: IBM introduces the personal computer ("PC" for short).
- 1984: Apple launches the Macintosh.
- 1985: Microsoft releases its Windows operating system.
- 1991: The World Wide Web becomes available to the public.
- 1998: Google launches Google Search.
- 2004: The launch of Facebook.
- 2007: Release of the first iPhone.
- 2010: Instagram comes online.
- 2014: Amazon introduces Alexa with the Echo.
- 2016: TikTok launches, rapidly gaining popularity.
- 2022: OpenAI releases the first version of ChatGPT.
- 2050: What will the future look like?

WHAT THIS MEANS FOR YOU: THE IMPORTANCE OF STAYING UPDATED

Advances in technology bring more possibilities and drive down the cost of tech. However, these advances also mean that devices like smartphones and tablets now only have a short lifespan, and people feel that they have to replace their devices regularly to keep up (not great for the planet or the pocketbook!).

It's not just the devices that evolve—so do the platforms. For instance, TikTok reached 100 million users in only nine months. Because things move so quickly, it can be a challenge to keep up. That's why it's important to develop digital skills early and keep them sharp throughout our lives.

DIGITAL SKILLS: THE NEW LANGUAGE OF OUR TIMES

Digital skills are crucial. They extend beyond how to use devices, apps, and the Internet to understanding how to use them responsibly and make smart choices.

Developing these skills is like learning a new language or mastering a musical instrument. It requires regular practice to stay up-to-date, especially as technology evolves.

A Day in the Life: Digital Skills in Action

To illustrate the importance of tech, let's imagine a typical day for a digitally connected person:

TIME	ACTIVITY
7:05 am	Wakes up with a smartphone alarm.
7:20 am	Asks Alexa to play a favorite song.
8:00 am	Messages a friend.
8:15 am	Browses social media over breakfast.
10:30 am	Researches online for a school project.
Noon	Organizes homework schedule in a digital planner.
2:30 pm	Messages parent for a ride home.
4:30 pm	Plays Fortnite with friends.
6:15 pm	Completes homework and submits it online.
7:30 pm	Watches a show on Netflix.
9:00 pm	Listens to an audiobook with a sleep timer.

This is just a snapshot—not every young person lives like this. But it highlights our increasing reliance on technology.

WHY DIGITAL SKILLS MATTER

Digital skills are as essential as reading and math to help us navigate our digital world. Whether at home, school, or work, technology is part of almost every aspect of our lives, from streaming movies to completing homework online.

TECHNOLOGY IN THE WORKPLACE

"Computer science empowers students to create the world of tomorrow."—Satya Nadella, CEO of Microsoft

Technology has changed the way we work. It's created new jobs (like app developers and social media influencers), and almost every job requires some digital skills (whether basic typing or more advanced skills like coding).

In the next chapter, we will explore how to build these skills and stay safe.

CHAPTER 2:

UNDERSTANDING DIGITAL SAFETY: HOW TO PROTECT YOURSELF ONLINE

The Internet is full of exciting opportunities. It's a portal to a world of knowledge, a platform for innovation and creativity, a window to limitless entertainment, and a place for connecting with friends and family. But it also presents potential risks. Understanding and navigating these hazards is what digital safety is all about.

WHAT IS DIGITAL SAFETY?

You've probably heard of "digital safety," also known as e-safety, online safety, or Internet safety. But what does it really mean?

Simply put, digital safety is about protecting yourself and your personal information in the online world. It's learning how to balance the resources and connections the Internet offers with the need to protect your digital identity and personal data.

Just as you wouldn't share personal details with a stranger on the street, you need to be cautious about what you share online, and with whom.

What Is Personal Data?

Think of personal data as your digital fingerprint. It's information that identifies you, including your name, address, school, and even your interests. This data is as valuable as gold for companies and advertisers. They use it to target you with their services and ads. There are two main ways your data can be shared:

1. **Voluntary Sharing:** This is when you share information publicly, such as when you post on social media, sign up for a new app, or enter your details into a shopping website.

2. **Involuntary Collection:** This is when sites or apps collect data about you without you actively giving it to them. They do this through cookies or tracking your activities online, like the posts you like.

DIGITAL SAFETY SKILLS

Developing strong digital safety skills will set you up for successful and safe online experiences. In this chapter, we'll look at some things to be aware of and some ways to protect yourself online.

THE IMPORTANCE OF PROTECTING PERSONAL DATA

Companies using your personal data to sell you things might not sound too bad. However, once your data is out there, you have no control over it. Companies can change their terms or even sell your data to other parties, who might have different ideas about what to do with it.

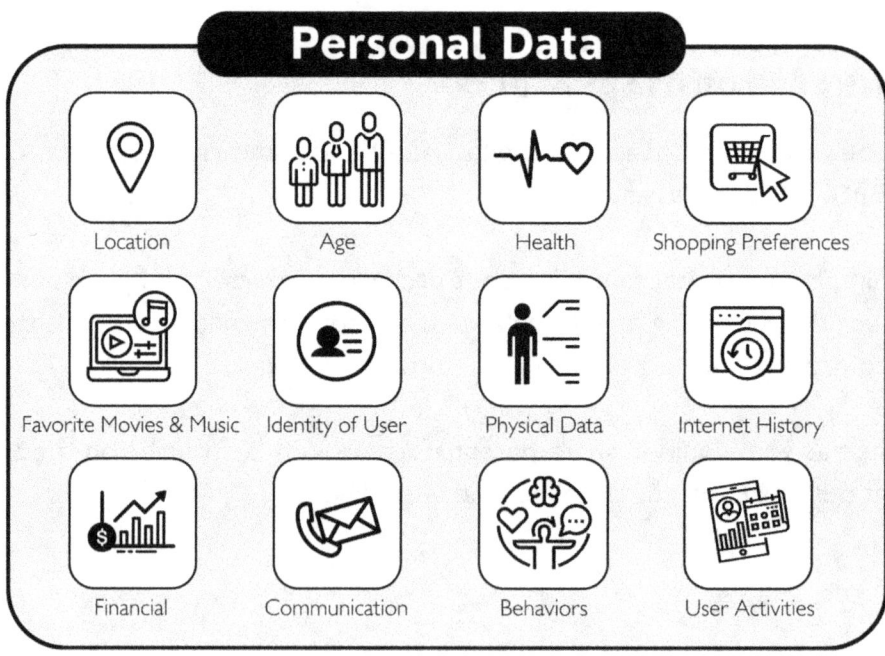

226   ESSENTIAL SKILLS EVERY TEEN SHOULD KNOW

DID YOU KNOW? Most social media platforms, like Facebook, Instagram, and TikTok, collect user information for advertising. When you create an account on these platforms, you agree to their terms and conditions, often allowing them to monitor your activities on their site.

What Kind of Information Do They Collect?
Think about the things you do on social media—those times you looked up an old friend or joined a group, or those direct messages where you shared personal experiences. All of these are tracked and recorded anonymously against your user ID.

Why Do They Collect This Information?
You might wonder why social media platforms are interested in these details. The answer is simple: It's all about creating a detailed profile of you. This profile isn't just a list of your likes and dislikes—it's a comprehensive picture of your interests, habits, and preferences. By understanding who you are, these platforms can tailor advertisements specifically to you, making them more effective and, ultimately, more profitable.

Your personal information is also highly attractive to hackers and scammers. If they get hold of it, they can try to "steal" your identity. Sounds impossible, right? After all, you're unique! However, identity theft is a very real and very serious issue. It occurs when someone uses your personal details without your consent, potentially opening bank accounts or applying for loans in your name.

The consequences of identity theft can be severe, impacting your future and leading to financial difficulties. Unfortunately, many victims of identity theft remain unaware of how their information was taken, and resolving these issues can be both stressful and costly.

What Is a Hacker?

The term "hacker" refers to someone using computer programming skills to illegally access another person's computer system. Once inside, they can access, retrieve, or manipulate any information stored on the system. This could range from personal data, like emails and photographs, to more sensitive details, including financial information.

THE THREAT OF ONLINE PREDATORS

Sharing personal information publicly, whether on purpose or by accident, can expose you to the risk of online predators. These individuals often create fake social media profiles to make themselves seem legitimate and hide their predatory behavior. They might use convincingly real or AI-generated profile pictures and slang to pretend to have interests that make them seem like young people.

Unfortunately, these people's intentions are rarely good. They might try to manipulate their victims into giving away personal information in order to steal money, or they might try to get victims to do dangerous things, like sending intimate photographs or meeting up in person. Sometimes, predators offer gifts or money to establish "trusting relationships." They can be very convincing and may work on a victim for months or even years.

It's crucial to remember that people you meet online are strangers, regardless of how friendly they may seem. Tell a trusted adult immediately if an online interaction feels suspicious.

HOW TO PROTECT YOUR PERSONAL DATA: ESSENTIAL TIPS FOR ONLINE SAFETY

Just like in the offline world, there are some simple steps that you can take to stay as safe as possible online.

1. Guard your personal information.

Would you share your deepest secrets with a stranger you met on the street? Probably not! The same caution should apply online. Always remember that your personal information should remain just that—personal. Never share sensitive details on the Internet with people you don't know.

2. Create strong passwords.

One of the most effective methods to protect your personal information is to use strong, unique passwords for each account. Avoid copying and pasting passwords. When you copy a password, it's stored in the clipboard, which can be accessed by any application with permission, potentially exposing your password.

Remember, sharing passwords, even with friends, is a risky move. Once a password is shared, you lose control over how and when it is used or who else it might be passed to.

Passwords to Avoid

A good password should be unique, complex, and hard to guess. A bad password is the opposite! Here are some examples of bad passwords to avoid:

- **Simple number sequences:** "123456" is a classic example of an incredibly easy-to-crack password. It's just a simple sequence of numbers.
- **Default passwords:** Using "password" as your password is as bad as not having one. It's one of the first guesses a hacker will make.
- **Keyboard patterns:** "qwerty" might seem clever, as it follows the top row of letters on the keyboard, but it's far from secure.
- **Repeated numbers with slight variations:** Using a short sequence like "11111" or "123123" is also risky, as it's simple and repetitive.
- **Personal information:** Passwords based on personal information, like birthdays, your address, or family member names, are easy to work out, especially with the amount of personal data available online.

3. Explore privacy settings.

Many users, including adults, are unaware you can adjust the privacy settings for devices, apps, and websites. Those cookies that websites keep asking about? Declining them can prevent the site from collecting and selling your information to third parties (usually advertisers). Customizing these settings takes a little time, but it's a valuable step in controlling who sees what about you.

What Are Cookies?

Cookies on your computers are a little different from the ones you eat! They are small files that sites place on your digital device to store information (such as your login information), so you don't have to sign in every time you visit. They also track what you look at, what pages you visit, and what you click on. Companies use this information to show you more relevant information and content. However, it's also sold to advertisers so they can target you with ads that match your interests.

4. Use a VPN.

A virtual private network (VPN) is an essential tool for online privacy. Just like an envelope protects the contents of a letter, a VPN shields your browsing activity, identity, and location.

It hides your IP address—your device's online ID that can reveal your physical location—safeguarding any personal data you transmit online.

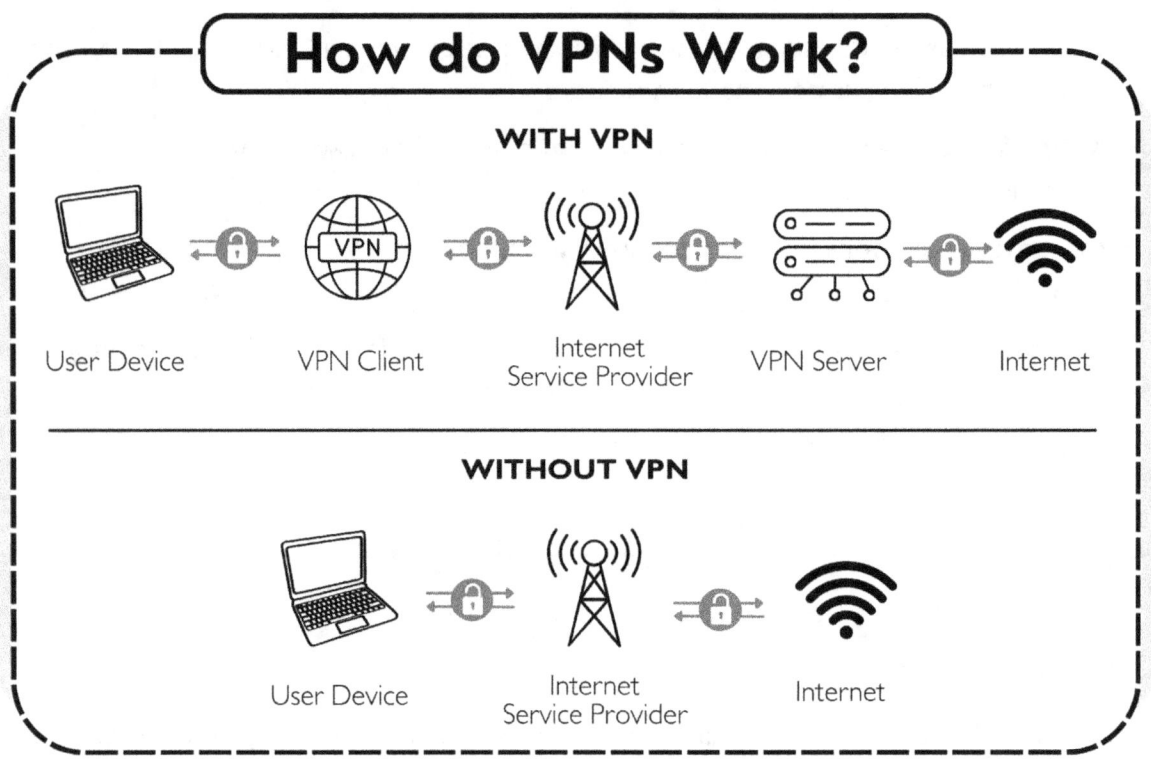

ONLINE SCAMS: A GUIDE TO STAYING SAFE ON THE INTERNET

Imagine this: You're online and come across something that seems important, like a message from your bank asking for your account details or a notification telling you you've won a prize for a competition you don't remember entering. You quickly enter your details, but something feels off. The "bank's" website doesn't look quite right…

You've just fallen for an online scam.

WHAT IS AN ONLINE SCAM?

Online scams are clever tricks used by certain people on the Internet to fool you into giving them your personal information, or even your money. They take many forms and are often very convincing.

Scams are designed to look real, making it hard to tell them apart from genuine interactions. Scammers use cleverly disguised emails, phone calls, images, or messages to mislead you into thinking they're someone they're not.

Even if you're smart with technology, online scams can still catch you out. Scammers use tricky methods to deceive you into revealing personal information, sending money, or downloading harmful software that can steal your data, including private details.

> **The Different Types of Scams**
>
> There are many different online scams, and scammers constantly develop new methods as people become aware of the threats. Some examples of common scams include:
>
> - **Phishing scams:** Scammers try to get you to give away personal information they can use for further scam activity.
> - **Ransomware/scareware scams:** Clicking a link or downloading a file locks up or threatens to damage your computer unless a ransom is paid.
> - **Friend/romance scams:** Scammers pretend to be interested in friendship or a romantic relationship to get money or information.
> - **Money transfer scams:** Scammers attempt to get you to send them money by pretending to be bank employees, family members, or even foreign dignitaries.
> - **Lottery scams:** A notice that you've won a competition or lottery takes you to a page where all the data you input is taken by scammers.

Scammers use technology to convince their victims that they're real. Email, telephone, chat apps, and social media are all common avenues of attack.

Email

Beware of emails claiming to be from your bank or other trusted organizations. They might ask you to click a link and provide account details or other personal information. These emails are not actually from the organization they say they are! They're from scammers trying to lure you into clicking links or responding, with the aim of stealing your information or accessing your bank account.

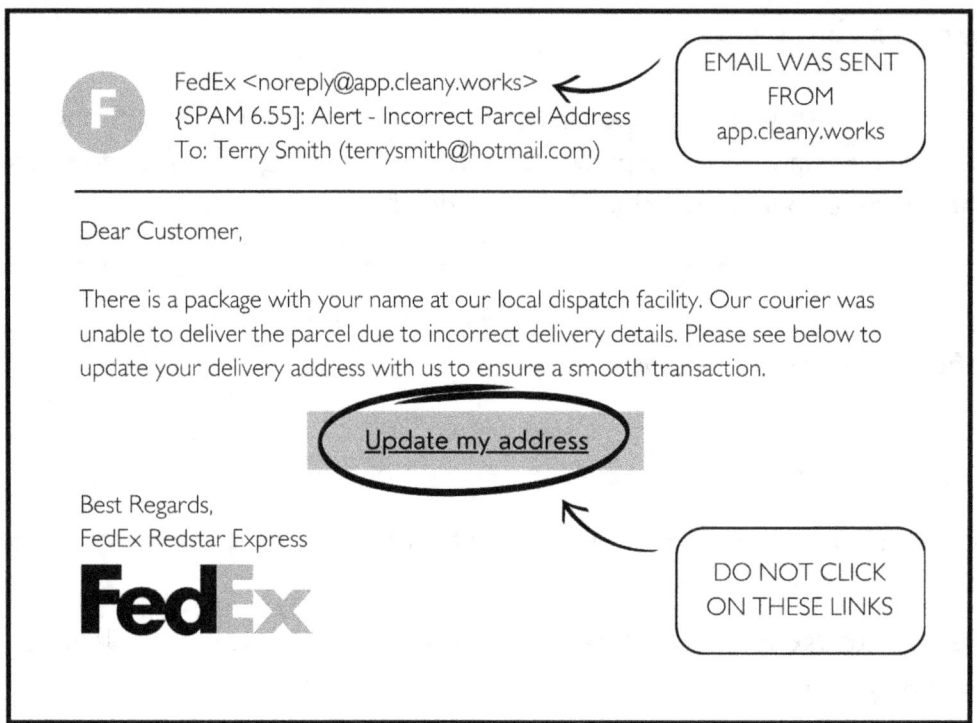

Telephone

Scammers also use phone calls, pretending to be from banks or other organizations. Their goal is similar: to get you to give away your personal details, usually so they can steal your money. If you suspect a phone scam, hang up immediately. You can always call the organization back using a trusted phone number.

Chat and Social Media

Scammers often use social media messages or apps like WhatsApp and iMessage. They send messages that appear to be from sources like PayPal or your bank, asking you to click a link or share personal information.

Scam Protection Tips

 BE CAUTIOUS WITH UNEXPECTED CONTACTS
Don't click suspicious links. Verify with the organization directly.

 SAFEGUARD YOUR INFORMATION
Never share personal details via email or phone. Legitimate organizations won't pressure you.

 EXAMINE EMAIL DETAILS
Look for mistakes or oddities in email addresses and domains.

 TRUST YOUR GUT
If something feels off, it probably is. Avoid suspicious links and offers.

 STAY UP-TO-DATE
Learn about new scam tactics and stay skeptical.

 DON'T RUSH
Scammers create urgency. Stop, think, and verify.

 PROTECT YOUR DEVICES
Use antivirus software and firewalls. Be careful with downloads.

 MAKE REGULAR BACK-UPS
Keep important data backed up to prevent loss from theft, damage, or viruses.

Tips to Protect Yourself from Scams

Scammers are always devising new ways to trick people, using sophisticated methods that can be hard to spot. But there are ways to protect yourself and stay safe, even as scams become more advanced.

1. **Be cautious with unexpected contacts:** If you receive a message or email from someone you don't know or a message that just doesn't feel right, don't click on any links. You can always double-check by contacting the organization's official contact.

2. **Examine email details:** Pay attention to the small things. Scam emails might have mistakes or seem a bit off. For example, the email address might look weird or not match the sender's name. Look out for letters replaced with numbers ("PayPa1," for example) or odd domain names.

3. **Safeguard your information:** Your personal details, like passwords and bank info, are precious. Never share them via email or phone call. If someone pressures you, hang up or don't respond. No legitimate representative of an organization will attempt to pressure you into giving away your details.

4. **Don't rush:** Scammers love to create a sense of urgency so their victims don't get a chance to stop and think. They might tell you an offer is only good right then to rush you into a decision

or that someone is hacking your bank account and they need to move your money to safety immediately. Remember, real opportunities don't need you to decide in a panic! Stop, hang up, and think.

5. **Protect your devices:** Use antivirus software and keep your computer's firewall on. These are your digital shields against unwanted intruders. Be aware of what you're downloading and from where—free online "goodies" are often nasties in disguise. "Free" items frequently come with a hidden price tag—often in the form of viruses or data harvesting by scammers.

6. **Trust your gut:** If something feels weird or too good to be true, it often is. Trust your instincts—if you're unsure about a link or an offer, it's better to be safe and avoid it. You can find lots of information about scams online, so do a quick search if you feel something is wrong.

7. **Stay up-to-date:** Scammers are quick to use the latest tech, like AI, for bad purposes. They might use AI to create fake videos (deepfakes) or to imitate someone you trust. So, it's important to keep learning and aware of the latest trends. Most importantly, always keep a healthy dose of skepticism. If something doesn't feel right, take a step back and think about it before acting.

8. **Make regular backups:** Always keep a backup of your important data and files. Whether it's to a physical external drive or cloud storage, having a backup means that if your device gets lost, stolen, damaged, or if you're hit by a virus, you won't lose everything.

. . . .

CYBERBULLYING: UNDERSTANDING AND TACKLING DIGITAL HARASSMENT

Cyberbullying, or online bullying, is an unfortunate reality in the digital world. It can happen anywhere online—through texts, social media, forums, or gaming platforms. Unlike offline bullying, cyberbullying doesn't happen face-to-face, although it can certainly spill over into the offline world.

Cyberbullying can happen at any time of day or night, and bullies can share materials (such as fake videos or doctored photos) widely and quickly. When you combine this with the "always online" nature of modern life, cyberbullying can be difficult to escape.

The intent of cyberbullies is often to be hurtful, spread hate, or cause public humiliation to their victims. Sometimes, though, people don't realize that their behavior is bullying. It's important to think carefully about your actions online and their potential consequences.

> **What Is Cyberbullying?**
>
> Cyberbullying can take many forms. Some of the most common include:
>
> - Sending rude or hateful direct messages (DMs) or messages in group chats.
> - Deliberately excluding someone from group chats.
> - Posting hateful or rude comments about someone on social media.
> - Circulating embarrassing or inappropriate images of someone on social media, email, or through messages.
> - Tagging someone in offensive content, such as nasty memes, with the intention of upsetting them.

The Internet can sometimes be like a mask, making bullies feel they can be mean without getting caught because they're hidden behind a screen. They don't see how their words or actions hurt someone, which might make them think it's okay to be unkind.

The reality is very different. Being mean online is never okay. It's just as bad as any other type of bullying. It can really hurt people, making them feel alone, sad, or even scared. Just because it happens online doesn't make it any less serious.

HOW TO DEAL WITH CYBERBULLYING

If you encounter online bullying, it's crucial to have strategies to deal with it:

- **Block the bully:** Immediately block the individual responsible for cyberbullying on the platform where it occurred.
- **Report the behavior:** Use the platform's reporting feature to report the cyberbully's actions.
- **Tell someone**: Talk about the situation with a trusted adult, such as a parent, teacher, or family member. There are also some useful resources at *www.stopbullying.gov*.
- **Involve your school:** Remember that teachers and school counselors can help, even if the bullying happens outside school hours.

Remember, you are not alone. Cyberbullying is serious, and you don't have to face it by yourself. Speaking up is a brave and important step towards stopping it.

MOBILE DEVICE SAFETY

With so many young people using cell phones these days, learning how to do so safely is key. Let's look at how you can enjoy your mobile device, stay safe, and keep your personal data private.

> ### What Is Geolocation?
>
> Geolocation, or GPS, is a feature that pinpoints your exact location. It's convenient for finding your way on a map or locating the nearest supermarket. However, this convenience comes with privacy risks.
>
> Social media apps like Snapchat often allow you to share your location with others. While this feature can make it easy and fun to meet up with friends or check where they are, it can also expose your location to strangers.
>
> Before you turn on geolocation, it's always best to check with your parents and limit sharing to your closest friends and contacts. Never share your location openly or with people you don't know well offline.

PHOTO SHARING AND GEOLOCATION

Photos are a big part of modern cell phone use. From capturing funny moments to asking a parent about a product or simply using fun filters for selfies, we take a lot of pictures!

However, with geolocation, photos posted publicly can give away a lot of information about where you live, the school you attend, and where you like to hang out. This might not seem like a big deal, but it's information predators can use to find you or use against you. The more information predators have about you, the easier for them to convince you they're harmless.

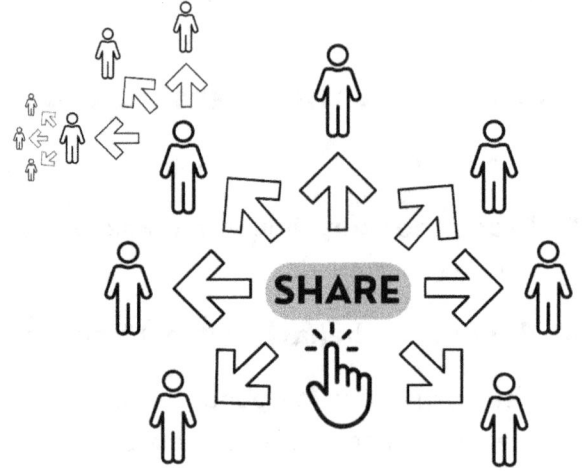

PERSONAL AND SENSITIVE IMAGES

If you share a photo online, it's out there forever and can quickly slip out of your control. It could be saved, forwarded, or even posted elsewhere by someone else, potentially making it impossible to remove entirely. This is particularly true for photos that contain nudity or other sensitive content, as they can lead to uncomfortable, embarrassing, or even harmful situations. They might be used in ways you never intended, affecting your privacy and well-being.

> **Tips on Sharing Photos Responsibly**
>
> 1. **Pay attention to what's in your photos.** This includes identifying features of your location that could inadvertently reveal where you are. Also, don't include people who haven't consented to be in your photo.
>
> 2. **Watch what you wear.** If you wear a school uniform, think twice before sharing a photo of it publicly, as it can reveal where you go to school.
>
> 3. **Check before you share.** Double-check photos for any personal information before sharing them online. This includes visible school names, signs, or other sensitive information.
>
> 4. **Turn off automatic geotagging.** Check the settings for your social media accounts and turn off auto-tagging. If you're unsure how to do this, a simple online search like "How to turn off photo geotagging on [social media platform name]" can guide you.
>
> 5. **Share photos and your location only with people you know and trust.** Avoid broadcasting your location to a broad audience you don't know personally.
>
> 6. **Be careful who you befriend.** Only connect with people you know in real life.
>
> 7. **Check which apps are using your geolocation.** In settings, go to app permissions and check which apps use your location.
>
> 8. **Turn off geolocation.** This will also improve your battery life!

Handling Pressure and Saying No

If anyone pressures you to share images that make you uncomfortable, trust your instincts and say no. You have every right to protect your privacy and personal boundaries. If something doesn't feel right, you should always feel able to refuse and end the conversation. Remember, your comfort and safety should always come first.

Even if you don't feel uncomfortable sharing photos, you should still exercise common sense. Don't send private or sensitive photos to anyone—doing so can have enormous unintended consequences for you and the person you send them to.

Seeking Help When You Need It

If you feel uncomfortable or unsafe because of photos or requests for photos, it's essential to seek help immediately. Talk to a trusted adult, such as a parent, teacher, or school counselor. They can offer support and help you navigate the situation safely and respectfully.

ALL ABOUT PASSWORDS

Creating strong passwords is your first line of defense in the digital world. Strong passwords act like fortified gates, keeping scammers and digital intruders at bay. Try this activity to help you understand what makes a strong password and how to create a secure and memorable one.

Step 1: Identifying Weak Passwords

First, examine the following list of passwords. Use a pen to circle the ones that might be easy for someone to guess:

1. password123
2. 50!!&*myjuice<99
3. 123456789
4. qwertyuiop
5. SigJ$>99!

Passwords are often vulnerable if they use common phrases, predictable letter patterns, or lack complexity. The best passwords incorporate a diverse mix of letters, symbols, numbers, and both uppercase and lowercase letters, and are impossible to guess.

Step 2: Creating a Strong Password

Now, let's craft a strong and memorable password for you. Follow these steps:

1. **Choose a base word:** Write down the name of your favorite animal or pet.
2. **Add a favorite thing:** Write down something that your chosen animal loves.
3. **Incorporate a number:** Write down your age or another memorable number.
4. **Mix it up:** Add an uppercase letter and one symbol.
5. **Combine elements:** Now, merge all these elements to form a unique sentence or string.

Example:

- Pet's name: Tag
- Loves: Cats
- Age: 10
- Uppercase and symbol: T and !
- Password: TagLovesCats10!

By using a blend of letters (both uppercase and lowercase), numbers, and symbols and ensuring the password is long, you can make it much tougher for someone to guess or crack your password.

Your Turn:

Now it's time for you to create your strong password. Follow the steps above and craft a password that's uniquely yours and tough to crack. If you don't have a pet, you can use some other person or thing in your life. Remember, a strong password is like a strong lock—it's a fundamental part of being safe and secure online.

- Pet's name: _____
- Loves: _____
- Age: _____
- Uppercase and symbol: _____

🔒 **PASSWORD:** _____

DIGITAL LIFE SKILLS FOR TEENS

CHAPTER 3:

DIGITAL CONDUCT: HOW TO BEHAVE RESPONSIBLY ONLINE

The Internet is constantly evolving, and we're still figuring out how to make it safe and useful for everyone. Each of us has a role to play in this process, learning and adapting as we go.

NAVIGATING THE ONLINE WORLD

As a young person, understanding how to behave online is a huge part of learning to live in the world.

WHAT IS ONLINE BEHAVIOR?

Online behavior is the way people act and the things they do online. Similar to offline behavior, our online actions and behaviors can have a big impact on our lives and the lives of those around us.

Offline, the consequences are usually good when we help others. Helping a neighbor find their lost cat brings smiles all around—the neighbor is happy, we're happy, and even the cat is happy! On the other hand, negative actions have consequences, too. They can lead to guilt or even trouble with teachers or parents.

WHY DOES ONLINE BEHAVIOR MATTER?

Part of learning to live in the world with others is understanding our behavior's effects on them. It's normal to make mistakes, and no one always gets it right. When we're face-to-face with people, we see the consequences of our actions. We have thousands of years of culture to guide us, and we can learn the rules from one another.

Online, things aren't always so simple.

Our online behavior has just as much of an impact as our offline behavior, but it's not always as easy to see its effects. Hiding behind a screen can make it seem like there are no consequences, but that's not true. How we conduct ourselves online can have far-reaching effects on our relationships, careers, and opportunities.

HOW CAN WE NAVIGATE ONLINE BEHAVIOR?

Although the online space is fairly new, and we're still working things out, there are accepted ways of behaving online that are useful to know. In this chapter, we'll look at how to navigate the online world safely and responsibly.

We'll explore:

- The ins and outs of "netiquette"
- How to manage your digital footprint
- How to use social media so it's safe and fun for everybody

NETIQUETTE 101

Etiquette is all about the rules we use to behave properly in situations and around others. Netiquette is the same, only on the Internet. Just like when we are offline, different parts of the online world have slightly different rules. But there are a few basic rules that apply pretty much everywhere. Knowing them means we'll have a much better time online, as will everyone around us.

UNDERSTANDING NETIQUETTE

Netiquette, like traditional etiquette, has evolved over time and continues to develop as we adapt to new forms of digital communication.

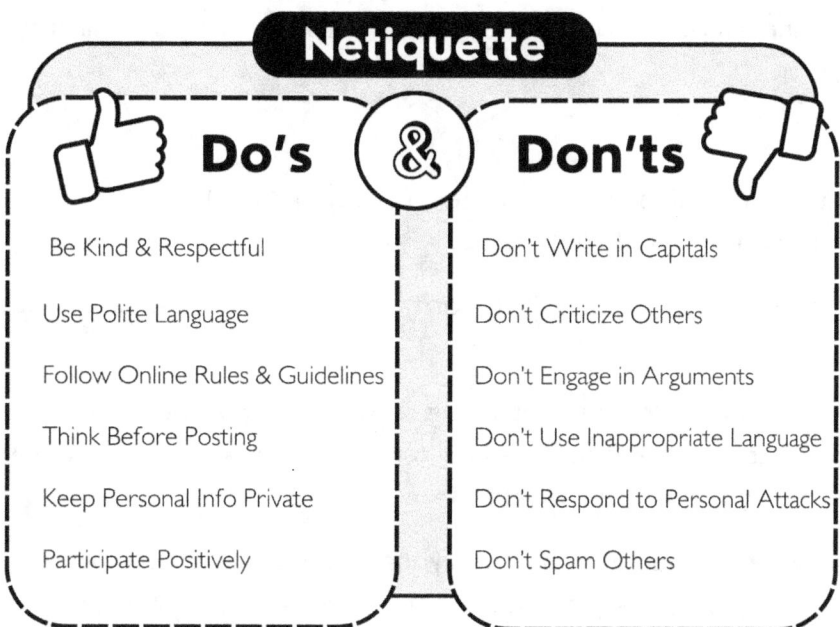

People don't behave the same way today as they did 200 years ago. Over time, what has been considered good or bad manners has changed. For instance, while you might get scolded for talking with your mouth full today, 19th century table manners accepted different behaviors. Similarly, the way a 19th century teenager interacted with their best friend was very different from how they would behave with a school teacher.

However, how we behave today isn't completely different from the past. Some actions are just as unacceptable now as they were 100 years ago. The same goes for online behavior. We've established rules that adapt to different situations, but some actions remain inappropriate or are considered bad manners.

Just like in the offline world, practicing good manners online helps things run smoothly and ensures people are treated fairly. Misunderstandings are less likely when people agree on what constitutes good behavior.

We are all responsible for how we act online, making it crucial to learn and practice good netiquette.

PRACTICING GOOD NETIQUETTE

Think about some of the social rules you follow in daily life. These likely include using polite phrases like "please" and "thank you," not interrupting people when they speak, and taking good care of items you borrow. While these rules might differ slightly depending on where you are, the basics apply everywhere and are important to master.

The same applies online. Here are some basic netiquette rules to help you navigate any online space.

Having Respect

- **Be kind:** Treat others online with the same courtesy and kindness as offline. Think about how you would like to be treated, then do that.

- **Keep it clean:** Use polite language that won't offend. Don't swear or call people names, even if you're joking.

- **Mind your tone:** Things don't always come across how you mean them to, especially when you are online. Try to be clear, direct, and polite in your interactions to avoid misunderstandings. Use emojis to make your meaning crystal clear.

- **Practice patience:** Remember that everyone communicates differently and has different strengths. Avoid correcting people's word choice, grammar, or spelling unless they ask you to.

Online Communities

- **Learn the rules:** When you join an online community, it will have a specific set of rules. Read them before engaging so you don't accidentally make a mistake.

- **Acknowledge others:** If someone asks you a reasonable question, reply honestly and in a friendly way. If you share someone else's work, make sure you credit them. That means adding their name when you share the work and not pretending it's your own.

- **Participate positively:** Aim to bring something good to the community you're taking part in. Offer helpful suggestions and share supportive comments where you can.

- **Take a moment to think:** Before you publish that post or send that comment, seriously consider any possible effects it could have—both on you and other people.

IDENTIFYING AND AVOIDING NEGATIVE BEHAVIOR

Not everyone follows good netiquette online. Similar to everyday life, some people like to cause trouble on the Internet for various reasons. Others may not realize their actions are disruptive, but the effect is often the same—people feel upset or hurt.

HOW TO SPOT BAD BEHAVIOR

Bad online behavior is often pretty easy to spot. Examples might include:

- Using inappropriate language
- Telling lies about another person or group
- Ganging up on one person or group
- Posting content that is intended to upset or hurt people

If you see these things happening online, it's important to take action. Remember, acting means reporting the behavior through the proper channels. Don't try to take on the perpetrators yourself!

What Is a Troll?

A troll is someone who purposely annoys or upsets other people. Sometimes trolls act this way because they find it funny, and other times they have nastier motives. Whatever their reasons, trolls want to provoke a reaction, and thrive on attention. Unfortunately, trolls are very common online. The only effective way to deal with them is to ignore, block, and report them.

TIPS TO DEAL WITH BAD BEHAVIOR ONLINE

Dealing with poor online behavior is an unfortunate reality, but it doesn't have to spoil your online experience. Here are some strategies to help you deal with negative behavior effectively.

1. **Keep your cool:** Don't get drawn into arguments or let people provoke you into responding. Breathe and take some offline time if you need to.

2. **Ignore trolls:** Trolls thrive on attention. Ignoring their comments or behavior can often defuse the situation and deny them the desired reaction.

3. **Rock that block button:** You're not obligated to engage with anyone. If someone is misbehaving, don't be afraid to block them. Most online platforms have this functionality, so use it!

4. **Report abuse:** If you see harassment, threats, or other forms of abusive behavior happening in an online space, report it to the platform administrators. Reporting abuse is anonymous, so don't be afraid that it will come back on you.

5. **Get help:** Tell someone if you're struggling with bad behavior online. Friends, family, and trusted adults can all help support you if things get unpleasant online.

6. **Document the evidence:** If you encounter negative behavior online, it's important to keep a record. Saving messages and taking screenshots can be helpful if you need to take action.

7. **Take breaks:** Taking occasional breaks from social media and other online platforms is always a good idea. By giving yourself breathing space outside of these platforms, you can prioritize your mental health and well-being.

RECOGNIZING AND DEALING WITH HARMFUL CONTENT

Wherever you go online, there's a risk of encountering harmful content. Knowing how to respond can sometimes be challenging, but it is important to take action. It's down to all of us to create and maintain an online world in which everyone feels safe and comfortable.

REPORTING HARMFUL CONTENT

Like other forms of negative online behavior, the best way to handle harmful content is to report it. Most online platforms have a reporting system, but it's not always obvious what to do. If you're unsure how to report harmful content on a specific platform, try searching online for "how to report harmful content on [platform]."

It's important to remember that reporting content is anonymous, and you won't get in trouble or face any repercussions. Reporting harmful content helps make the Internet safer and more enjoyable for everyone. If you're unsure whether something you see counts, but you feel it might, it's best to report it and let the platform decide.

What Is Harmful Content?

The term "harmful content" can cover a lot of things. Generally speaking, it's any content that could cause damage or distress. Harmful content might include things like:

- **Illegal activity:** Anything that breaks any laws or encourages breaking the law
- **Hate speech:** Using words to attack or talk badly about members of a particular group (like race, ethnicity, sexual orientation, or gender)
- **Discriminatory language:** Using words to exclude members of a particular group (race, ethnicity, sexual orientation, gender, and so on)
- **Images of violence or abuse:** Pictures or videos (real or created) that show violent or abusive behavior
- **Misinformation:** Any type of content that aims to distort or obscure the truth
- **Scam materials and malware:** Any content that tries to trick users into falling for scams or downloading computer viruses or other dangerous software

YOUR DIGITAL FOOTPRINT – THINK BEFORE YOU CLICK

Everything we do online leaves a trace. That's not always a bad thing, but it is important to keep in mind when doing anything online.

WHAT IS A DIGITAL FOOTPRINT?

A digital footprint is a record of everything we do online—the sites we visit, the content we post, the comments we make—and much of it remains long after the feed moves on.

A digital footprint is like a tattoo. Once it's there, it's pretty much permanent. Trying to erase a tattoo is very difficult, and there are usually traces left behind. The same goes for a digital footprint—even if we remove the content, it can pop up unexpectedly.

There are two types of digital footprints:

- **Passive:** The cookies and trackers that collect as we move around the Internet.

- **Active:** The things we put out there voluntarily (or involuntarily)—messages, comments, videos, etc.

You control most of what you add to your active footprint—whatever you (or your friends) post online becomes part of it! You also have a fair amount of control over your passive footprint. In this section, we'll look at how to control both.

WHY SHOULD YOU CARE ABOUT YOUR DIGITAL FOOTPRINT?

Have you ever been absolutely certain about something, only to change your mind later on? Maybe you were a huge fan of a band when you were younger, but now you're not so keen on them (maybe they're even a bit embarrassing!). Or perhaps you once hated chocolate ice cream, but now it's your favorite.

It's a normal part of life to change your mind and opinions, and we all do things that we might later regret or feel embarrassed about. It's no different online. Things that we post can come back to haunt us!

Although you can "delete" a post from your social media accounts, it may still exist online—it just becomes invisible to you and other users, which is usually enough. But what if someone took a screenshot or shared the post before you deleted it? Then, you have no control over what happens with it.

> ### Real-World Consequences of Online Behavior
>
> Imagine you're online one evening, browsing TikTok and chatting with friends. A newcomer in your friend group points out a TikTok creator from your school that they dislike. They persuade everyone to leave silly comments on the creator's posts.
>
> To you, the comments seem harmless and fun. Unfortunately, the creator doesn't feel that way and reports your whole group to TikTok and your school. You receive discipline at school, and the incident goes on your permanent record.
>
> Years later, when you apply for college, your top choices reject you because of the blemish on your record. One thoughtless action can permanently impact your digital footprint and cause unintended consequences, even years later.
>
> Of course, this is an extreme example of how poor online behavior can have unexpected and unpleasant consequences. However, the takeaway is to think before you act and consider how it might affect the "future you."

HOW TO MANAGE YOUR DIGITAL FOOTPRINT

To avoid your digital footprint causing problems, it's important to manage it mindfully. Here are three things to remember to help you keep on top of it.

1. Explore your privacy settings.
Every social media platform and website that you can log on to will have a privacy settings section. It might be called "preferences," "settings," or something else. When you find it, go through the settings and activate those that give you the most privacy. That means opting out of sharing information where possible, keeping viewers of your posts to contacts only, and not allowing people you don't know to comment/send messages. Check these settings regularly.

2. Think twice, post once.
Before you post anything online or even send a message, think carefully. Ask yourself, "Would I be okay with everyone seeing this?" If the answer is "no," it might be better not to post it.

3. Remember that once you've posted something, it's out of your control.
People can take screenshots and share your posts if they want to, so don't count on being able to post something and then delete it. Don't post it if you aren't happy with it being out there forever.

WHAT TO SHARE AND WHAT TO KEEP TO YOURSELF

If you're unsure whether to post or share content online, consider what it contains. Some types of content are almost always safe, and others are nearly always a bad idea. Remember that sharing a post is the same as posting it—you align yourself with the content.

- **Safe:** Posts about your achievements and positive experiences, as long as they don't have any personal details like your address, school, or location. You can always use photo editing software to remove these details.

- **Not safe:** Anything showing personal details, like your address, school, or location; posts showing illegal or harmful activity, or other kinds of bad behavior; and private photographs of yourself or others.

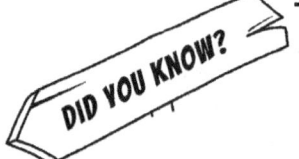

Here's a good rule of thumb: **If you're unsure whether something is appropriate to post, don't post it!** You can always decide to share it later if you change your mind, but you can't take it back once it's out there.

What is Appropriate to Post?

To help decide if something is appropriate to post, ask yourself:

1. Who will see it?
2. Would I be comfortable if my parents, teachers, or friends saw it?
3. Does it reveal personal or others' information?
4. Could it hurt someone's feelings?
5. Would I be proud to show it to my future self?
6. What do I hope to achieve with this post?

Now, it's your turn: Think about what's safe and respectful to share and what's not.

Safe to Post...	Not Safe to Post...

USING SOCIAL MEDIA RESPONSIBLY

Social media hasn't been around that long, but it plays a massive role in modern life. From the early days of IRC channels, MSN Messenger, and Angelfire web pages (ask your parents!) to chatrooms and Myspace, Facebook, WhatsApp, Snapchat, and TikTok, we live in the social media age.

What Is Social Media?

Social media is any online platform where users can create and share content with others. That content might be simple messages (WhatsApp, for example), multimedia posts (like Instagram), or short-form videos (as with TikTok).

Social media platforms use "algorithms" to decide what content to show individual users.

> **What Is an Algorithm?**
>
> An algorithm is a set of instructions that computers follow to solve problems or complete tasks.
>
> Humans also use algorithms in our daily lives! Think about getting ready for school in the morning. Chances are, you get up, get dressed, and eat breakfast the same way each day. You can think of each step as a different algorithm in your "Getting Ready for School" program.

HOW DO SOCIAL MEDIA ALGORITHMS WORK?

Have you noticed that if you look at something on social media—cute bunny videos, for example—more of that type of content comes up in your feed? That's a social media algorithm at work. You get shown more cute bunny videos because the algorithm thinks they're what you're into—and who doesn't want more of what they love, right?

A social media algorithm aims to keep you engaged—keeping you on the platform and interacting with content for as long as possible. It does this by tracking what you do on the platform (and often across other platforms) and how you engage with content. It notices what you stop scrolling to look at, what you scroll right past, what you "like," what you comment on, what you share…everything.

By tracking what you engage with, the algorithm works out how to keep you engaged and interacting on the platform. It's important to note that the algorithm doesn't know or care what you actually enjoy, what makes you happy or sad, or what is healthy. Its only aim is to keep you on the platform. As long as you interact with content, it's doing its job.

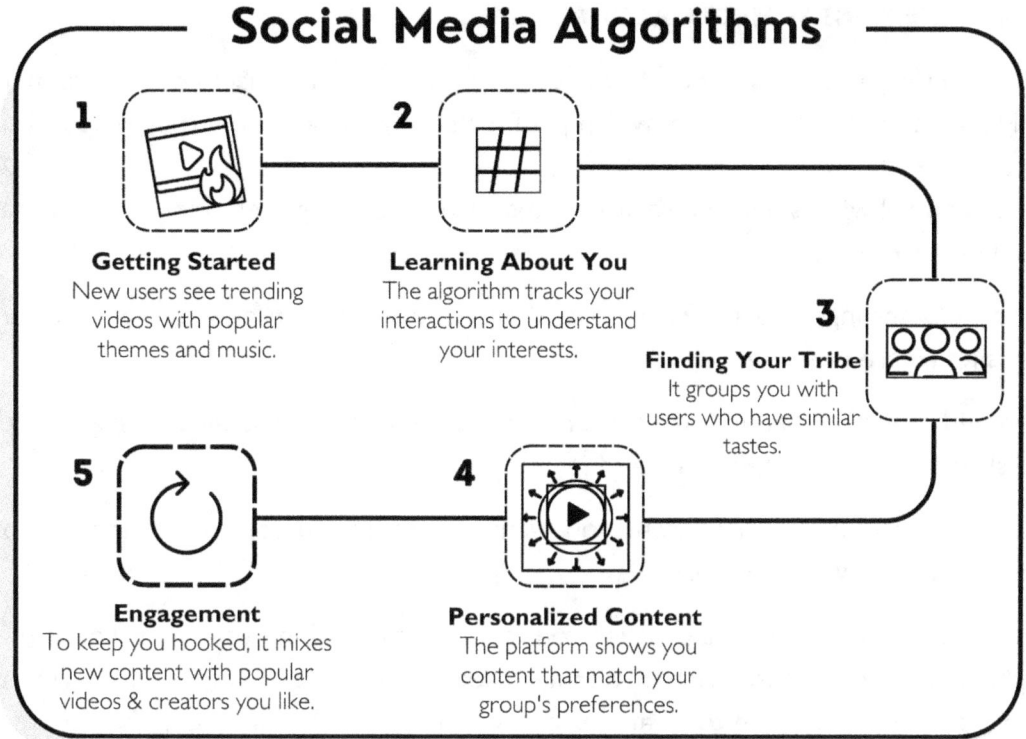

HOW MIGHT SOCIAL MEDIA ALGORITHMS CAUSE TROUBLE?

There is a lot of discussion about social media algorithms, their effects, and whether they are potentially dangerous. Let's explore some of the ways that social media algorithms might cause problems.

- **Creating echo chambers:** When people only see content that reflects their worldviews, they often forget that other people have different opposing ideas. This is particularly true when it comes to politics or elections.

- **Spreading misinformation:** Algorithms are computer programs that prioritize high-engagement sensationalist stories over true factual ones, resulting in the spreading of fake news.

- **Boosting harmful content:** As with misinformation, algorithms promote content that gets a lot of engagement. Social media algorithms may automatically promote dangerous, divisive, and extremist content that gains engagement.

- **Using addictive techniques:** These algorithms have been designed to keep people engaged and stop them from leaving. Personal recommendations, notifications, and autoplay features aim to keep you scrolling, and they're almost impossible to resist.

HOW TO MANAGE SOCIAL MEDIA ALGORITHMS

Ultimately, social media companies decide what systems they use, and users don't have much control over that. However, users can control which platforms they use and how they respond to content.

It's difficult to control what social media algorithms show you completely. However, you can manage the situation in a few ways:

1. Use site/app settings and preferences to limit data collection and opt out of personalized advertising where possible.

2. Engage with content that you like rather than content that you dislike. Engaging with content you dislike only means seeing more of it.

3. Follow new accounts with content you want to see, and unfollow or block accounts with content you don't want to see.

4. If you start seeing content that makes you feel uncomfortable, reset your social media feeds. The process is different for each platform, so search for "reset [name of platform] algorithm" for each platform you'd like to clean up. It's a good idea to do this every six months or so.

> ### Privacy Settings Check-Up
>
> Review your privacy settings for every social media platform regularly to ensure they're as strong as possible. Opt out of personalized ads and data collection where possible. Ask a trusted adult for help if necessary.

WHAT DOES RESPONSIBLE SOCIAL MEDIA USE LOOK LIKE?

Using social media responsibly is simple. It means:

- Being mindful of the content you post, share, and engage with
- Using privacy settings to keep yourself safe
- Interacting with others respectfully and safely

THINKING BEFORE POSTING

Remember that everything you say and do online can affect you and others. Sometimes, these consequences might happen immediately, but other times, they might come up years after the original post. Your words have weight.

What you say online impacts others, often in ways you might not intend. Online communication can easily lead to misunderstandings, so that joke you think is funny might not be well received by everyone.

Think about how it would make you feel to see something negative about you or one of your friends. It would hurt, right? Even a joke can be hurtful, whether the teller intended it that way or not.

A responsible social media user aims to uplift others rather than bring them down. Consider posting positive content that brightens someone's day instead of negative things that might upset people.

The Pause Principle

Before you post anything, pause and ask yourself, "Is this something I'd be okay with everyone seeing, even years in the future?" If the answer is "no," it's probably a good idea to hold off. The future you will thank you!

Your posts might be seen by future colleges, employers, and others, so it's important to post things that reflect positively on you.

UNDERSTANDING ONLINE VS. OFFLINE RELATIONSHIPS

It's common for people to have friends that they met online, and who they may never meet in the offline world. Online friendships are not necessarily bad but come with an extra layer of uncertainty. The possibility of being deceived is real, and it's much harder to judge people's intentions online than offline.

It is vitally important to keep your wits about you when making online friends. Anonymity and the potential for people to lie about their identity mean that not everyone is who they say they are or has your best interests at heart.

Friend or Faux?

Sometimes, a person might pretend to be your friend for their own reasons. This can happen offline and online, but it's harder to spot on the internet—especially if you don't know what warning signs to look for. Some red flags that might suggest someone isn't who they claim to be include:

- **Suspicious behavior:** The person avoids voice or video calls and doesn't provide additional photos to prove their identity.

- **Unrealistic profile:** Their social media profile seems too "perfect" or too good to be true.

- **Pressure tactics:** They may press you to give personal information, send pictures, or do things you don't want to do.

- **Inconsistent information:** The details they give about themselves don't line up, or they frequently change their story.

- **Fake photos:** They refuse to show their real face, instead using stock images, AI-generated photos, or other people's photos. You can use Google image search to check the authenticity of their photos.

These are not necessarily signs that a person is lying about their identity, but they're indicators that they may not have your best interests at heart. Don't be afraid to set boundaries about when and what you want to discuss. A real friend won't push you into giving information or try to get you to do things you don't want to.

If you feel uncomfortable in an online conversation, whether with someone you've just met or a person you've known for a while, it's important to tell a trusted adult.

Influencer Real Talk

Do you have any favorite TikTok, Instagram, or YouTube creators? Chances are, you follow at least a few people who make content about something you're interested in. Whether it's pop music, makeup, wrestling, mountain biking, or reading, there's content out there for every passion.

> **What Is an Influencer?**
>
> An influencer is someone who creates content on social media that appeals to specific audiences or focuses on particular topics. These individuals earn money by gaining followers and partnering with companies to promote products. A well-known example is MrBeast, who began posting videos on YouTube in 2012 and now has hundreds of millions of subscribers.

Influencers are not new—people have been influencing each other for a long time. However, social media influencers are unique in that they can connect with people across the globe.

While it may appear simple, being a successful influencer involves significant effort and consistency in producing engaging content.

Many influencers only share the best parts of their lives, making it seem like they live perfectly, without any troubles. This isn't the whole truth. They often show a "perfect" version that's carefully crafted for their audience, as this is part of their job.

While it can be fun to see someone engaging in exciting activities, remember they experience the same frustrations and challenges as everyone else—they just don't share those bits online. This selective sharing of "perfection" can sometimes make us feel like our own lives are lacking or don't measure up in comparison. It's important to remember that what we see is not always the complete picture.

SETTING UP A SOCIAL MEDIA PROFILE SAFELY

Social media is an easy and fun way to keep in touch with friends and family and meet new friends. But it's important to set up your profiles safely and securely. Don't worry—it's simple when you know how!

How to Create a Safe and Engaging Profile

Your Screen Name

Be creative: Choose something related to your interests and hobbies, your pet's name, or something you love.

Don't get personal: Avoid using too much personal information, like your full name, location, or school.

Your Profile Picture

Use a picture that you find fun and expressive, but doesn't give away any personal information. It's okay to show your face, but avoid including anything that shows where you live or go to school. Always double-check the background of your photo to ensure it doesn't give away too much information.

Your Content

Before you post or share anything online, think carefully about whether it's a good idea. If you decide to go for it, ensure no personal details are visible in the post. Feel free to share information about what you love and enjoy doing, but don't share anything that could reveal where you live or go to school.

Managing Interactions

Adjust your privacy settings to prevent messages from people you don't know, if possible. This helps protect you from potential predators posing as friends.

If this isn't an option, be cautious when responding to messages or accepting friend requests from strangers. Remember, you don't have to respond to every request. Your safety is more important than what a stranger thinks of you.

If you receive messages from anyone—known or unknown—that make you feel uncomfortable or concerned, report them and tell a trusted adult.

Social Media Dos and Don'ts

Do:
- Get to know the privacy settings and check them regularly.
- Use different strong passwords for all your accounts.
- Think before you post, comment, or share.
- Be selective about who you talk to.
- Be kind and respectful.
- Report any inappropriate or harmful content.

Don't:
- Share personal information.
- Share your passwords.
- Meet people offline.
- Accept requests or respond to messages from people you don't know.
- Be a troll or a bully.
- Pretend to be someone else.
- Get drawn into online arguments.

CHAPTER 4:

COMMUNICATING IN A DIGITAL WORLD: HOW TO INTERACT EFFECTIVELY ONLINE

What's the one thing that all living things have in common? You might have heard of the seven common characteristics of living organisms—movement, respiration, sensitivity, growth, reproduction, excretion, and nutrition—but something else ties us all together, from tiny ants to humans: **Communication.**

THE EVOLUTION OF COMMUNICATION

Humans have developed incredible ways to communicate over hundreds of thousands of years. But the communication we take for granted today, like speaking on a phone or messaging friends, is just a recent development. Let's take a look back and see how communication has changed over the years.

> **What Is Communication?**
>
> Simply put, it's the passing of information from one organism to another—and there are many different ways to do it. From speaking, dancing, howling, and growling to changing color or wafting chemical signals through the air, the world around us buzzes with creatures of all kinds sending messages!

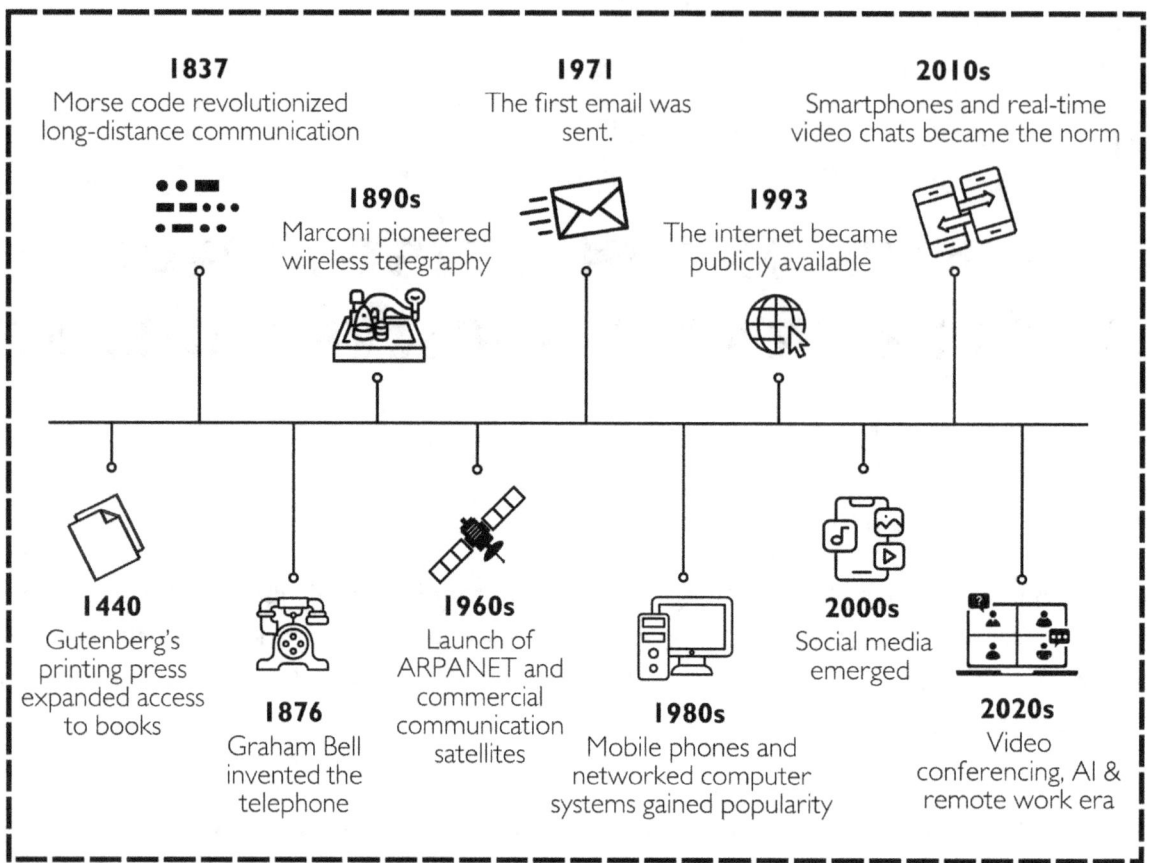

THE DIGITAL REVOLUTION

As you can see from the timeline, communication technology made massive strides between the 19th and 21st centuries. In just over 200 years, humans went from sending messages via carrier pigeons to instant messaging and Zoom calls!

This leap began with the discovery and application of radio waves in the late 1800s. People realized that detailed information could be sent and received almost instantly over long distances, setting the stage for the instant information culture of the present day.

With each new development in the communication timeline, people had to learn new skills. When the telephone was introduced, that meant learning how to make and receive calls. This might seem simple today, but imagine if you'd never seen a phone before. Fast-forward to today, and there are many more communication technologies to learn.

> **DID YOU KNOW?**
>
> When the telephone was invented, there was much discussion about how to answer when picking up the phone and how to end the call. To us, saying "Hello" and "Goodbye" seems obvious, but back then, people were still working it out.
>
> Alexander Graham Bell, the inventor of the telephone, thought a jolly "Ahoy!" would work best as a greeting, while others favored "Speak." Pretty quickly, "Hello" became the most popular choice.
>
> Early phone books recommended saying, "That is all," and hanging up to end the conversation. Maybe people thought it seemed rude or abrupt, but "Goodbye" won out.

MASTERING EMAIL

Communication is fundamental to modern life, and it's constantly evolving. That means it's a great idea to continually improve your communication skills!

With that in mind, let's look at some common communication technologies. Although you might not need to use all of these daily, having the skills is helpful, as you never know when you might need them.

Email has existed for more than 50 years, going from a novelty to a basic form of communication. Today, many (although certainly not all) people use email for work, business, or other "official" purposes.

EMAIL WRITING

Writing an email is like writing a letter (ask your grandparents!). Just like letter writing, there are accepted ways to email correctly. Because emails are often sent in a work environment, the tone tends to be quite formal, although they're usually a little more laid-back than a letter. Most of the time, the person sending the email knows the receiver but may not be close friends.

When writing an email, the first thing to consider is what you are trying to say. Then, think about who you are saying it to. These two things will help you choose the best tone, greeting, and sign-off.

> **What Is "Professional" or Formal Language?**
>
> You'll see this term a lot. It's best to use professional language whenever you talk or type with someone you know in a formal context, like a school teacher, a college professor, a colleague, or an employer. This means being clear and to the point, using proper spelling and grammar, and avoiding slang.

CRAFTING THE PERFECT EMAIL

Writing a good email that effectively conveys your message is pretty simple when you break it down into a few key components. The trick is to keep it clear and to the point.

- **Subject:** This short sentence summarizes what the email is about. For example, "Question about Spanish homework."

- **Greeting:** Start with a polite greeting. The exact wording depends on who will read the email (the recipient) and how well you know them.

    Unless you know the recipient very well, it's best to use a formal greeting like "Dear [name]," including any titles like "Dr." or "Professor." If you're unsure, It's usually better to be too formal rather than too informal.

    If you're writing to a close friend, you'll probably start with "Hi [name]," "Hello," or just their name.

- **Body:** This is where your message goes. Aim to keep it short, while still providing all the relevant details. Be careful not to ramble! Organize your points clearly so they're easy to read and understand. The following format works well:

    1. Start with your main point or question.

    2. Explain why it's important.

    3. Add any other necessary details.

- **Sign-off:** The sign-off wraps up your email. The way you sign off should match the tone of your email and your relationship with the recipient. For someone you don't know well, stick to formal sign-offs, like "Yours faithfully," "Respectfully," or "Best regards." For people you know in a formal setting, such as teachers, "Sincerely" or "Thanks" works well.

For emails to friends, family, or other people you're close to, you can use a more relaxed expression, like "Bye for now," "See you soon," or "Have a great weekend."

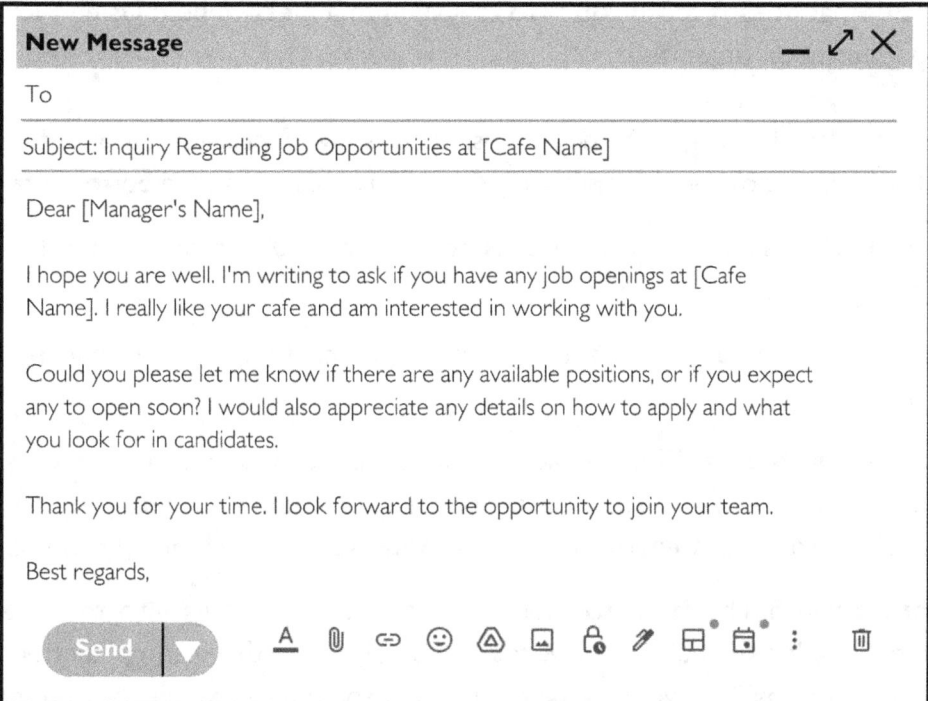

Replying Options
CC and BCC: When replying to or sending emails, you'll see the options "CC" and "BCC." Most of the time, you can ignore these options, but here's what they stand for:

- "CC" is short for "carbon copy," you use it if you want to send a copy of your email to another person to keep them in the loop. Using CC signals that the person copied in doesn't need to respond. With CC, everyone in the email chain can see the email addresses of those to whom the email has been sent and those who have been copied in.

- "BCC" stands for "blind carbon copy." It works like CC, except the email address of the person copied in is hidden.

Reply all: To reply to an email, just hit "Reply," type your message, and send. Sometimes, though, if you receive an email from a group and want to share your response with everyone, you can "Reply all." This sends your message to all the original recipients, including those who have been CC'd.

MANAGING YOUR INBOX

A disorganized inbox has become a joke among almost everyone with an email address. With potentially hundreds or even thousands of emails pouring in daily, keeping an inbox tidy can be a real challenge. But that doesn't mean you have to give in to a messy inbox! Using a few tricks makes it easy to keep your inbox organized.

1. **Unsubscribe:** Avoid signing up for email subscriptions. If you receive promotional emails you're no longer interested in, look for an "unsubscribe" link. This is usually at the bottom of the email.

2. **Delete:** Delete emails you don't need as soon as possible to stop them from piling up in your inbox.

3. **Search:** If you need to find a particular email, search for it rather than scrolling through your inbox.

4. **Use folders and labels:** Choose ways to categorize emails and make folders and labels so you can find them quickly and easily. Categories might include particular projects, friend groups, or interests. You can set categories and labels in the settings area of your inbox.

5. **Set filters:** Email filters can automatically sort incoming emails into their relevant folders based on the sender, subject, or keywords you set. Look in the settings section of your inbox to set filters. Your email provider will already use a spam filter, which you can manually change in the settings.

6. **Embrace the archive:** Use the archive function to keep important emails without cluttering your inbox.

7. **Do regular inbox maintenance:** Set aside time each day or week to go through your inbox, organize emails, respond to messages, and clear out clutter.

8. **Limit your notifications:** Reduce email notifications (or even turn them off) so you're not constantly interrupted by incoming emails. Instead, check your inbox at regular times.

9. **Respond promptly:** Respond to emails immediately so the unanswered ones don't pile up in your inbox.

HANDLING SPAM AND PHISHING

Some emails that find their way into your inbox will be spam or phishing attempts. At best, these emails are a waste of time and space. At worst, they're dangerous.

> ### What Is Spam?
>
> "Spam" is any unwanted or excessive electronic communication. It's those emails you get three times a day from a website you visited once, and the constant stream of emojis your friend puts in your group chat. Spam is annoying but usually harmless. However, it can sometimes be dangerous. It might contain links to harmful downloads or phishing attempts.

HOW TO DEAL WITH SPAM

- **Use a spam filter:** The best way to deal with spam is to use a good email filter. Most email providers already have one set up, and you can tweak it to your liking in the settings.

- **Avoid opening spam emails:** If an email looks suspicious, don't open it.

- **Mark messages as spam:** If a spam email gets through to your inbox, mark it as spam. This will help your spam filter become more effective.

HOW TO RECOGNIZE A PHISHING ATTEMPT

"Phishing" is when a scammer tries to trick you into giving away sensitive or personal information. The goal is to gather enough information to get into your accounts, usually to steal money.

Phishing attempts can be very sophisticated and hard to spot. It's best to treat any email or message that asks you to log into an account or send details as suspicious. If in doubt, do not follow any instructions. Check online for similar scam messages.

PayPal, Amazon, Facebook, and other such accounts are prime targets for phishing scammers. Never follow links from emails. Instead, type in the proper URL address yourself. Banks will never ask you to send information by message or email.

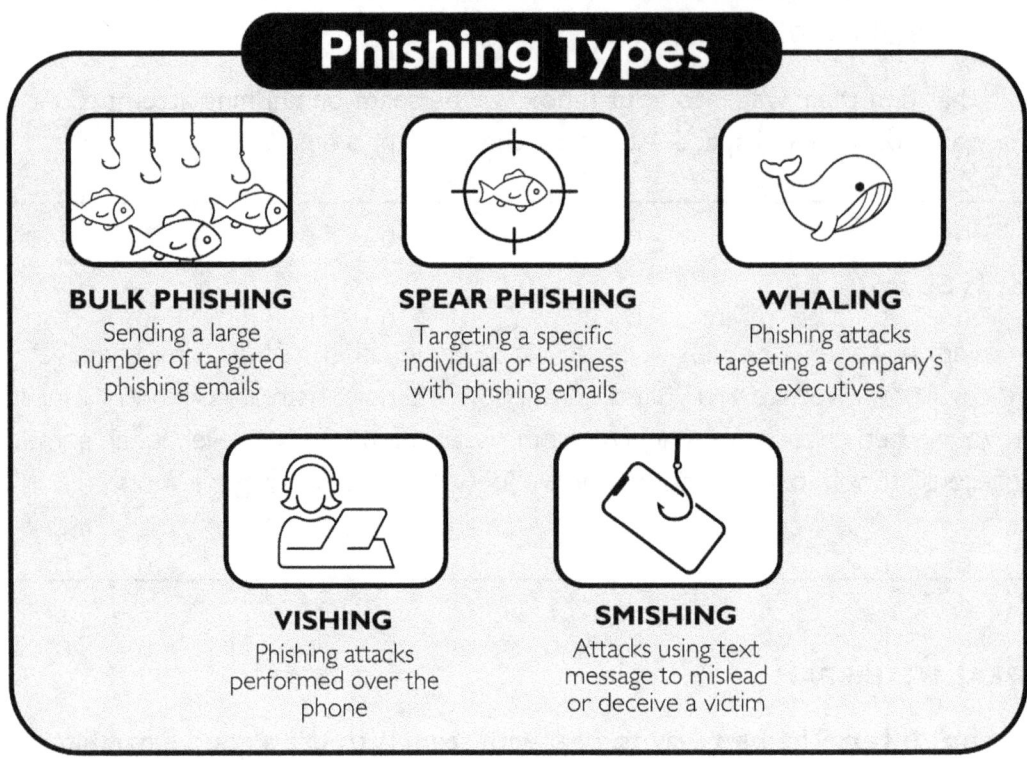

Be wary of messages telling you you've won a prize or have a limited time to respond. These are almost always phishing or other scam attempts. Scammers often try to invoke a sense of urgency or panic in their victims so that they won't stop and think. Scammers do this because it works—so always take time to think about what you're doing.

VIDEO CONFERENCING

It's very common these days to use video conferencing instead of face-to-face meetings. Faster Internet speeds and improved video technology have made these tools accessible at home. The COVID-19 pandemic accelerated this trend and made working and schooling from home a necessity. While face-to-face interaction is back in many areas, the ease of video conferencing means it's here to stay.

How to Video Conference Like a Pro

Video conferencing is quite simple when you get the hang of it. The best way to ensure that things run smoothly is to set up your equipment and space before the call. Here are a few pointers to help you.

1. **Set up in a quiet spot:** Choose a quiet area with minimal background noise and distractions. Ensure other people know not to disturb you while on the call. Keep pets out of the room, unless you know they'll be welcome on the call.

2. **Dress appropriately:** You might be at home, but that doesn't mean video conferencing in your pajamas is a good idea. Wear clothes that you would wear if you were attending the meeting offline to give a good impression and help you feel prepared.

3. **Arrange your camera:** Set up your space so that you appear face-on in the middle of the screen. Aim to appear one or two feet from the camera—not too close or too far away. You can check how your setup looks in the video settings of your conferencing software.

4. **Choose your background:** Use an area with as little going on in the background as possible to avoid distracting other participants. A neutral wall is ideal. Avoid using novelty in-app backgrounds unless you're talking with your friends, as they can give the wrong impression. Make sure no personal details are visible in your background.

5. **Fix the lighting:** Choose a well-lit area, ideally with two or three light sources in different places. Try to ensure that you are evenly lit and that there are no dark shadows. Close the curtains or blinds if too much light comes in through a window.

6. **Use headphones:** Headphones can help you to concentrate on the conversation and avoid distractions. They also improve the audio quality and help to reduce background noise. Make sure your headphones have a built-in microphone.

7. **Test your tech:** Before the meeting, check that your Internet connection, webcam, microphone, and necessary software are working. Also, test your audio and video settings—look in your video conferencing software's "Settings" or "Preferences" section. Give yourself enough time to tackle any problems—half an hour should do it.

VIDEO CONFERENCING ETIQUETTE

Once you're set up, it's time for the call. Follow these tips to make a great impression.

PHONE ETIQUETTE

The term "smartphone" is a bit misleading. Yes, smartphones make calls. But is that what people use them for most of the time? Probably not. Most of us use them for messaging, browsing the Internet, social media, and shopping more than for actual phone calls.

Interestingly, a surprising number of people struggle with speaking on the phone. Maybe it's because we're so used to texting or using video calls, where the rules and social cues are a little different.

How to Make and Receive Phone Calls
The good news is that, by being prepared (and with a little bit of practice), it's easy to develop phone skills.

1. **Make a plan:** Before the call, note down the points you want to make or questions you want to ask.

2. **Pick your time:** Aim to call when the other person is likely available and happy to talk. Check their time zone and call according to theirs, not yours. If it's 5 pm for you but 1 am for them, it's better to call earlier in the day!

3. **Say hi/introduce yourself:** If you know the person you're calling, start the call by saying, "Hello, it's [your name]. How are you?" If you don't know them, go with, "Hello, my name is [your name], and I'm calling about [your reason for calling]."

4. **Be polite:** Use polite language and a friendly tone throughout the conversation. Respect the other person's time and avoid interrupting them while they speak.

5. **Pay attention:** Listen carefully to what the other person is saying. If it's an important call, take notes to remember what was said.

6. **Speak clearly:** It can be harder to understand what people are saying on the phone, as there are no visual clues. Make sure to speak at your normal speed and volume, and keep the microphone near your mouth.

7. **Stay focused:** Try to stay on topic. If you notice the call going off track, gently guide it back on topic.

8. **Be careful with information:** Don't publicly discuss sensitive or confidential information (your own or other people's) where others might overhear.

9. **Sign-off politely:** Thank the other person for their time and make any plans for follow-up actions or calls. Finish with a friendly "Bye!"

ONLINE MESSAGING

Texting and online messaging are great ways to stay in touch, regardless of the apps you use. But as with every form of communication, there are good and not-so-good ways to use them.

Texting Done Right

Everyone has their texting style and preferences, and it's OK to text however you like. That said, there are a few things to bear in mind.

Using Emojis

It can be quite difficult to convey exactly what you mean when texting, especially if you're making a joke or writing something that could be interpreted in different ways. That's what emojis are for! Emojis are a great way to ensure your meaning is understood—if you use them right.

Emojis are best used in casual situations, like messaging with friends. Avoid using them too much, unless you know that the person you're texting with likes to use them a lot, as some people find them annoying. Also, bear in mind that many emojis have specific meanings. If you want to use a particular emoji and aren't sure what it means, look it up online first.

Responding Mindfully

When texting, sometimes you chat back and forth quickly, and other times, there might be longer breaks between messages. Some people reply immediately and are happy with a constant stream of messages, while others prefer to respond at a time that suits them better.

There's no right or wrong way to text, but respecting the other person's time and preferences is essential. Don't expect an immediate reply all the time. Sometimes, people are too busy to respond or need time to think about what you've said. At the same time, don't leave someone hanging "on read" for too long, or they may feel you're ignoring them.

When to Call Instead

If you need to discuss something urgent or confidential—or feel you are in danger—it's best to call instead of texting.

GROUP CHATS

Group chats are a fun way to chat with a bunch of friends. They're great for sharing jokes or sorting out plans for hanging out, but they're not the right choice for every situation.

Group chats are best for lighthearted conversations or for planning specific events. If you need to discuss something you'd rather not have everyone in the chat know about, use direct messaging instead. It's also important to be mindful of other people's privacy.

Group Chat Behavior

DO	DON'T
• **Use Appropriate Language:** Help everyone feel comfortable. • **Be Respectful:** Treat everyone with kindness. • **Include Everyone:** Avoid private jokes and exclusion. • **Think Before You Send:** Pause and consider before posting. • **Follow the Rules:** Read and adhere to them. • **Set Boundaries:** Mute notifications during specified times. • **Report Issues:** Report mean or inappropriate content.	• **Don't Invite Strangers:** Keep group chats for friends, family, and known people. • **Don't Spam:** Avoid sending lots of messages, emojis, or stickers at once. • **Don't Argue:** Disagree calmly and respectfully. • **Don't Be Afraid to Leave:** Exit the group if you feel uncomfortable or need a break. • **Don't Be a Cyberbully:** Avoid excluding people, being nasty, and name-calling. • **Don't Spread Gossip:** Avoid talking behind others' backs or sharing screenshots. • **Don't Share Personal Info:** Never share addresses, phone numbers, or passwords in an open group chat.

EMPATHY IN THE DIGITAL AGE

Digital communication can sometimes feel a little "soulless." It can be easy to forget that the people we're talking to are people with feelings, just like us. Offline, it's easier to see whether a person is laughing, smiling, or crying, which helps us decide what to do or say next. Understanding how our actions affect others online can be a lot harder.

BEING THERE WITHOUT BEING THERE

If someone you know is struggling, it's important to be there and help them. Our lives and relationships are strengthened and richer when we do this for each other. But what about if you're not physically in the same place?

It's still possible to be there when you're not there. Sometimes, people even find opening up to be easier with a little physical distance. Supporting a friend online is not so different from helping them offline—it comes down to listening. Here are a few tips on how to be a supportive friend. They'll work wherever you are (or aren't!).

1. **Listen actively:** Pay full attention to what the other person is saying, and don't interrupt. Don't check your phone or do other things on your computer. Show your friends you're listening to them by making eye contact—look into the camera.

2. **Show understanding:** Acknowledge what your friend says as their truth, even if you see things differently. Don't argue with them about what they're experiencing or feeling.

3. **Don't judge:** Avoid giving your opinions or advice unless your friend asks.

4. **Let them know they're not alone:** Even if you're on different sides of the world, make sure they know you're there for them.

5. **Respect their boundaries:** Sometimes people don't want to talk, and that's OK. Don't press them, but let them know you're there when they are ready. Then, offer to do something else together instead, like playing a game.

6. **Check in**: Don't wait for your friend to get in touch. Let them know you're there by dropping them a message or voice note now and again and arranging calls or hangouts with them.

LOOKING AFTER YOURSELF

Although it's important to be there for the people around us, both online and offline, we also need to look after our mental health. Sometimes, supporting others can be too much. If you feel overwhelmed or can't give a friend the support they need, respectfully tell them.

WHEN TO GET HELP

If your friend tells you they're being bullied, threatened, or made to feel unsafe, encourage them to get help from a trusted adult. Don't be afraid to tell a trusted adult yourself if necessary.

CHAPTER 5:

FINDING AND HANDLING INFORMATION: SMART STRATEGIES FOR THE DIGITAL AGE

The Internet is like a massive digital library where the answers to all your questions are just a few clicks or taps away. While that's pretty awesome, it's very easy to get lost! There is a lot of irrelevant stuff in the world's biggest library, so finding your way is an important skill.

THE INTERNET – YOUR DIGITAL LIBRARY

The Internet puts a world of information at your fingertips. People have unlimited access to information and knowledge for the first time in history, without leaving the comfort of their homes. It's a powerful resource, but, as you probably know, "with great power comes great responsibility." Learning to navigate the online world is essential to thrive in it.

MASTERING WEB SEARCHES

Just like in a library, you need to know what you're looking for and how to find it to find what you want online. That means perfecting the art of the search query or search term.

There are many ways to ensure you get valuable results when searching online. Here are a few tips to help you get the most out of your searches.

1. **Use a reputable search engine.** Google is the most commonly used, but other options exist, such as DuckDuckGo and Bing.
2. **Use specific keywords:** Try to be as specific as possible. For example, if you're looking for information on Marvel comics from between 1980 and 1990, search for "Marvel comics

between 1980 and 1990" rather than just "Marvel comics." The more you narrow it down, the better your results will be.

3. **Use quotation marks:** Quotation marks help you search for exact phrases. Using "" around your search phrase will search for those exact words in that order, so you'll get better results.

4. **Use filters:** Search engine filters let you narrow down results by date, location, and content type to find more relevant information.

5. **Use advanced search operators**: If you want to get super specific, try some advanced search operators. Here are a few examples:

   a. **"–" (Minus sign):** Use this to exclude terms you don't want in your search results. For instance, if you type "Marvel comics–Spider-Man," you'll get results for Marvel comics without much about Spider-Man.

   b. **"OR":** This lets you search for one thing or another. So, if you're unsure, you can look up "Spider-Man OR Batman" to find information on both.

   c. **"define:":** If you want to know what a word means, use "define:" followed by the word, and you'll get its definition.

   To discover more advanced search commands, search [advanced search commands] on your favorite search engine!

6. **Check the search suggestions:** As you type your query, look at the autocomplete search suggestions. You might see the exact phrase you're looking for, or notice something you hadn't thought of.

7. **Search by voice:** Most search engines allow you to search using your voice, which can be faster than typing and more convenient if you're out and about.

8. **Image search:** Your searches don't have to be text-based. You can also upload an image or image URL. This can be handy when seeking information on a particular item, place, or person.

UNDERSTANDING SEARCH RESULTS

Once you've got your search results, you need to know how to interpret them. You'll get a few different kinds of results, and some are more useful than others.

Sponsored Results

Sponsored listings usually appear at the top of the results page and are often marked as "sponsored." This means someone has paid the search engine to show their site or product, hoping to get more visitors. When you click on a sponsored listing, the advertiser usually pays the search engine a small fee for bringing you to their site.

While sponsored results are not necessarily bad, it's important to note that not all sponsored listings are trustworthy. Scammers often create fake sites and have them sponsored to trick people into visiting them, so watch out.

Organic Results

These are the results that have not been paid for. Their order is based on how well the search algorithm thinks they fit your search term and how much value they provide. The closer a website is to what you're looking for, the higher you should see them in the results.

Assessing Website Credibility

Not all websites are trustworthy. Even if a site looks slick and professional, there may be reasons to doubt its credibility. Learning to determine whether a website (or a newspaper, book, or any other source online or offline) is credible is crucial.

> **What Is Credibility?**
>
> Credibility means being trustworthy and reliable. It's usually earned over a long period of time by telling the truth and acting without underhanded or shady motives. People build credibility by working hard and honestly within their fields of expertise, and publications (newspapers, news sites, and so on) build credibility by behaving truthfully and honorably. Lying, cheating, and being deceptive are easy ways to lose credibility.

How to Assess Credibility Online

Don't believe everything you read. When you're online, keeping your critical thinking cap on is crucial! Use these tips to help you understand whether something you see online is trustworthy.

1. **Consider the content:** Look at the content closely. Check for errors and mistakes, or things that seem "off." Does the content seem one-sided, or is it trying to get you to take a particular view? Are there any experts or reputable organizations involved, or any citations? Is the language trying to provoke anger or negativity toward a specific group?

2. **Check the sources:** Look at where the information comes from, who made it, and when. Sometimes, people use their platforms to cause trouble or push an agenda, even if they pretend otherwise. Information from trusted sources, such as educational institutions, government websites, and reputable news outlets, is generally trustworthy. Blogs, TikTok videos, and social media posts are often personal opinions—that doesn't make them wrong, but they should not automatically be treated as fact.

3. **Look for signs of trustworthiness:** A professionally made website isn't automatically trustworthy, but it is something to look for. Other things to look for include people using their real names for their content, quotes, references, citations from trusted organizations, and honesty about the site's goals and funding.

4. **Check the domain:** Websites with domains (the bit in the address after the ".") like .gov (government websites) and .edu (educational institutions) are generally more credible than those with generic domains like .com or .biz.

SPOTTING FAKE NEWS AND BIAS

Having such easy access to information has a lot of advantages, and it's great that people today can have their perspectives heard by millions of others around the world. However, not everything that ends up online should be taken as fact.

Some people have particular reasons for promoting certain ideas, some like telling lies, and some want to cause trouble. Other times, the truth at the center of the story is spun into something completely different.

> **What Is Bias?**
>
> In this context, "bias" means treating a particular person or group more favorably or worse than another. A bias favoring a group means treating them better, and a bias against a group means treating them worse. Biases are not always obvious and can exist deep in society and people's behavior.

HOW TO IDENTIFY FAKE NEWS AND BIAS

It's vital to learn how to distinguish between reliable information, information that could be suspect, and false information. It's not always easy, but some reliable techniques will help you. These tips build on the methods mentioned above for determining whether a source is credible. Always use those as a baseline.

1. **Use your critical thinking skills:** Being able to tell the difference between fact, opinion, and lies is vital to thriving both online and offline. Consider why information may be presented the way it is and keep your mind open to different perspectives.

2. **Read the headline:** Headlines are supposed to attract attention, but if they use wildly exaggerated language, make wild claims, or use all caps or exclamation marks, there's a good chance they're not to be trusted.

3. **Check for supporting sources:** Real news will have reliable sources to support its claims. Look for links to scientific studies and quotes from experts and research them. Quotes and studies can be misrepresented, so it's important to look at the original source.

4. **Don't believe everything you see:** Images and videos are easy to manipulate. Always check the sources of images and videos, and be wary if no source is given or the source lacks credibility. You can use reverse image search to check where else images have appeared online.

5. **Check the date:** Sometimes, people present old news as recent. Always check the date of a story or piece of content and consider why someone might want to present it as more recent than it is.

6. **Always fact check:** Go through the content for anything presented as a fact and check it against other trusted sources, like government or educational institution websites. The more cross-checking with other sources you do, the better. Check that the author or creator of the content is who they say they are, and that they are being honest about their credentials. Use reliable fact-checking websites like Snopes.com to investigate claims.

THE LURE OF CLICKBAIT

With so much content vying for Internet users' attention, "clickbait" has become a common way to get views. Unfortunately, as an Internet user, it's often a waste of time.

What Is Clickbait?

Clickbait is unremarkable content with a sensational title or thumbnail (often both). The idea is that the title and thumbnail are so irresistible to anyone who sees them that they just have to click and view the content. Usually, the content is not nearly as interesting as it pretends to be.

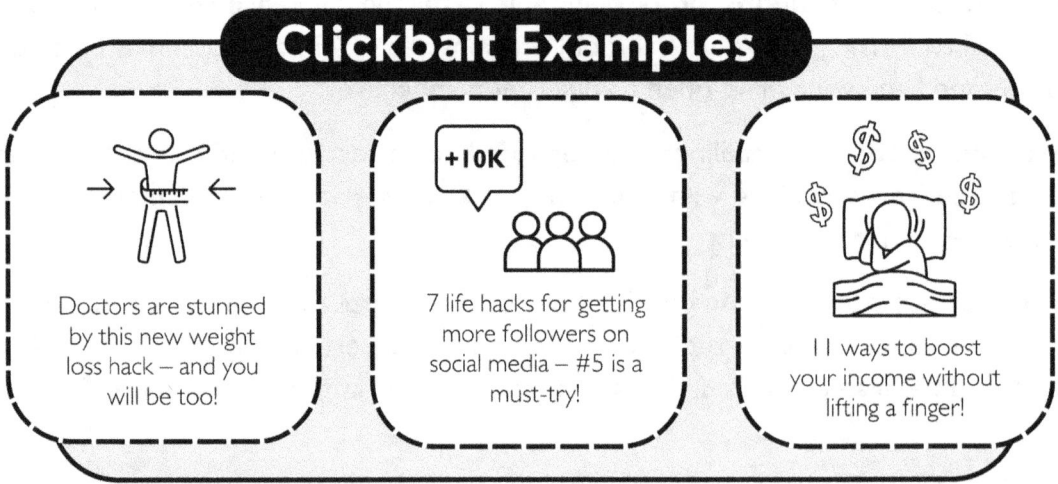

RECOGNIZING CLICKBAIT

Clickbait uses a few tricks to grab your attention. Here are some ways to spot it:

- **Angry headlines:** Sometimes, headlines are written to provoke anger or disbelief without telling the reader the story. For example, "You Won't Believe What This Terrible Person Did!"

- **Secrets and gossip:** If you see something like "Discover This One Trick to Reveal the Secret to Eternal Life!" it's probably clickbait. They promise big secrets, famous people doing incredible things, or discoveries to get you to click.

- **Question headlines:** Headlines that ask unrealistic or remarkable questions and often don't have great answers are usually clickbait. For example: "Do You Know This One Secret to Winning Fortnite?" sounds great, but unfortunately, it likely won't have the great answer it promises.

- **Eye-catching images:** Clickbait often uses images that have little to do with reality. Often, these images are AI-generated, showing celebrities in crazy situations or people doing impossible things.

Being able to tell what is clickbait from what isn't helps you avoid wasting time on content that's just trying to get you to click without offering anything real or valuable.

NAVIGATING THE WORLD OF AI

AI has been in the news in recent years. AI technology is playing an increasing role in many aspects of life, and this trend will likely continue. Learning how to understand this technology and make it work for you will be vitally important in the coming years.

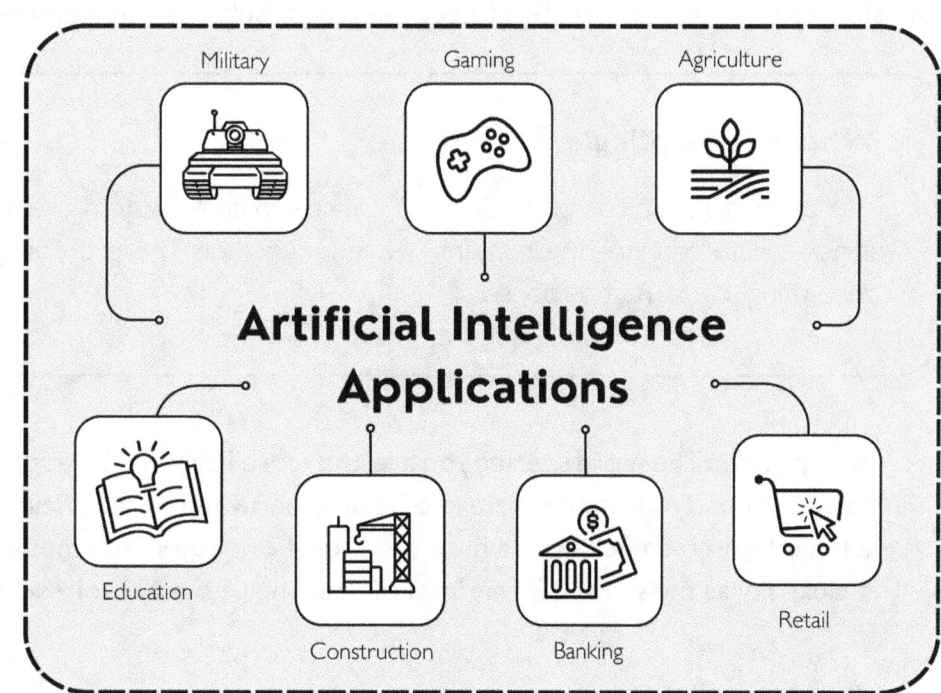

> ### What Is AI?
>
> "AI" stands for artificial intelligence. It is software designed to process information and "think" like a human, only faster. The term has been around since the mid-20th century, but technology has only recently caught up to the name.
>
> Modern AI technologies combine, compare, and reshape existing information into new forms. This could involve working with huge amounts of data from deep space to construct models of the universe, or creating new images by processing every image on the Internet. Machine learning is the process whereby AI learns from the data we feed it.
>
> AI can work with huge amounts of data much faster than humans, and can perform many "human-like" tasks, like spotting patterns and categorizing objects. At the moment, though, AI technology can't have ideas or think new thoughts—it can only work with what we feed it. In the future, that might change!

HOW TO PROMPT AI EFFECTIVELY

Interacting with AI systems can be a lot of fun and make things like planning and researching faster and simpler than ever before. But to get the best results, you must know how to prompt.

> ### What Is Prompting?
>
> A prompt is a specific type of text you provide to an AI system, like a chatbot or an image generator, to produce the content you're looking for. The prompt guides the AI tool in generating the correct response.

1. **Be specific:** The more specific you are, the more likely you'll get the AI's output to match your expectations. For instance, instead of saying, "Show me a green field full of cows," try, "Show me a large, lush, green field with a herd of 17 longhorn cows, with mountains in the distance, under a clear sky as the sun sets." This level of detail helps the AI tool visualize exactly what you want.

2. **Give examples:** Include examples that closely match what you're looking for. For instance, for the "cows in a field" example, you might provide photos of the specific type of cows or the mountains you're looking for. This helps the AI tool understand the style you're seeking.

3. **Try different formats:** Experiment with questions, statements, and instructions to see how they affect the results. For instance, "How many people have been to the moon?" might prompt a chatty, informal response. "List all the people who have been to the moon" will likely prompt a simple list. Experimentation is key!

4. **Break it down:** Tackling large or complex tasks in parts rather than all at once is more effective. For instance, if you're asking an AI to produce a detailed image, focus on one part at a time—cows, then fields, then mountains, then sky. Once you're happy with each part, instruct the AI to combine them into one image.

5. **Build on results:** If the output isn't what you want, use it as a stepping stone for the next prompt. For instance, if the AI produces an image of a small brown cow with short horns, your next prompt might be, "Make the cow bigger and the horns two feet long." The AI model uses your prompts to understand and improve its outputs.

6. **Be realistic:** Remember that AI technology cannot think or create anything for itself. It operates with the information it has been trained on. In other words, don't expect it to come up with anything startlingly original! Use AI tools to enhance your work and productivity rather than relying on them to do all the work.

THE ACCURACY OF AI

Although AI technology is impressive, it isn't perfect and can make mistakes. If you're using a system like ChatGPT or Bard, don't take what it says as fact. These systems are trained on billions of pieces of information, and not all of it is true. The AI doesn't know the difference, so it's up to you to check.

The AI's results might be outdated, error-ridden, or completely wrong. When an AI system produces false results, we call it "hallucinating."

AI, PLAGIARISM, AND COPYING

Remembering that AI does not generate original ideas or create new concepts is crucial. It is brilliant at rearranging information, but, unlike humans, it cannot create its own novel content.

A human has produced every piece of data that goes into an AI system, so although the output may be unique, it is never original. For this reason, it's important not to use AI to generate anything that is supposed to be your own work, such as schoolwork or exam answers. Generating work with AI and submitting it as your own is dishonest and could get you into big trouble.

> **What Is Plagiarism?**
>
> Plagiarism means taking someone else's work and pretending it's your own. It can be anything from copying an essay found online to taking quotations from a book without crediting the author. Plagiarism is very serious and can lead to getting in trouble in school, losing your credibility, and even being prosecuted.

UNDERSTANDING OWNERSHIP AND COPYRIGHT

Online, it's easy to access pretty much any kind of media content you like. Movies, games, music—it's all out there. To ensure that the people who create the content are treated fairly and paid for their work, we have laws in place about how we can get content, and how we can use it.

INTELLECTUAL PROPERTY, COPYRIGHT, AND YOU

When a person creates something, whether it's a film, book, piece of music, or one of the many other kinds of creations, that work is that person's intellectual property. This means they have legal rights to it. Intellectual property is protected by law, and stealing or using someone else's intellectual property without permission is illegal.

The rules that cover intellectual property are called copyrights. By creating something original, a person automatically has a copyright—they don't need to register the creation with anyone. If someone takes that work and pretends it's theirs without permission, that breaks copyright laws. So, if you write a story and someone else takes it and publishes it as their own, they're breaking the law!

FAIR USE

One exception to copyright is "fair use." This is where someone uses a small part of a copyrighted work in a way that doesn't negatively affect the original work. In these cases, there is no need to get permission. Generally, it's best to get permission from the copyright holder and credit them if you use their work.

WHERE TO FIND CONTENT

The Internet is full of places to find content legally. For music, there's Spotify, YouTube, Apple Music, and many other sources. Films are available from Netflix, Amazon, and many other providers. Steam is a great place to find games, and you can buy books from online booksellers like Amazon.

These platforms ensure that creators receive payment for their work and are acknowledged as the original creators. Sharing people's work in other ways without getting permission or paying for it is illegal, so always use the proper sources.

PRODUCTIVITY AND ORGANIZATION

Like in the offline world, organization is crucial for working efficiently. Searching for an item in a messy room is challenging, and clutter can distract you from focusing. Similarly, your digital life becomes much more manageable when it's well-organized!

USING CLOUD STORAGE

Over the past decade, cloud storage has become a standard way to store digital data. Files stored in the cloud can be accessed easily from any internet-connected computer, allowing instant sharing without requiring direct computer-to-computer connections.

Before cloud storage, data had to be stored locally—on individual computers—and shared by file transfer or email. Using the cloud makes it much easier and faster to collaborate on projects, and saves storage space for individuals. Many cloud storage services exist, like Google Drive, Dropbox, and Microsoft OneDrive. They all work in a similar way: You upload your files to the cloud, where they are stored securely, and then you can access them from anywhere with an internet connection.

One popular cloud storage example is Google Photos. If you sync it with your phone, any photo you take automatically uploads to Google Photos, where it's stored on Google's servers. You can access these photos anytime and from anywhere through your account.

ORGANIZING DIGITAL FILES

Managing digital files is an ongoing job, and organizing as you go is best. Once you get into the habit, it'll be with you for life. The following tips will help you get started.

How you create folders, use tags, and do other similar things will depend on your operating system (Windows, MacOS, Linux). Here are a few general pointers.

1. **Create folders:** Make folders to group related files together so you know where to look for them. You can even use different colors for different subjects or types of files.

2. **Use descriptive file and folder names:** Although you might think you'll remember what's in a particular file or folder, you will likely forget after a while. Use names that tell you what's inside—you'll thank yourself later.

3. **Sort and delete regularly:** Take some time now and then to review your files and remove old ones if you don't need them.

4. **Use tags and metadata:** File tags are information about a file that helps you categorize and organize it more easily.

5. **Organize your bookmarks:** Using folders and subfolders for your browser bookmarks makes it much easier to find them when you want to.

What Is the Cloud?

"The cloud" is a simple way of describing the huge network of computers that makes the Internet run. Although the term suggests that "the cloud" doesn't have much of a physical existence, in reality, all the information is held in huge server farms (a special type of computer). When many of these computers are linked together, they can do things that individual computers can't.

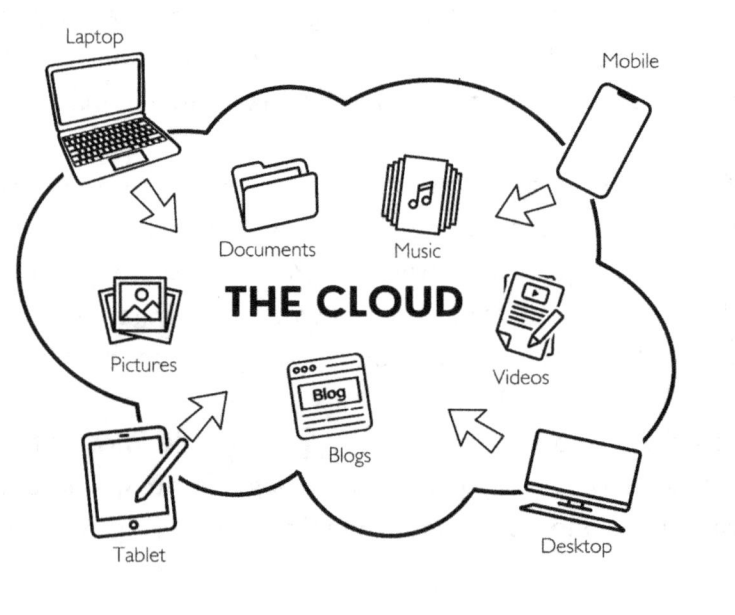

286 Essential Skills Every Teen Should Know

BACKING UP

Have you ever spilled a drink on your computer—or seen someone else do it? If so, you probably heard, "I hope you've got a backup!" Having a backup means keeping extra copies of your important files. That way, if one set gets damaged—say, by a soda spill—you have another set safe and ready to go.

It's crucial to back up your files regularly. This involves copying them to a different type of storage, so you have at least two copies in separate locations. If one gets damaged, the other is still available. For example, you might keep your main files on your laptop, back them up to a cloud service like OneDrive, and use a USB stick for an additional layer of security. This protects your data if your laptop gets soaked in soda or eaten by a dog.

DOWNLOADING AND SHARING FILES

Files can hold nasty surprises, such as viruses, so it's crucial that you only download files from trusted online sources. It's a good idea to ask an adult before downloading anything so that they can check the source. If you're being offered something for free, be suspicious. "Free" often comes with a hidden cost!

It's also very important not to plug anything into your computer that you find or that was given to you by someone you don't know. Viruses can be passed from USB sticks and other devices. If someone needs to share a file with you, ask them to use the cloud. Likewise, if you need to share files with someone else, use cloud storage or email.

CHAPTER 6:

DIGITAL COMMERCE: HOW TO BE A SAVVY ONLINE SHOPPER

Online shopping makes it simple to get virtually any item you like from anywhere in the world. The Internet is not only the world's biggest library, but also the world's biggest department store! In one afternoon, you can choose a new outfit, purchase school supplies for the coming term, stock up on Japanese food ingredients, and more. It's like having every shop you could ever want to visit, all in one place.

MASTERING THE ART OF ONLINE SHOPPING

Of course, as with the rest of life online, digital commerce requires a bit of know-how to get the most out of it. In this chapter, you'll learn everything you need to know about digital commerce, online shopping, and making purchases online.

There is a dizzying variety of online shopping stores and platforms available. If you think about the many stores in the biggest shopping mall, that doesn't even come close.

WHERE TO SHOP ONLINE

Some shopping websites are online versions of bricks-and-mortar stores, such as Target, Best Buy, and The Home Depot. Others are huge online-only platforms where you can find pretty much anything. Some popular online shopping platforms to explore include:

Amazon
- **Good for:** Pretty much anything you can think of. Amazon carries a wide range of products, from electronics, clothing, and books to groceries and more.

- **Key features:** Huge selection of goods and sellers. Prime membership includes faster shipping and access to Prime Video. Robust customer review system. Use voice commands to shop with Amazon Echo.

eBay
- **Good for:** Many new and used items, including clothes, electronics, collectibles, and more, at price points to suit various budgets.
- **Key features:** Auctions and "Buy It Now" listings. Huge range of items from individual sellers and businesses. Rare finds and vintage items.

Etsy
- **Good for:** Handmade, vintage, unique jewelry, clothing, art, and crafts.
- **Key features:** Items from independent sellers and small businesses. There are lots of one-of-a-kind finds in this community-driven marketplace.

Depop
- **Good for:** Pre-loved fashion items, vintage clothing, accessories, and rare finds.
- **Key features:** Users sell and buy items directly to and from each other. Lots of rare and unique finds. Huge range of items and prices. Strong focus on community.

Steam
- **Good for:** Video games of all kinds, from AAA releases to small indie games.
- **Key features:** Huge variety of games. Lots of different price points. Easy for creators to sell their games. Works across different operating systems.

MARKETPLACES VS E-COMMERCE SITES

It's important to distinguish between online marketplaces and e-commerce sites when shopping online, as they offer different shopping experiences.

Online Marketplace	E-Commerce Sites
Lots of individual sellers or small businesses.	Usually owned and operated by one company selling directly to customers.

The marketplace deals with payments and sometimes handles delivery and customer service.	The company handles everything, from payments to customer service and delivery.
Sellers have little control over how their "storefront" looks. The marketplace controls everything.	The company has complete control over how its website looks.
Examples: Ebay, Amazon Marketplace, Etsy, Depop	*Examples: Nike.com, Apple.com*

PAYMENT METHODS

Once you've found what you're looking for, you have to pay for it.

There are many different ways to pay for online purchases, each with advantages and disadvantages. Here, you'll find a brief explanation of some of the most commonly used payment methods.

Credit Cards

Credit cards let you pay with money you borrow from the issuing bank. Rather than money coming from your account, the bank lends you the money for the purchase. Then, you pay it back over a specific period.

Pros:
- **Fraud protection:** Very strong protection in case of fraudulent payments. If you notice a charge you didn't authorize, or if the item you receive is faulty, the credit card company can help you recover your money.

- **Rewards and benefits**: Credit card companies provide cashback, discounts, travel miles, and other perks to encourage spending. These rewards can lead to savings, good deals, and occasional freebies.

- **Build up credit history:** A good credit history makes getting products like loans and mortgages easier when you're older. Using a credit card responsibly is a simple way to build your credit history.

- **No-interest period:** If you pay off your credit card debt within a specified time, you might not pay interest. This can be a useful way to purchase large-ticket items you can't afford outright, such as a new TV.

Cons:
- **Interest charges:** Credit cards charge interest on unpaid balances after the no-interest period ends. This means you'll pay more than the original purchase amount if you haven't paid it off in time.
- **Risk of overspending:** It can be tempting to spend more than you can afford with a credit card, as you don't see the money coming out of your bank account.
- **Fees:** Some credit cards have extra fees attached, making them very expensive.
- **Debt:** Credit cards are a form of debt. If you don't keep up with your payments, the interest rate can increase and spiral out of control. This can also affect your credit score, which means you may be unable to borrow money for things like a house or car when you're older.

> ### What Is Interest?
>
> When you borrow money from a bank, you must pay it back with a little extra. This extra is called interest, and is how the bank earns money from the loan. Interest rates are usually a percentage known as the annual percentage rate (APR), which indicates how much interest you'll pay over a year.

Debit Cards

Debit cards let you pay for things with money directly from your bank account. You must have money available in the account to use a debit card. If you don't have the money, your purchase will be declined.

Pros:
- **Debt-free:** The money comes straight from your bank account, so no debt or borrowing is involved.
- **No interest:** No debt means no interest!
- **Convenient:** Debit cards are accepted everywhere and are quick and easy to use.

Cons:
- **Weaker fraud protection:** It can be harder to reverse fraudulent payments than with a credit card.
- **Limited rewards:** Most debit cards don't come with rewards or cashback.
- **Overdraft fees:** If you spend more money than you have in your account, you'll likely be charged an overdraft fee.

Digital Wallets (PayPal, Apple Pay, Google Pay, etc.)

Digital wallets, like Apple Pay or PayPal, combine the convenience of debit cards with the security of credit cards. When you open a digital wallet account, you enter your payment card details. After that, you never have to enter those details again to make payments—you simply use your wallet.

Pros:
- **Security and privacy:** The digital wallet stores and protects your information. This means you don't have to enter and share your card details every time you make an online purchase. Digital wallets use the latest technology, making fraudulent charges much more unlikely.
- **Convenience:** Making payments is easy and smooth, no matter where you shop online. Add your items to the cart, choose your digital wallet at checkout, and the payment will be made using the card linked to your wallet. It works on many websites and apps, making shopping faster and more secure.

Cons:
- **Transaction fees:** You might be charged for particular types of transactions, like sending money abroad.
- **Technological dependence:** Digital wallets work with devices like smartphones and smartwatches. They cannot be used without those devices.
- **Ease of use:** Digital wallets make spending incredibly convenient, but sometimes they're almost too easy to use. It can be tempting to tap, pay, and not think about the money being spent, which might lead to overspending.

Buy Now Pay Later (BNPL) Services (Splitit, Klarna, Four, Flex etc.)

BNPL services allow you to purchase and receive items and pay for them later, often in installments (the cost is divided into several smaller parts).

For instance, imagine you find a jacket you love that costs $100, but you only have $20. Using BNPL, you don't have to pay the whole amount up front. Instead, you can divide the payment into smaller parts (often interest-free) over a certain period. So, if you get $20 every month, you could choose to spread the cost over five months.

Pros:
- **Pay in installments:** BNPL makes purchases more affordable in the short term by splitting payments into smaller parts.

- **Interest-free period:** These services often charge no interest on payments for a fixed period.

- **Convenient:** It's usually quick and easy to get approved for BNPL services.

Cons:
- **BNPL is debt:** Remember, using BNPL means taking on a short-term loan. Essentially, you are borrowing money to make your purchase.

- **Fees and penalties:** Missing payments or defaulting (stopping paying altogether) will lead to extra costs, which can spiral out of control.

- **High interest rates:** Many BNPL services charge very high interest rates outside the interest-free period. If you miss payments, the purchase cost can significantly increase, sometimes making you pay much more than the item's original price.

- **Risk of overspending:** BNPL makes it tempting to buy more than you can afford, since you don't have to pay the full amount immediately.

- **Promotes unnecessary spending:** BNPL services are often linked to fast fashion and other impulse-buy sites, encouraging spending on things you might not need.

	👍 PROS	👎 CONS
Credit Cards	• Fraud protection • Rewards and benefits • Build up credit history	• High potential interest charges • Risk of overspending • Fees • Debt
Debit Cards	• Debt-free • No interest • Convenient	• Weaker fraud protection • Limited rewards • Overdraft fee
E-wallets	• Security & privacy • Convenient	• Transaction fees • Technological dependence • May be too easy to use & spend
Buy Now Pay Later	• Pay in installments • Interest-free period • Convenient	• BNPL is debt • Fees & penalties • High interest rates • Risk of overspending • Promotes unnecessary spending

UNDERSTANDING DIFFERENT PAYMENT TYPES

There are several different ways to make payments online. The simplest is a single payment for a one-off purchase, while more complex types include subscriptions and recurring fees. Understanding what kind of payment you're signing up for before purchasing online is essential.

Single Purchases

Single purchases are a one-off transaction where you pay for a product or service when you purchase it. Once you've paid and the transaction is complete, you have a legal right to the product or service. You'll either receive it straight away (in the case of a digital purchase) or your item will be shipped to you. For example, when you buy a game through Steam, you choose the game, enter your details, click "Pay," and the game is yours to download.

In-App Purchases and Virtual Currencies

In-app purchases are purchases you make in a particular app or platform for use within that environment. Platforms often use their own "virtual currency," which you have to buy with real currency or earn in the app. For instance, in Fortnite, you use real money to buy the virtual currency "V-bucks," which you can use to purchase in-game items.

It's vital to think carefully before making in-app purchases. These systems are designed to encourage users to spend more, and it's easy to run up a huge bill. Always check with a trusted adult before making any in-app purchases, pay attention to what you are clicking on, and avoid linking payment accounts to apps, if possible.

Subscriptions and Recurring Payments

Recurring payments and subscriptions are purchases that happen automatically at a specific time, usually once per week, month, or year. They are used for ongoing access to products or services, such as streaming services or subscription boxes, and continue until the user cancels the subscription. These types of payments are increasingly used for software such as Microsoft Office and Adobe Photoshop.

"Buy now pay later" services also use recurring payments, but the payments end when the total owed is paid off.

Subscriptions are a simple way to make recurring payments for products and services you want to use regularly. However, it's easy to end up with many subscriptions you don't need or want, or find yourself paying out more than you can afford.

To avoid oversubscription issues, regularly review your subscriptions and cancel any that no longer work for you. Use phone alerts to remind you what payments are scheduled and when, and check bank statements regularly for any subscriptions you've forgotten about.

UNDERSTANDING DIGITAL CURRENCIES

Digital currencies, often known as cryptocurrencies (or "crypto" for short), are modern money that only exists in digital form. They are different from regular (or "fiat") money in that they are not controlled by any centralized authority, but instead are "decentralized" and secured by blockchain technology.

Decentralization

While the Federal Reserve controls the US dollar, the most famous digital currency, Bitcoin, is not controlled by any one organization—it's decentralized. Every transaction with Bitcoin is recorded on the blockchain (basically an enormous list) for everyone to see. The idea is that this keeps the system transparent and secure.

Using Cryptocurrency

People use cryptocurrencies like Bitcoin to send money online and occasionally to pay for goods and services offline. Many view them as alternative investments, similar to commodities like gold or silver, rather than as traditional financial currencies for everyday purchases.

What Are the Risks?

Using or investing in digital currencies is very risky due to their extreme volatility. The value of these currencies can fluctuate dramatically—a single cryptocurrency "coin" might be worth $50 one day and just $1 the next, meaning if you bought it at $50 and sold it at $1, you would lose $49.

Digital currency regulation is still in its early stages globally, and it's unclear how the laws and rules around them will develop. In some regions, these currencies are even banned, raising doubts about the practicality of using digital currency for most people at this time.

SECURING YOUR TRANSACTIONS AND RECOGNIZING SCAMS

It's crucial to ensure your transactions are secure when shopping online. This means keeping your payment information hidden to prevent it from being stolen during the transaction, protecting you from potential fraud. Unsafe transactions can allow thieves to use your information for their purchases or sell it to others.

Shopping websites use various methods to protect their customers. The most important step is to stay alert and ensure the website uses the best security technology. Once you know what you're looking for, it's easy to check. If a site doesn't appear secure, stay away. No item is worth the risk of a scam or theft!

When making purchases online, here are key practices to keep you safe:

1. **Shop at reputable sites:** Stick to well-known retailers and research unfamiliar websites before purchasing. If in doubt, don't use them.

2. **Check for the "S" in URLs:** Shop only on sites that show "https://" in the URL and a padlock symbol in the address bar, indicating a secure TLS certificate.

3. **Use secure payment methods:** Credit cards and reputable third-party payment services like PayPal offer strong protection against fraud.

4. **Enable two-factor authentication (2FA):** This adds an extra layer of security by requiring a special one-time code each time a payment is made.

> ### What Is a TLS Certificate?
>
> Without getting too deep into technical talk, TLS certificates (often known as SSL certificates) show that a site is safe to visit. With a TLS certificate, you can be sure that any data sent through the website is encrypted (scrambled into a tough-to-crack code) and hidden from anyone who might want to steal it.
>
> Your browser automatically checks for a TLS certificate when you visit a website, so you don't need to do anything. Look for the "S" and the padlock in the address bar. If you get a warning saying the certificate is out of date or not valid, stay away from the site.

Unfortunately, the online world is also full of scammers looking to make an easy dollar at your expense, so being vigilant is key.

1. **Check for authenticity:** Legitimate businesses pay attention to their online presence. Spelling mistakes and poor-quality images are big warning signs.

2. **Do your research:** Investigate sellers thoroughly, check customer support details and read customer reviews, especially negative ones. Also, look for additional ratings on review sites like Trustpilot.

3. **Protect your personal information:** Never give out sensitive information like passwords, banking details, or Social Security Numbers.

4. **If it seems too good to be true…:** It probably is. Be skeptical of offers that are too good to be true. They are usually scams in disguise.

5. **Stay vigilant:** Treat being online like walking on the street — stay alert and cautious. Report anything suspicious to the authorities and stay up-to-date on scams and best security practices.

• •

Making Informed Decisions

Successful online shopping requires understanding product descriptions, reviews, and terms and conditions. Without this basic knowledge, making informed decisions can be challenging. As with many topics in this book, these skills are applicable in various situations, both online and offline. It's well worth paying them some attention!

FINDING THE BEST DEALS

With so many choices available online, finding the best deal can feel overwhelming. However, there are effective strategies to streamline your search. Use these tips to find great deals, every time. Always exercise caution and stay alert. While there are genuine bargains out there, remember: if it seems too good to be true, it probably is!

1. **Use price comparison sites:** These websites, such as Shopzilla, Google Shopping, and PriceGrabber, simplify comparing prices across different platforms. They allow you to use filters to refine your search and provide real-time information to ensure you see the most up-to-date prices.

2. **Learn to search effectively:** Sharpen your search skills to pinpoint the best deals. Be specific with your search terms, include words like "discount" or "sale," and use special search operators like quotation marks to search like a pro.

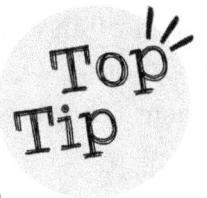 **Top Tip:** For big-ticket items, search using the manufacturer's serial number instead of the product name. This can help you compare prices more accurately across different sellers.

3. **Time it right:** Shop during sales seasons, such as Black Friday, Cyber Monday, and end-of-season sales, to take advantage of the best deals, especially on electronics and clothing. Also, buying off-season, like purchasing summer clothes in winter, will often save you money.

4. **Use vouchers and discounts:** Sites like RetailMeNot, Coupons.com, and Honey offer discount codes for a wide range of products. Check the voucher details, apply it at checkout, and save.

5. **Take advantage of loyalty programs and cashback offers:** Many sites and platforms have loyalty programs that offer savings or rewards on regular purchases. Signing up for email alerts can also provide exclusive discounts. Cashback sites like TopCashback can also help you get money back on your purchases.

COMPARING PRODUCTS

When deciding whether to make a purchase, it's crucial to consider various aspects and compare multiple options. Here's what to keep in mind:

Features and Specifications

Ensure the product meets your specific needs. For instance, if you need a table for a certain corner, confirm the dimensions to fit that space.

Focus on essential features. For instance, if you're buying a smartphone, these might include a foldable design and an AI-assisted camera.

These are the product's features. Specifications include details like the size, weight, and color. These will help you understand the product better and determine whether it matches your requirements.

Value for Money

The cheapest item isn't always the best choice. While everyone loves a good deal, it's essential to consider the overall value an item offers. Ask yourself: How long will it last? Is it reliable? Can it be repaired?

Very cheap items, especially electronics, may have a short lifespan and often cannot be repaired. Although the initial cost is lower, you may end up replacing them sooner, which can be more expensive over time. These items are also terrible for the environment. They are hard to recycle, so they often end up in landfills once they break.

When shopping for clothing, consider the "cost per wear" value. For example, a jacket that costs twice as much might be better value if it lasts three times longer. Always consider the durability and longevity of the item.

Customer Reviews

Always read reviews of an item before making a purchase. Look for both positive and negative points, and pay special attention to reviews from customers who used the product in ways similar to how you plan to use it. Keep in mind that not all reviews or reviewers are trustworthy. Despite this, reviews can still provide a useful general sense of a product's quality.

Expert Opinions

There are lots of websites and videos where experts test and review products. If you're considering a technical or high-value item, it's a good idea to explore these resources to get expert insights. However, be cautious—some review sites earn money from the companies whose products they review, so it's important to check the credibility of the reviewers before fully trusting their opinions.

Return Policies and Warranties

Always check the return policy and warranty terms before buying a product. These are crucial for knowing what to do if the item fails to meet your expectations. Beware of cheap items from faraway places; it can be expensive and complicated to return an item, and there may be no warranty.

DECIPHERING REVIEWS

Customer reviews are invaluable when deciding whether to buy a product. But not all reviews are equal. When evaluating an item, consider both the positive and negative feedback. It's tempting to overlook negative reviews if you're attracted to a product, but that's not usually a good idea.

Spotting Fake Reviews

Some sellers and businesses pay people to write fake reviews of their products, or negative reviews about competitors' products. It's challenging to spot fake reviews, but here are some things to look out for:

- **Repetitive patterns:** If reviews share the same pattern, details, or similar overly positive or negative comments, they might be fake.
- **Single review accounts:** Reviewers who have posted only one review or multiple reviews for the same company are suspicious.
- **Excessively positive or negative:** Generic reviews that are excessively positive or negative without clear details about the product could also be fake.

These signs suggest that the reviews may not be genuine.

Verified Purchase Reviews

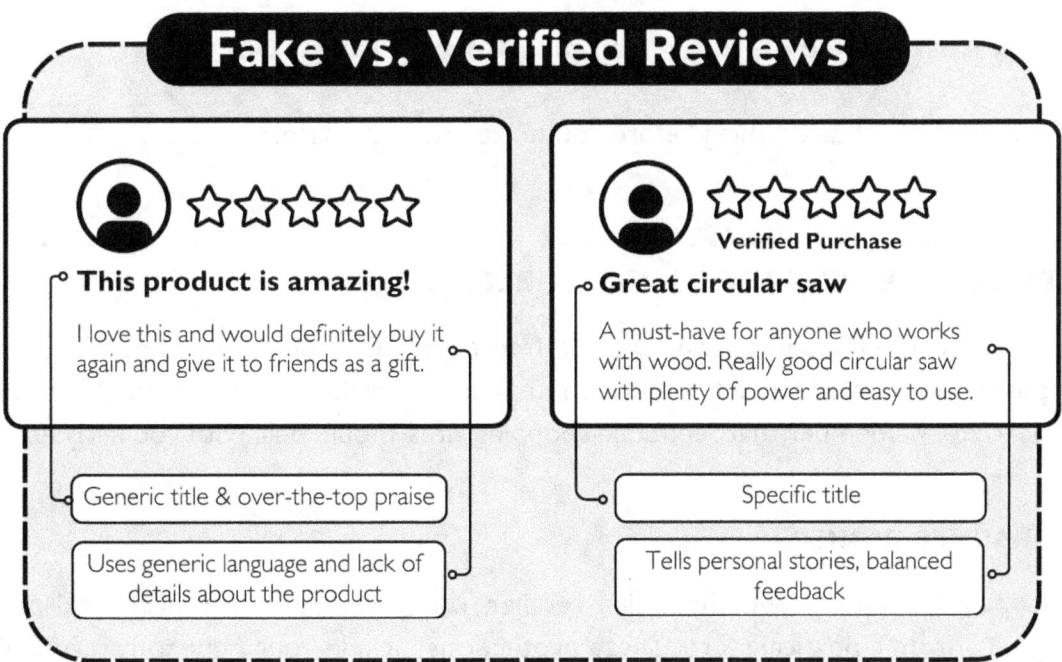

To combat fake reviews, many sites mark reviews as "Verified Purchase" to confirm the reviewer actually bought the item. While these reviews are generally more trustworthy, be aware that some companies pay individuals to purchase and review products, so they are not foolproof.

CALCULATING THE TOTAL COST OF A PURCHASE

Before making a purchase, it's crucial to understand its total cost. While most websites display this information clearly, it's wise to calculate it independently as well, just to be certain.

1. **Check the item price:** The base price of the item is typically prominently displayed.

2. **Include shipping costs:** While shipping may sometimes be free, often it must be added to the item's cost. Shipping fees are usually found on a dedicated page of the site or in the terms and conditions.

3. **Account for taxes:** Additional taxes might apply to your purchase. Check this information and add the appropriate amount to your total.

4. **Apply any discounts:** If you have a discount voucher or code, deduct the amount or percentage from the total.

5. **Calculate the total:** Combine the item's price, shipping costs, and taxes, then subtract any applicable discounts. The final number is the total cost of your purchase.

So, **Total Cost = Price of Item + Shipping Costs + Taxes–Discounts**

Always double-check everything before you make your purchase!

AFTER PURCHASE – SUPPORT AND PROBLEM SOLVING

Shopping online is often a smooth and trouble-free experience. But sometimes, things go wrong. Because there's no physical store to return an item to or visible staff to talk to, it can be hard to know what to do. Remember that reputable shopping sites should deal with you fairly and honestly.

YOUR CONSUMER RIGHTS

When shopping from a trustworthy online retailer, you generally have similar legal protections as when buying from a physical store. These protections include your right to return faulty items, cancel certain types of orders within a specific timeframe, dispute incorrect or unauthorized charges, and expect fair treatment and privacy protection from businesses.

The specific rules and regulations depend on your location and the site from which you've made your purchase. Understanding these rights is crucial for making informed purchasing decisions.

USING SELF-HELP RESOURCES

If you need help with a product, start by exploring the self-help resources available. Most online retailers provide FAQs and tutorials on their websites—these can be great for resolving common problems.

User forums can also be handy. The communities around certain products or companies often know more and offer better solutions than official customer support. Before posting a new question in a forum, make sure to check if it has already been addressed; chances are, someone else has faced the same issue!

REACHING OUT FOR HELP

If you can't resolve an issue using the self-help resources, your next step is to contact customer support. You can find contact information on the business's website.

If the business offers live chat, it's a quick way to get help. Emailing customer support is a good option if you're not in a hurry. For direct interaction, consider using phone support if available.

When contacting support, be prepared with all the details about your issue. This includes your order number, product name or number, any error messages, and a detailed description of the problem. Providing complete information helps the support team resolve your issue more efficiently.

MANAGING MONEY AND ONLINE BANKING

Online banking allows you to access and manage your money electronically. It makes sending money, paying for items, and moving money between your accounts quick and easy. You can access your online banking accounts 24 hours a day, seven days a week—as long as there's an Internet connection—making it incredibly convenient. Additionally, modern banking platforms use the most up-to-date encryption methods, ensuring your transactions are safe and secure.

HOW TO SET UP AN ONLINE BANK ACCOUNT

Setting up an online bank account is straightforward but usually requires the help of an adult.

1. **Choose a reputable bank:** Start by researching banks and financial service providers in your area. Consider their security measures, customer reviews, and the services they offer. Check whether the bank operates solely online or also has physical branches, which can be useful for face-to-face interactions.

2. **Sign up for online banking:** Visit the bank's website and follow the instructions to sign up. You'll need an adult to assist you, along with personal details like your name, address, and Social Security Number. Depending on the bank, you may need to open a bank account first, or you might be able to sign up for an account and online banking simultaneously.

3. **Create a strong password:** It's crucial to use a strong password for all your accounts, especially for banking. Use a mix of upper and lowercase letters, numbers, and special characters. Refer to the password creation guide in Chapter 1.

4. **Download the app:** For mobile access, download your bank's app and log in with your details. Do this over a secure Wi-Fi connection, not in a public place. Once set up, your online bank account is ready to use.

CHAPTER 7:

FINDING BALANCE: HOW TO MANAGE SCREEN TIME AND WELL-BEING

The Internet has become such an important part of everyday life that it often seems more appealing than the offline world. It's easy to get swept up in the digital world and overlook the incredible experiences the offline world has to offer! In reality, many of life's most important moments take place away from the screen with friends and family, outdoors, and in nature.

THE QUEST FOR DIGITAL EQUILIBRIUM

You've probably heard the sayings "too much of a good thing" and "moderation in all things." These expressions emphasize the importance of balance. Having a good thing all the time—even when it is brilliant, like ice cream or the Internet—can lose its appeal and make for an unbalanced life.

Having a mixture of interests and activities is essential to prevent this imbalance. Just as a varied diet is crucial for physical health, engaging in a range of activities is beneficial for overall well-being. While the idea of having ice cream for every meal might seem tempting, it wouldn't be healthy, and it might also—believe it or not—get boring pretty quickly. The same applies to all aspects of life, including spending time online. It's healthy and useful in the right dose, but too much is just that—too much.

THE BENEFITS OF BALANCE

Maintaining a healthy balance between online and offline time is crucial for every part of your life, from mental health to personal relationships. Finding the right balance can significantly improve your quality of life.

Spending too much time online has been linked to poorer mental and physical health in young people. By balancing this with offline experiences, you can enjoy "real-world" pleasures and get the best of both worlds.

MANAGING YOUR SCREEN TIME

You've probably heard a lot of talk about "screen time," especially concerning the amount young people spend on screens and whether it's too much. However, it's important to recognize that not all screen time is created equal, and whether it's "good" or "bad" is not a simple issue.

> **What Is Screen Time?**
>
> Screen time is the time people spend looking at electronic devices with screens. This includes smartphones, games consoles, TVs, tablets, cinema screens, and anything else with a screen.

There are three basic types of screen time:

- **Educational:** Screen time spent on activities where you're learning something. This includes schoolwork, language apps like Duolingo, or doing research.

- **Recreational:** Time spent on entertainment. Watching TV, playing video games, and scrolling through social media without interacting much are all examples of recreational screen time.

- **Social:** Time spent communicating directly with other people. Things like video calls, messaging through apps, and interacting with people through social media are social screen time.

THE IMPACT OF TOO MUCH SCREEN TIME

There's nothing intrinsically wrong with screen time. As part of a balanced lifestyle, it can play an important role in learning, socializing, and communicating. However, excessive screen use can have negative consequences, mainly because other aspects of life get ignored or forgotten.

Negative effects of screen time include:

- **Poor sleep:** Using screens before bed can disrupt sleep, making it difficult to fall asleep and stay asleep. Lack of quality sleep can negatively affect mental and physical health.

- **Physical health problems:** Sitting for long periods can harm your bones and muscles and increase the risk of obesity. Staring at screens for too long can also strain your eyes.

- **Mental health problems:** Rates of depression, anxiety, and stress are on the rise among young people. Although they are not solely caused by screen time, spending too much time on screens, especially on social media, can lead to less interaction with others, heightening feelings of loneliness and worsening mental health concerns.

- **Weak social skills:** Not engaging in enough face-to-face conversations can weaken your ability to communicate and collaborate with others, impacting your social skills. Social skills are like muscles—they need exercise to stay strong!

SETTING HEALTHY LIMITS

There's no need to panic about screen time, but setting limits and boundaries for yourself and encouraging your friends and family to do the same is a good idea. Use these tips to help you create a healthy balance between online and offline time.

1. **Create a weekly screen schedule:** A schedule can help you manage your screen time and maintain a healthy balance. Decide on a schedule that suits you, with specific time slots for different screen time activities. For example, consider limiting evening screen time to one hour before dinner.

2. **Use screen time monitoring apps:** There are many apps available that can tell you how long you spend on your devices and how you spend that time. Many digital devices have these features built-in—check the settings for "Digital Wellbeing Controls" or similar. These apps and features can help you understand your screen time and stay accountable.

3. **Establish screen-free zones:** Work with your family to choose specific parts of your home as screen-free zones to encourage more face-to-face interaction. Bedrooms and dining rooms are a good choice.

4. **Lead by example:** Modeling healthy screen time behavior will help others do it, too. Encourage your friends and family to find a healthy balance and suggest activities you can do together that don't involve screens.

HOW TO CREATE A PERSONAL SCREEN TIME PLAN

Making a plan is a great way to create a healthy balance between screen time and screen-free time. It will help you understand what you want from your screen time and what you'd like to focus more on off-screen.

Ask yourself these questions to help you build a plan tailored to your life.

- **How much screen time do I get currently?** Use monitoring apps or features to track your screen time. If you can't use an app, use a timer and a notebook. Be honest with yourself and record it all.

- **What do I do with my screen time?** Use those apps to understand precisely how you spend your time online. Again, be honest with yourself. You might be surprised how long you scroll through Instagram or other social media feeds!

- **What do I want to do with my screen time?** Work out your priorities for screen time. You probably have schoolwork, friends you want to speak with, or other things you want to do online. Make those the things you use most of your screen time for.

- **What's my schedule?** Based on your answers to the previous questions, establish a schedule that includes limits for each type of screen activity. Even a flexible schedule should have clear boundaries to help manage your screen time effectively.

- **What would I like to do more of?** Consider activities you enjoy that don't involve screens, such as spending time with friends, playing sports, or reading. Plan to use the time you save from reduced screen use for these interests.

MANAGING NOTIFICATIONS AND DISTRACTIONS

App notifications can be useful, but too many can become overwhelming and distract you from important tasks or conversations. Here are some tips to help manage them.

1. **Switch them off:** Most apps allow you to turn off or limit their notifications. Dive into your app settings and turn off notifications for apps you don't need constant updates from. Just remember to leave important ones, like banking apps, active.

2. **Use "do not disturb":** Mealtimes, bedtime, and deep conversations with friends are ideal times to use your device's "do not disturb" function, which silences all but the most urgent notifications. Your device will continue to function normally—it just won't interrupt you.

3. **Try "focus mode."** Similar to "do not disturb," "focus mode" quietens your device so that you can concentrate on other things. Depending on the situation, you can customize it to allow notifications from certain apps or contacts.

4. **Out of sight, out of mind**: When you're not using your phone or tablet, place it somewhere out of sight. This reduces distractions, and the temptation to check it frequently diminishes when it's not within easy reach.

TIME FOR A DIGITAL DETOX?

Spending too much time online or glued to screens can lead to some serious downsides. It's vital to monitor its impact on you and consider taking a break if digital life becomes overwhelming.

RECOGNIZING WHEN SCREEN TIME IS BECOMING A PROBLEM

Sometimes, you might feel the effects of too much screen time, but other times, the signs are less noticeable. Knowing the symptoms of addiction and digital burnout is crucial. Here are some red flags to watch for:

- **Preoccupation with screens:** Constantly thinking about screen time and struggling to focus on anything else.

- **Neglecting responsibilities:** Putting off essential things to spend more time on your devices/gaming/watching TV.

- **Losing control:** Feeling like you can't stop checking or using your devices, even if you want to or have tried to.

- **Using for longer than intended:** Losing time and neglecting other parts of life by spending more time on your devices than you mean to.

- **Feeling bad, mentally or physically:** If you notice any decline in how you feel mentally or physically, it could be a sign that you're spending too much time on your devices.

SIGNS OF DIGITAL BURNOUT

Ignoring signs that digital use and screen time are causing problems can lead to digital burnout. Burnout is a serious health condition in which the body and mind go into a kind of exhausted shock after being exposed to stress for a long time. Don't ignore these symptoms if you notice them in yourself or if others notice them in you.

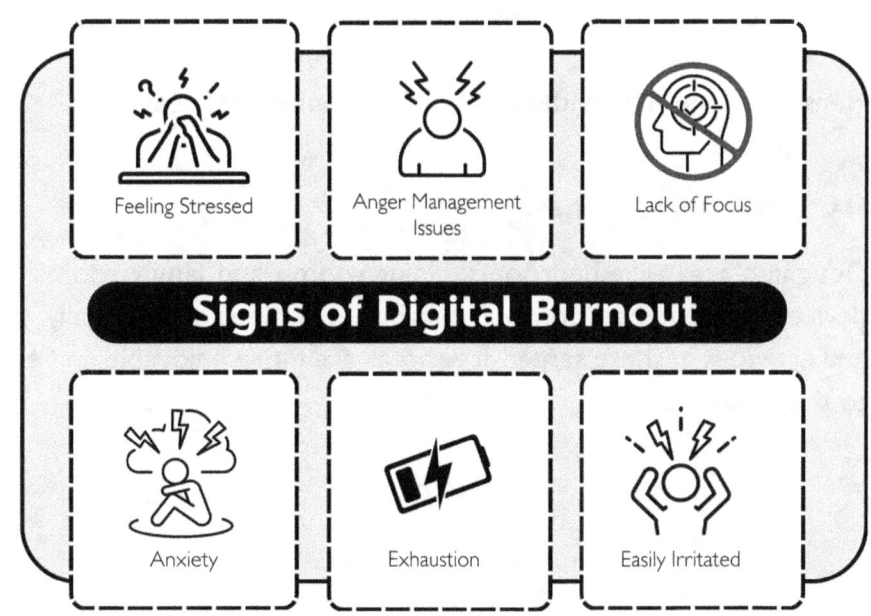

Speak to a healthcare professional, or, if that isn't an option, to a trusted adult, then take steps to reduce your screen time. Use the strategies in this chapter to help manage your digital exposure.

Symptoms of burnout include.

- **Feeling exhausted:** Feeling very tired, even after getting enough sleep, with little or no energy for basic activities.

- **Lack of motivation:** Losing interest in things you once enjoyed and feeling indifferent about many aspects of life.

- **Struggles concentrating:** Difficulty focusing on routine tasks and everyday conversations.

- **Mood swings:** Sudden mood swings for no apparent reason, or frequently feeling cross, angry, or irritable.

- **Physical symptoms:** Headaches, eye strain, sore muscles, digestive issues, and other physical symptoms without an obvious cause.

- **Avoiding people:** Not wanting to be around others and avoiding social situations.

- **Problems sleeping:** Difficulty falling asleep or staying asleep, frequent waking during the night, bad dreams, and feeling tired even after sleeping.

DIGITAL DETOX STRATEGIES

A "digital detox" is a great way to take action when you notice you're spending too much time with devices and screens. When trying digital detox strategies, it's a good idea to tell other people you trust so they can help you and offer support. They might even join you!

Here are some simple ideas to try with your digital detox.

Try Screen-Free Zones

Designate areas like bedrooms, dining rooms, and family rooms as screen-free zones. Eliminating devices from the bedroom will improve your sleep. Additionally, you might find that conversations and activities in these screen-free areas are more enjoyable and engaging when people aren't glued to their phones.

Use Your Screen Schedule

You might not want to (or be able to) stop using devices completely, instead, consider establishing a structured screen schedule to help regulate your screen time. You'll need self-control here, but remember, it's for your own good!

Create Tech-Free Habits

Introduce small, enjoyable habits that don't involve using screens into your day. Whether having breakfast without your phone, writing in a notebook on the way to school, or stepping outside into nature, these activities contribute to a more fulfilling real-world experience.

Get Outside

Green spaces, fresh air, and sunlight are all proven mood boosters. Spending time outdoors is the perfect way to get offline. Hiking, biking, playing sports, or simply walking around are all great ways to improve your mood and reduce stress. You don't have to be out in the countryside (although it's great if you can be)—even a walk around the block will positively affect your body and mind.

Embrace Analog Activities

Explore the endless array of enjoyable and engaging activities that don't rely on devices or screens. From crafting and learning a musical instrument to journaling and photography. Not only is it fun to try new things and work on skills, but you'll also often have something to show for it!

Prioritize the People in the Room

Have you ever been talking with someone, and they suddenly get a notification on their phone and immediately break off the conversation to check it? It's annoying, right? Phones and notifications are designed to attract attention—and they do. But ignoring real people in favor of our devices can be annoying and hurtful. Over time, it can lead to weaker, less fulfilling relationships.

Pay attention to the people in the room. Listen to them when they speak, and concentrate on giving thoughtful replies. Keep your phone out of the conversation, and don't shy away from interacting because it's easier to look at a screen—social skills take practice, and if you don't use them, you'll lose them!

HEALTHY HABITS BEYOND THE SCREEN

A healthy, balanced lifestyle isn't just about controlling your screen time. It's essential to consider other aspects of well-being as well! Building healthy habits from a young age is a wonderful way to increase your chances of enjoying a long, happy, healthy life—and who doesn't want that?

PHYSICAL ACTIVITY

Humans are designed to move. Staying active keeps bodies and minds strong and healthy, so getting as much physical activity as possible is important. Try these tips to help you increase your daily movement:

1. **Move often:** Whatever you're doing in your day, try to find ways to incorporate some movement. If you've been sitting for a while, walk around for a minute. Do some stretches while watching TV or working at your computer. Walk up the stairs instead of using the elevator. Look out for ways to move more in daily life.

2. **Do things you enjoy:** Walking, swimming, soccer, flying a kite—it doesn't matter what you do; what matters is that you enjoy it. Try out different activities until you find something you love. It doesn't have to be a sport. All kinds of movement count—even dancing around your bedroom!

3. **Set goals:** Goals make it easier to cultivate good habits. Try setting a goal like 30 minutes per day of continuous movement and see where it takes you. Update your goals when needed, and keep them realistic so you don't set yourself up for disappointment.

4. **Make a schedule:** Schedules help you achieve your goals and do more with your time. Try scheduling a daily movement session at a sensible time and sticking to it.

5. **Get other people involved:** Exercising with others can be more fun than going it alone, so round up some friends and get moving!

NUTRITION AND SLEEP

Food and sleep have a massive influence on overall health. Prioritizing healthy eating and sleeping will help you develop good habits and set you up for success, so follow these tips.

1. **Eat a balanced diet:** The more variety in your diet, the better. Eating many different foods, with a focus on vegetables, whole grains, and healthy fats, will give you all the nutrients you need.

2. **Eat mindfully:** Listen to your body—eat when you're hungry and stop when you've had enough. Pay attention to what you're eating and avoid doing other things at the same time, like watching TV or talking on the phone.

3. **Prioritize sleep:** Aim to get seven to nine hours of sleep per night. Sleeping is one of the body's essential processes, so don't put it off to do something else!

4. **Create a bedtime routine:** It can be easier to fall asleep when you have a routine that lets your body know it's bedtime. Taking a warm bath, getting into your pajamas, and reading a book for 15 minutes are all good ways to wind down.

5. **Avoid screen time before bed:** Using devices and watching TV can make the brain too alert to fall asleep. Try to avoid screens for at least an hour before bed.

MENTAL WELLNESS

Looking after your mind is just as important as looking after your body. The two are strongly connected, and you might find your mood improves when you look after your body. But there are also a few things we can do to nurture our minds.

1. **Avoid digital overload:** Use the tips and strategies in this chapter to help you manage your digital life.

2. **Practice your hobbies:** Doing things you enjoy is a great way to relax and unwind. Experiment with a mix of activities, and make sure some are offline.

3. **Connect with others:** Make time for the people in your life, even if you find social situations difficult. Connecting with others is one of the best ways to look after your mental health.

4. **Practice mindfulness:** Pay attention to the present moment and what you are doing. Notice the sensations and feelings. For instance, if you are drawing, concentrate on the pencil in your hand and the feeling as it touches the paper. Try not to obsess over the future or worry about the past. Instead, appreciate each moment as it comes.

5. **Get help if needed:** If you feel like you're struggling with your mental or physical health, tell a trusted adult. Don't keep it to yourself—people are ready and willing to help.

EMBRACING THE OFFLINE WORLD

Now that you know how to strike a healthy digital balance, it's time to get out there and explore the offline world. There's so much to do and see! Sometimes, offline activities seem more difficult to get into than online ones. That's all the more reason to do them—when things are a challenge, that's when we learn and grow.

FINDING JOY OFF-SCREEN

Offline activities might not provide the immediate feel-good hit that online activities can. Still, over time, you'll likely find that they give you more fulfillment, enjoyment, and long-lasting pleasure. Here are a few ideas to get you started.

1. **Take your hobbies further:** Find ways to get deeper into whatever interests you. That could mean attending conventions, reading books, visiting museums, or talking with others who share your interests.

2. **Discover new interests:** Try new activities, even if you're not sure you'll like them. Sometimes, you'll be surprised! And you'll learn a lot about yourself with each new activity you try.

3. **Embrace uncertainty:** Embrace the unknown. For example, avoid looking at the menu online before you visit a new restaurant. When you go on a trip, walk around without using Google Maps. Try not to worry about not having everything planned out.

4. **Try volunteering:** Helping in the community is a great way to connect with others and feel more involved with your local area. Look for open days or welcome sessions with local groups that interest you.

SCREEN-FREE SOCIALIZING

Humans are social animals, and we thrive in the company of other people. But offline socializing can be nerve-racking when you're not used to it. The good news is that it gets easier with practice. If you're looking for ideas on how to up your offline socializing game, try these tips.

1. **Plan outdoor adventures:** Socializing is easier when there's a focus, so organize group trips into the great outdoors. You don't have to go far—the local park is fine. Just take some friends along!

2. **Attend local events:** Once you start looking, you'll find that most places have a lot going on. Local festivals, markets, music, and art events are perfect for exploring with friends and family and meeting new people.

3. **Host a game night:** Get your friends and family involved in a group game night. You could play board games, card games, physical games like charades, or a mixture of game types.

4. **Join clubs or groups:** Themed groups are an easy way to meet people who are interested in similar things. There are groups for everything you can imagine, from crochet to camping, so check out your local options.

TAKE TIME IN NATURE

The sights, sounds, and smells of the outdoors affect the human body in ways scientists are only just beginning to understand. What we do know is that spending time in nature has many benefits, including improved mood, reduced stress and anxiety, and better quality sleep. Try these ideas to immerse yourself in nature.

1. **Take a nature walk:** Simply walking through a natural environment benefits the body. Watching the birds, counting the different kinds of plants and bugs, or just enjoying the feeling of the air on your skin—it's all good!

2. **Go camping or stargazing:** A starry night sky is a wonder everyone should see as often as possible. In towns and cities, a few stars might be visible, but the night sky is spectacular out in the wilderness. Camp in areas with as few buildings as possible. There are even "dark sky" reserves where you're guaranteed a fantastic view of the night sky.

3. **Get near the water:** Swimming, kayaking, or sunbathing on the shore (don't forget your sunscreen!) are all wonderful ways to enjoy nature. Explore your local seashore, lake, or pond; just check for safety information and take friends along with you!

4. **Tend your garden:** Growing and looking after plants is a rewarding way to spend time outdoors. If you have a garden at your house, ask if you can take ownership of a patch. Growing plants in pots on a balcony or indoors is just as much fun if you don't have a garden.

CONCLUSION

We've reached the end of this voyage of digital discovery. Take a moment to pat yourself on the back! If you don't remember everything you read, don't worry—you can dip into this book whenever you need to for a quick refresher.

Throughout this book, you've learned all about:

- The history of digital communication, how it came about, and why it matters.
- How to stay safe online, including how to spot scams and keep your bank account safe and secure.
- Netiquette, how to conduct yourself online, and look out for others.
- How to communicate effectively in different digital situations, from video calls to group chats.
- How to search, shop, and spot fake news successfully.
- How to stay healthy mentally and physically and find the right balance between online and offline.

To break it down, you might say that the three main takeaways of this book are:

- Respect yourself and other people online (and offline!).
- Keep your wits about you online (and offline!).
- Stay curious and keep learning.

WHAT'S NEXT?

Developing strong digital skills is one of the best gifts you can give yourself, and it's never too late or too early to start. These skills will stay with you for life, but it's important to practice to keep them sharp. Think of this book as the first step in a lifelong journey of digital understanding, and use it to build from as you grow.

To keep your digital skills in top shape, the best thing you can do is to keep working on them. Because the digital world moves on so quickly, it's pretty common to be up-to-date and on top of everything one minute and then feel lost and left behind the next.

To prevent this, follow tech trends and develop your skills wherever and whenever you can. Podcasts, newsletters, and forums are all great ways to stay up-to-date with what's going on. By incorporating your digital skills into your daily life responsibly and healthily, you'll set yourself up for success.

THE END...AND THE BEGINNING

Now that you've got this incredible digital skills toolkit, it's time to use it! The next time you do anything online, think about how to use what you've learned to make your experience safer, more fun, and more valuable.

Why not share what you've learned with your friends and family? You might be surprised at how many people you can help with their digital skills. Remember that it is down to all of us to make the digital world a better place for everyone.

Good luck on your digital journey. May it be a long and fruitful one!

Your friend,
Ferne Bowe

THANKS
FOR READING MY
BOOK!

I truly hope you enjoyed the book and that the content is valuable now and in the future.

I would be grateful if you could leave an honest review or a star rating on Amazon.
(A star rating is just a couple of clicks away.)

By leaving a review, you'll help other parents discover this valuable resource for their children. Thank you!

To leave a review & help spread the word

www.ingramcontent.com/pod-product-compliance
Lightning Source LLC
Chambersburg PA
CBHW081707100526
44590CB00022B/3687